Schooled in Fear

Schooled in Fear

Lessons Learned about Keeping Students and Staff Safe

Deborah Lynch

ROWMAN & LITTLEFIELD
Lanham • Boulder • New York • London

Published by Rowman & Littlefield
A wholly owned subsidiary of The Rowman & Littlefield Publishing Group, Inc.
4501 Forbes Boulevard, Suite 200, Lanham, Maryland 20706
www.rowman.com

Unit A, Whitacre Mews, 26-34 Stannary Street, London SE11 4AB

Copyright © 2017 by Deborah Lynch

All rights reserved. No part of this book may be reproduced in any form or by any electronic or mechanical means, including information storage and retrieval systems, without written permission from the publisher, except by a reviewer who may quote passages in a review.

British Library Cataloguing in Publication Information Available

Library of Congress Cataloging-in-Publication Data Is Available

ISBN: 978-1-4758-2980-8 (cloth : alk. paper)
ISBN: 978-1-4758-2981-5 (paper : alk. paper)
ISBN: 978-1-4758-2982-2 (electronic)

∞™ The paper used in this publication meets the minimum requirements of American National Standard for Information Sciences—Permanence of Paper for Printed Library Materials, ANSI/NISO Z39.48-1992.

Printed in the United States of America

Contents

Preface vii

Introduction ix

1 School Shootings by Students 1
2 Intruder Violence 17
3 Aggression and Intimidation 31
4 Bullying and Cyberbullying 55
5 Suicide and Suicidal Behaviors 71
6 Sexual Harassment and Abuse 93
7 Teen Dating Violence 111
8 Gang Violence 131
9 Violence against Teachers and Staff 149
10 Reflections on Lessons Learned 161

About the Author 175

Preface

I am a mother and a teacher. I have taught for over twenty years in urban elementary and high schools and am now a college professor of school leadership. One of my guiding principles has been from the Paideia reform group, which advocates that the quality of schooling to which students are entitled is "what the wisest parents would wish for their own children."

Over the years I have seen many disparities between the quality of schooling between my students and my children, but none more so than the issue of school safety. I never worried about the safety of my children while they were in school, even after Columbine. Their schools, in a relatively safe middle class neighborhood, were characterized by calm, order, and discipline. There were no metal detectors, school security officers, or other modern-day efforts to keep violence out. My kids walked to and from school without fear, and I did not fear for them.

Fear was a different story for my students, however. At both the Chicago elementary and high schools where I taught in the 1990s and 2000s, over 90 percent of the children lived in poverty. For many of them, going to school meant taking their lives in their hands. There were students who were afraid to stay after school for desperately needed extracurricular activities because they feared going home in the dark. They feared of crossing gang lines as they went to the bus stop. Sadly, there was a lot of fear inside the school as well. Students who were intimidating and aggressive, some staff members so intent on rule enforcement that they forgot they were working with children, a substantial amount of theft, the threat of gangs, and very few resources for students who were at risk were just some of the challenges our students had to deal with.

I often felt helpless in the face of such challenges. The only thing I felt I could do at the time was to be the very best teacher that I could possibly be and support my students academically and emotionally—in every possible way. Today I know that there is so much more that my colleagues and I could have—and should have—done to at least make the school a safer, better place for those great, deserving kids.

Since the Columbine shootings, and the more recent Sandy Hook shootings, suburban and rural families are experiencing the fear that many urban parents in struggling communities have felt for a long time. They are more fearful than ever before about the safety of their children in school and out, despite the fact that, for many kinds of school violence, rates have declined, as have our overall violence rates.

This book is an effort to synthesize what has been learned about keeping schoolchildren safe in the years since Columbine changed everything. It synthesizes information I wish had known. It provides detailed overviews of the various types of school violence and an analysis of the research base on effective policies, approaches, and programs.

While not exhaustive, it is a comprehensive look at the types of school violence and hard lessons learned. This volume is for anyone, who, like me, is interested in ensuring that our schools are safe—or safer. It is for anyone searching for ways to address this issue to make judicious use of precious resources in determining and effectively implementing the best fit for their school.

It is also an effort to share state-of-the-art knowledge on school safety so that *all* children can see their school as the place they belong, the place they feel protected and loved. It is my small contribution to helping make every school a place that the wisest of parents would wish for their own children.

—Deborah Lynch

Fall, 2016

Introduction

School shootings. Intruder violence. Cyberbullying. Gang activity. These phrases strike fear in the heart of any parent and concerned school leader. In this uncertain and dangerous world of terror attacks inside and outside of schools, parents of school-aged children continue to be afraid for their children's safety. In a recent Gallup Poll (McCarthy, 2015), 29 percent of U.S. parents say that they fear for their child's safety at school. This number spiked after the Columbine high-school shootings and has averaged 29 percent ever since, as seen in figure 0.1.

The U.S. students themselves have reported that violence and school safety are the biggest problems facing their schools (figure 0.2).

Gallup also reports that these fears are not without reason, as, for example, the number of school killings in the United States between 2000 and 2010 was one less than the number in dozens of other countries combined. Yet, according to the National Center for Education Statistics, school violence reached a peak in 1993 and has been declining. Not everyone agrees. If parent and student perceptions are any indication, there is still so much more to be done.

While school shootings are especially tragic, statistics indicate that few children are killed at school. They are much more likely to be victims of other types of violence, which have very serious and detrimental effects: physical violence, sexual violence, relationship violence, bullying, and cyber violence. Exposure to such violence has a tremendous impact on the emotional health and well-being of students. It is known to cause depression, anxiety, and fear—even post-traumatic stress—with long-lasting and damaging effects. It also has a negative impact on learning and the entire school climate.

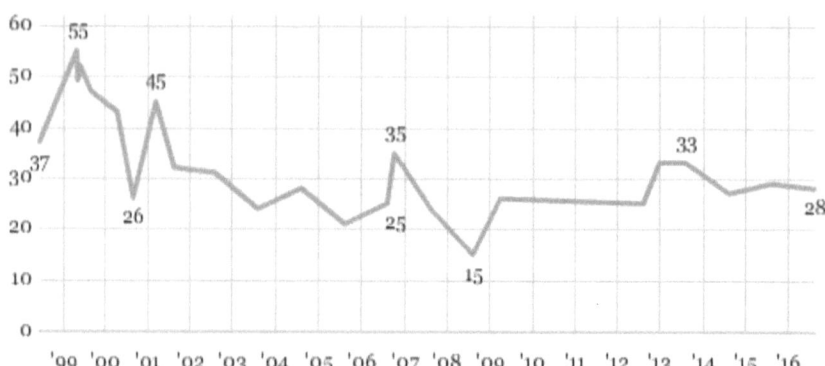

Figure 0.1 U.S. Parents' Concerns for Their Child's Safety at School. The line indicates the percentage of parents who said that they feared for their child's physical safety at school. Based on parents of K–12 children. Note: 1977 result of 24% not shown. *Source*: Copyright 2016 Gallup, Inc. All rights reserved. The content is used with permission; however, Gallup retains all rights of republication.

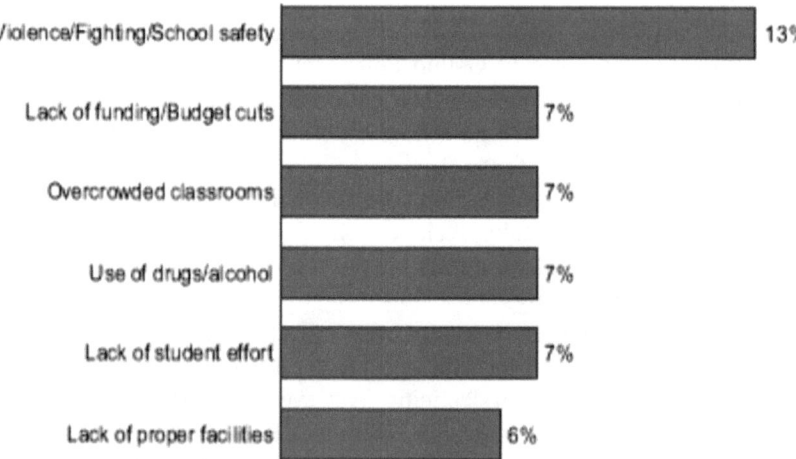

Figure 0.2 U.S. Students, Aged 13–17, Give Their Perceptions of Schools' Biggest Problem (Gallup Youth Survey, 2005). *Source*: Lyons, Linda (2005). Copyright 2016 Gallup, Inc. All rights reserved. The content is used with permission; however, Gallup retains all rights of republication.

Here are other key findings from recent *Indicators of School Crime and Safety* and Centers for Disease Control and Prevention (CDC) *Youth Behavior Risk Surveillance* reports:

- In 2010, 43 percent of public schools reported the presence of one or more security staff at least once per week, and 28 percent reported security staff routinely carrying guns
- In 2012, schools reported 689,000 crimes to police, or 15 per 1,000 students
- During the 2013–2014 school-year, 65 percent of public schools recorded that one or more incidents of violence had taken place, an estimated 757,000 crimes
- Roughly 8 percent of boys brought a weapon to school in 2013 (the same number who were threatened or injured with a weapon at school), with blacks and Hispanics more likely to be threatened or injured
- In 2015, students aged 12 to 18 were victims of 850,000 nonfatal crimes including 363,700 thefts and 486,400 violent victimizations
- Forty-six percent of U.S. schools reported twenty or more violent acts annually
- Urban schools have higher incidence of teen violence, with 23 percent of students reporting gang problems in their schools
- Ten percent of urban teachers report being threatened with injury by students
- Middle schools have the highest rates of bullying and sexual harassment, with almost one-third of students reporting being victims of school bullying.

In the past, school violence meant a fight on the playground, with fisticuffs and black eyes and detention as a consequence. Today it involves assault rifles and, too often, death as a consequence. What is happening? Why is it happening? And how can schools, working together with parents and the community, effectively respond—even prevent—such occurrences in today's schools? Doing so requires understanding the types of violence and exploring the causes, contexts, and correlates of the problems.

This book seeks to answer those three questions by taking an in-depth look at the many different types of school violence, using case studies of each type, to identify lessons learned from what happened, how it happened, and why. Each type of school violence addressed here has its own set of considerations and prevention approaches, which will be explained in detail in each chapter. Implications for education professionals, parents and community members, law enforcement, and the medical and mental health communities will be addressed, as well as the legal implications and ramifications.

So much more is now known about how to prevent the various types of school violence identified here. The CDC states emphatically that school violence *can* be prevented, that prevention efforts *can* reduce violence and improve the overall school environment.

The systematic use of research-based prevention strategies can reduce risk factors and promote protective factors. Such approaches include surveillance, deterrence, instructional programs, threat assessment, counseling, mediation, and much, much more, depending on the unique needs of each school.

This work presents a detailed discussion of each of these types of school violence: its descriptions and prevalence, causes and correlates, context and impact. Each chapter details the many perspectives on each one: those of education professionals, parents and community members, law enforcement, and the medical and mental health communities. What each constituency can do to address each type of violence is presented, along with a detailed analysis and critique of the evidence-based models, approaches, and programs designed for preventing, responding to, and recovering from them.

We can make schools safer. The CDC even says that we can prevent school violence. Our children are counting on us to get this right. Their very lives depend on it.

REFERENCES

Lyons, L. (2005). *Teens say safety issues top problem at school*. Gallup Poll. Retrieved from http://www.gallup.com/poll/20173/teens-say-safety-issues-top-problem-school.aspx

McCarthy, J. (2015). *Three in 10 U.S. parents worry about child's safety at school*. Gallup Poll. Retrieved from http://www.gallup.com/poll/184853/three-parents-worry-child-safety-school.aspx

Chapter One

School Shootings by Students

Eric Harris and Dylan Klebold did not plan a school shooting. Their original plan was to blow up 600 of their friends and others. Their carefully laid plan to do that, cold-bloodedly dubbed NBK for Natural Born Killers, in the works for over a year, failed. Instead, they shot up the school, which resulted in thirteen deaths that day (twelve students and one teacher).

It happened in Littleton, Colorado, in unincorporated Jefferson County. It was April 20, 1999, though they originally planned it for the April 19 anniversary of the Oklahoma City bombing to outdo that catastrophe. The killers, Harris (described later as a cold, calculating, homicidal psychopath) and Klebold (described later as hotheaded, depressive, and suicidal), were originally thought to be goths, loners, and victims of bullying. After their original plan failed, they went on their shooting spree, exchanging gunfire with police, and then committed suicide in the school library. This one tragic event changed the way schools and school safety have been viewed ever since.

OVERVIEW AND RECENT HISTORY

School shootings are very rare, contrary to popular opinion and the often overwhelming media focus. Fewer than 1 percent of homicides of school-age children happen at school. According to the 2013 National Crime Victimization Survey, the chance of a student dying in a car accident is 575 times greater than being killed at school. Only about one in two million children who die, die by homicide or suicide at school each year. This compares to victimization rates of thirty-three thefts and twenty-two violent crimes per one thousand students.

While these statistics illustrate that other kinds of problems in American schools are far more common than school shootings, the high-profile shootings that have occurred in schools over the past twenty years have resulted in increased fear among students, parents, and educators. The impact of the media coverage of high-profile tragedies remains, as seen in the large percentage of American parents who remain concerned about their children's safety at school. Due to this fear, it is estimated that $4.9 billion will be spent on school security by 2017, compared to $2.7 billion in 2012.

School fatalities were on the rise in the late 1980s. They peaked in the 1990s. By then there was an alarming rise in school shootings in rural and suburban schools where they were once considered just a problem in urban schools with gangs. This came after a particularly deadly increase in youth crime in general. It, too, had risen in the 1980s. Juvenile homicide more than doubled. It peaked in the early 1990s and reversed by the end of the decade. Many believe that this increase was because of the proliferation of crack cocaine, gangs and guns.

News media accounts tended to concentrate on the apparent spate of school shootings occurring during the late 1990s and early 2000s. The often 24/7 coverage of these incidents contributed to the general impression that school shootings were an alarming and increasing social problem. During this time, Princeton University professor John DiIulio described the rise of a new breed of offenders, the super-predator. The super-predator was described as a youth who had no respect for human life and no sense of the future.

This term, although now discredited, spread rapidly and resulted in much legislation focused on prosecuting more juveniles as adults and incarcerating them for longer periods. These changes had no effect on juvenile crime, however, and treating youth as adults and extending the punishments turned out to be no deterrent. According to Cornell (2006), youths were *more* likely to commit future crimes than their peers as they solidified their identities as criminals.

In 1994, Congress passed the Gun Free and Drug Free Schools Act. This required schools to expel for one year students in possession of firearms at schools. It allowed modification on a case-by-case basis, but this was not always the case. Cornell describes a *Harvard* (2000) report on zero tolerance, which concluded that it permeated our schools and employed a brutally strict disciplinary approach that embraced harsh punishment over education. By 1997, fully 80 percent of schools had zero tolerance policies on the books, yet as an example of the policy gone haywire, only 5 percent of students expelled under these policies possessed a weapon.

As a result of the Columbine tragedy, zero tolerance policies became almost universal. Two decades of research now conclude that those policies were not only extreme, but ineffectual as well. During the heyday of zero tolerance, 43 percent of students who were suspended were punished for insubordination, indicating how much schools went overboard with these policies. These policies have also had a proven, disproportionate, and negative impact on disadvantaged minority students.

There are documented cases where even kindergartners were being expelled for bringing little plastic toy figures holding guns. In fact, both the American Academy of Pediatrics (AAP) and the American Psychological Association (APA) have issued statements effectively condemning zero tolerance policies, given their harmful effects. They have instead called for students to be disciplined on a case-by-case basis and in a developmentally appropriate manner.

RESEARCH ON SCHOOL SHOOTERS

This section reviews three key studies done on school shootings and lessons learned: (1) the Newman (2004) study of rampage shootings; (2) Langman's (2009a) study of ten school shooters; and (3) the 2002 Department of Education (DOE)/U.S. Secret Service Safe School Initiative analysis of thirty-seven incidents with its recommendations.

Newman (2004) Study of Rampage Shootings

One highly publicized type of school shooting is the rampage shooting. One of the major characteristics of rampage shootings, according to Newman (2004), is that the target is generally symbolic in nature. What matters in those instances is not exacting revenge on particular people, but making a statement with violence: it may not matter who the ultimate victims are. School rampage shootings are thought to be distinct from other forms of violence because of the relatively safe rural setting in which most of these events have occurred and the lack of specified individual target.

Rampage shootings are among those that have attracted the most public attention. These are expressive, nontargeted attacks on a school institution. An institutional attack takes place on a public stage before an audience and is committed by a member or former member of the institution. It involves multiple victims, some chosen for their symbolic significance or at random. This final condition signifies that it is the organization, not the individuals, that is important, say these researchers.

Newman interviewed more than 150 individuals impacted by two different school shootings. They developed a comprehensive, multipronged theory of school shootings. Their theory consists of individual-level and school-level factors. In particular, they present four necessary but not sufficient factors that combine to produce school shootings:

- The individual views himself/herself as a social outcast
- The individual has a psychosocial problem, but not necessarily mental illness
- Cultural scripts that support violence as problem solving must be available
- The school must have poor surveillance systems to prevent potential shooters and guns must be easily accessible.

Their analysis emphasized the rage that fills school shooters and the fact that it is harbored by many young people today, especially boys who, they say, are on the losing end of what they call "the fierce competing adolescent for respect and masculine identity."

This study concluded that there are no policy solutions that reduce the risk of a school shooting to zero, but that the following issues need to be addressed to reduce the risk:

- The fragmentation of documentation within schools (e.g., in the discipline office, the social worker's desk, the teacher's file), which leave no one with the whole picture of threat or danger
- Team teaching, which has the potential to enhance and deepen teacher-student relationships, enabling better identification of problems
- Parent-teacher relationships that address both behavior and academics, to support parents in supporting their children
- Mental health staff and not metal detectors, as identification and prevention and treatment are more effective than punitive measures
- The presence of school security officers who can build positive relationships with students and can be sources of information on prevention and behavior management
- Making sure every student is connected to at least one adult in the building, as such trusting and caring relationships can be protective buffers for students
- Rewarding more than just sports participation and providing a range of activities so that all students have a place in the school and a way to bond with others and feel a sense of belonging.

Langman's (2009a) Study of School Shooters

Based on his work as a psychologist and his study of ten school shooters, Langman developed a typology of the school shooter. He found that school shooters were either psychopathic, psychotic, or traumatized:

Psychopathic—Langman describes Eric Harris as having the characteristics of this profile. He was cold, calculating, and manipulative. Though he was good looking, intelligent, and had friends, he felt superior to everyone. He was sadistic and narcissistic. He felt entitled and full of rage. He preyed upon his partner Klebold's weaknesses to fuel his rage and execute his plan. Here is an example of his writings and thought processes:

> WWII, Viet Nam, Duke and Doom all mixed up together ... a revolution to fuck up things as much as we can ... I want to leave a lasting impression on the world ... if there is any way in this fucked up universe we can come back as ghosts ... we will haunt the life out of anyone who blames anyone besides me and V (Dylan's nickname was Vodka) ... we will move to some island somewhere and if there isn't such a place, we will hijack a hell of a lot of bombs and crash a plane into NYC with us inside firing away as we go down ... just something to cause more devastation.
>
> —Eric Harris's journal entries (n.d.)

Psychotic—Dylan Klebold, on the other hand, was depressed, paranoid, and suicidal. Though he too had friends, he described a tremendous amount of rejection and anger in his journals. He is thought to have had some schizophrenic traits (e.g., disorganized thinking patterns). He had an extremely poor self-image, and was described as the follower to Harris' lead. Here are some of his thoughts:

> Farther and farther distant ... that's what's happening ... me & everything that zombies consider dear ... just images, not life. Soon I will be at peace I hope ... I've always had a thing for the past—how it reacts to the present & the future—or rather vice versa. I wonder how/when I got so fucked up ... Sadness seems infinite, & the shell of happiness shines around. Yet the true despair overcomes it in this lifetime ... The pain multiplies infinitely never stops. Yet I'm here, STILL alone, still in pain.
>
> —Dylan Klebold's journal entries (n.d.)

Langman says that the psychotics he studied realized that they were misfits. They struggled socially and felt isolated. Dylan Klebold had fallen desperately in love, for example, but felt he could never achieve intimacy. Langman says they raged against the cruelty of their fates, of being born impaired, and believed they could never be like other people.

Traumatized—In March 2005, Jeffrey Wiese went on a rampage shooting in Bemidji, Minnesota. He acted alone, though he had discussed the plan with his best friend and cousin. He entered his school and killed five students, a teacher, and a security guard, then shot himself. Jeffrey had been verbally and physically abused by an alcoholic mother and many of her boyfriends. His father had committed suicide during a standoff with police. His mother suffered an auto accident and brain damage, which left her in a nursing home. He was then in and out of the foster care system and had previously made several suicide attempts. He had no indication of either psychosis or psychopathy.

> My mother would hit me with anything she could get her hands on ... would tell me I was a mistake, and she would say so many things that it's hard to deal with them or think of them without crying ... I have friends, but I'm basically a loner inside a group of loners ... I'm excluded from anything and everything they do. I'm never invited. I don't even know why they consider me a friend or I them ... right about now I feel as low as I ever have ... I'm starting to regret sticking around. I should've taken the razor blade express last time around. Well, whatever, man.
>
> —Jeffrey Wiese's journal entries (2005)

Trauma's consequences, Langman says, include anxiety, depression, hostility, shame, despair, and hopelessness. These are features of post-traumatic stress disorder (PTSD). People who are traumatized often have a reduced capacity for feeling emotions and often feel isolated from others. They may feel constantly threatened and have mild symptoms of paranoia and hypervigilance. They often become self-destructive through substance abuse, self-mutilation, or social suicidal urges. And sometimes, as in this case, they become violent.

Physical and sexual abuse, often the causes of childhood trauma, can have devastating consequences, including anxiety, rage, depression, and suicide. Trauma affects one's identities and relationships. Due to the trauma, these children may have a sense of being damaged and have trouble relating to others. Their ability to trust people is affected, as is their ability to feel love and connected to others. Their worlds were unpredictable.

Parental alcoholism and bad tempers meant that the traumatized boys Langman studied never knew what each day would bring. They moved from one family member to another and back again or from one foster home to another. Stability was unknown. Some endured cruel, degrading sexual abuse. They lost parents to separation, jail, and death. They were depressed to the point of contemplating suicide. Life was overwhelming. Life was unfair and the world was cruel and people could not be trusted. On top of it all, they were angry. Angry at life. Angry for living in hell. Despite all these they were not crazy or evil, just wounded, he says. They were so badly wounded, that they sought a way to end their misery.

Langman says that the factors that contribute to school shootings are a complex mix of genetics, family, environment, personality traits, psychiatric symptoms, and peer relationships. More than three-fourths of the shooters he studied had difficulty coping with a major change or loss of status prior to the event. More than half had a history of feeling extreme depression and nearly 75 percent threatened or tried to commit suicide.

Langman found that nine of the ten shooters suffered from deep depression and suicidal thoughts. He says it is that combination of suicidal and homicidal thoughts, which is particularly dangerous—and hard to prevent—if the killers do not care what happens to them. The correlates he found between shooting and violence and psychotics included being male, substance abuse, lack of compliance, and taking medication.

Langman describes what all ten school shooters he studied had in common:

1. Lack of empathy: due to reasons such as anger, feelings of victimization, desperate insecurity, hallucinations, emotional impairment, or trauma, which leads one to not feel anything, just numbness
2. Existential rage
3. Existential anguish—social deficits, psychotic symptoms, history of suicidal thoughts
4. Extreme reactivity—overreaction to normal peer activities due to emotional instability and vulnerable identities: psychopaths had fragile narcissism; psychotics had poor social skills and paranoia; traumatics had hypervigilance, PTSD, and emotional instability. All had depression and self-loathing and were carrying a storehouse of resentment built up over years. They had chronic bitter exaggeration and distorted memories of past suffering
5. Shame, anger, and failure of manhood—they had fragile male identities; like Newman, Langman found that this was a powerful factor among school shooters
6. Fantasizing makes the task become easier to execute and turn off one's feelings. (Langman, 2009b, p. 11)

U.S.–DOE–Secret Service (2002) Study

The study by the DOE and the Secret Service (2002) identified thirty-seven incidents of targeted school-based attacks, committed by forty-one individuals over a twenty-five-year period. It defined school shooting as the intentional killing of at least three victims in a single incident by those under nineteen years old. The report concluded, as did Newman, that shootings at school seemed to be a general kind of revenge against an undifferentiated target. It also found that before they occurred, the shooters had told someone about their plan and that they displayed some behavior that caused others to be concerned about them. And in fully three-fourths of the cases, other students knew about the plan.

This study found that bullying played a key role in more than two-thirds of the cases. Some attackers received intense bullying over a long time. The report also found that potential school shooters at the K–12 level nearly always telegraphed their intentions. This is a tendency that federal law enforcement experts call "leakage." Prior to most of the shootings studied, the shooter told someone about the plan. Almost every shooter engaged in some type of behavior that caused others to be concerned.

Also, more than three-fourths had difficulty coping with a major change or loss of status prior to the event. More than one-half had a history of feeling extreme depression. Nearly 75 percent threatened or tried suicide. The shootings at school were chosen for a particular purpose and not related to gangs or drugs. All were committed by boys, two-thirds had one or more persons killed, firearms were the primary weapon, and they were planned.

Though the report concluded that there is no accurate or usual profile, it did have some key findings:

1. There is no accurate or useful profile of students who have engaged in targeted school violence
2. Incidents of targeted violence at school are rarely sudden, impulsive acts
3. Prior to most incidents, other people know about the attackers' idea and/or the plan to attack
4. Most attackers did not threaten their targets directly before advancing the attack
5. Most attackers engaged in some behavior prior to the incident that caused others' concern or indicated a need for help
6. Most attackers had difficulty coping with significant loss or personal failures and many had considered or attempted suicide
7. Many attackers felt bullied, persecuted, or injured by others prior to the attack
8. Most attackers had access to and had used weapons prior to the attack
9. In many cases, other students were involved in some capacity
10. Despite prompt law enforcement responses, most shooting incidents were stopped by means other than law enforcement intervention. (p. 10)

Other researchers have drawn similar conclusions to the above studies. Blame is identified frequently as a factor. The individual perceives that others are to blame for his personal problems—the mass killer sees himself not as the perpetrator, but as the victim.

Cullen, author of *Columbine* (2009), notes that the two biggest myths about school shooters are that they were loners and that they snapped. A staggering 93 percent plan their attacks in advance, he notes, citing the Federal Bureau of Investigation's (FBI) finding that the path toward violence is an evolutionary one with signposts along the way. And, finally, most perpetrators shared a critical experience: 98 percent had suffered a loss or failure that they perceived as serious and the trauma seemed to have set anger in motion.

Since Columbine, school officials and communities understand that there is a real obligation on the part of schools to take additional measures and provide more training on how to guard against bad things happening in schools. Staff needs to be trained to recognize students with signs and symptoms of psychological problems, to work more closely with local law enforcement, and, once identified, help these students and their families secure the necessary counseling services.

MULTITIERED APPROACHES

As we will see through this book, no matter what type of school-related violence is under consideration, experts recommend a public health approach using a three-tiered model. This public health model includes three overlapping tiers that collectively represent a continuum of interventions that increase in intensity to meet individual student needs (Sugai, 2007).

The first tier is referred to as the universal or primary level because all individuals in a given population (e.g., school, classroom) are recipients of interventions designed to prevent particular emotional, behavioral, or academic problems. The second tier, referred to as the selected or secondary level, is composed of more intensive interventions for those students who do not adequately respond to universal interventions. The third tier, referred to as the indicated or tertiary level, is characterized by highly individualized and specialized interventions for those students who do not adequately respond to universal and selected levels of prevention and intervention.

Tier 1, or primary prevention, strategies focus on the approximately 80 percent of students who do not have serious problems in a given area. Tier 2 or secondary interventions target the 5 to 15 percent who are at risk for the particular behavior in question. And finally, Tier 3 or tertiary interventions address the 1 to 5 percent of the student population who demonstrate intense problems in the area of focus.

Universal prevention programs are aimed at reducing risks and strengthening skills for all students in the school. Through universal programs all members of the target population are exposed to the intervention. Universal prevention approaches include a set of activities that may offer benefits to all. Examples include social emotional lessons that are used in the classroom and taught by teachers or counselors. These might include strategies for responding to reporting bullying, or classroom meetings among students and teachers to discuss emotionally relevant issues related to violence or conflict resolution.

Tier 2 or secondary interventions are of greater intensity as compared to the universal or selective levels of intervention. Indicated interventions incorporate more intensive supports and activities for those who are already displaying certain behaviors or who are showing early signs of behavioral, academic, or mental health consequences.

Tier 3 or tertiary interventions can include individual counseling, cognitive behavioral intervention programs, cognitive behavior intervention for traumatized students, family therapy, wraparound case management, and multisystemic therapies.

Primary/Universal Approaches for All Students

Violence Prevention and Emergency Planning

The Columbine High School shootings heightened attention to the need for schools—and law enforcement—to be better prepared to respond to armed assailant situations. Subsequently, schools focused primarily on lockdown practices, while law enforcement focused on improving tactics to find and stop the assailant as quickly as possible. It has been found that school administrators and teachers cannot easily distinguish high-risk youth from students with low risk. School shooters are not distinguishable from many of their peers and this results in two types of errors: mistaken classification of students and waste of resources.

Many school-wide violence prevention programs have been found to be effective and often high-risk students benefit the most. Each subsequent chapter will highlight a detailed example of a research-based and proven school-wide violence prevention program addressing the nine types of school violence covered.

When it comes to school shootings and intruder violence, the U.S. DOE recommends expanding the lockdown-only approach commonly used by schools (i.e., confining students and staff to their rooms). Its 2013 guidance recommends expanding that to an options-based lockdown approach that allows school staff to make more independent decisions about how to protect their students depending on evolving circumstances (e.g., evacuate the building rather than stay locked in a classroom). These recommended approaches include adapting the "Run, Hide, Fight" model that was originally developed for adults in response to workplace violence as part of a school-wide Emergency Operations Plan.

Threat Assessment

In 2002, the Secret Service and DOE recommended that schools train threat assessment teams. The best defense is early detection; thus, they strongly recommend the creation of threat assessment procedures. There are different kinds of threats: low, moderate, and high. Chapter 4 goes into greater detail on threat assessment and on preventing and responding to an active shooter situation.

According to the FBI, the more detailed the plan, the greater the risk. Threat assessment focus on students who pose a real threat: those making plans, drawing diagrams, leaking word of the plan, obtaining a weapon, and engaging in target practice. Schools need early detection systems: for example, training students to recognize warning signs, and teaching the difference between snitching and reporting. One is tattling and one is keeping people safe. Reporting a friend may be difficult, the report notes, but it may save a life. It is important to have multiple methods for students to report their concerns as well as educating the staff.

Warning Signs

Cullen asks, what should adults look for? Confessions. More than 80 percent of school shooters had confided their intentions. More than half told at least two people. While most threats are idle, the key is specificity, he advises. Vague implied and implausible threats are low risk. The danger is heightened when threats are direct and specific, identifiable, and indicate plans to carry them out. The FBI compiled a specific list of warning signs, including symptoms of both psychopathy and depression: manipulation, intolerance, superiority, narcissism, alienation, rigidity, lethargy, dehumanization of others, and externalizing blame (O'Toole, 1999).

Surveillance

Unlike most killers, school shooters are not concerned with hiding their identities so the security camera does not stop an attack. For example, there were cameras at Columbine and Red Lake. And metal detectors at Red Lake. The shooters simply shot at police and security guards and walked right in. They did not care what happened to themselves. A trained and prepared staff is vital, as is a school culture that promotes trust, respect, and safety.

School Culture and Climate

It is vital that all involved take safety seriously, including student's and staff's physical and emotional safety, advises the FBI. Maintaining a positive school environment with initiatives such as peer assistance programs, helping parents, mediation programs, teaching conflict resolution skills, stress management, and enhancing positive peer relationships can help create a culture and climate where all feel connected, respected, supported, and safe.

Cultures steeped in harsh discipline and zero tolerance are not effective at reducing violence. The main problem with punishment is that it does not prevent school shootings. Troubled students need attention and support, not punishment, expulsion, and rejection. As we have seen, when students commit school shootings, they typically do so at their own schools to make a statement.

Secondary and Tertiary Approaches

As we saw, nine out of ten shooters studied by Langman suffered from deep depression and suicidal thoughts. He notes that classic psychopaths are said to be untreatable. They like who they are and see no reason to change. The psychopathic school shooters and potential shooters are not necessarily like this, he asserts. Their narcissism is an attempt to compensate for their inadequacy. Their rage is a response to their social and personal frustration. There are, he believes, opportunities for intervention.

Depression can be treated. Self-esteem can be improved. Social skills can be developed. Empathy can be learned. A child who presents as a potential psychopathic school shooter is not a lost cause. Langman also says that traumatized kids who are potential school shooters can be treated. They need to process the impact of their traumas on their identities, their relationships, and their attitudes toward life. They need to develop healthy coping skills that allow them to deal with stress without becoming dangerous.

Potential psychotic shooters need to have their psychotic symptoms treated with medication and individual therapy. They also need help with their depression, their emotional isolation, their poor self-esteem, and their social deficits.

Langman posits that many school shooters were driven by a sense of desperate hopelessness. In treating potential shooters, a primary task is to develop hope for the future. If they can see a way out of their crisis besides homicide and/or suicide, then they are less likely to become violent.

Depression is a pervasive problem, affecting as many as 8 percent of adolescents. Paranoia, alienation, and acute social anxiety are hallmarks of emerging mental illness. Any events that cause stress, humiliation, frustration, depression, or rage can add fuel to the fires that are already burning inside. By creating positive peer cultures, reducing student conflict and harassment, and taking steps to improve the social connectedness of students, schools can be proactive in preventing school shootings, he advises.

LAW ENFORCEMENT APPROACHES

Columbine not only instilled fear in the heart of every parent and school administrator in the country, it also changed everything with regard to the way that schools address such violence. Caldwell (2012) describes Columbine as the giant wake-up call. All police training for these events has changed.

In 2003, the Department of Homeland Security released the active shooter protocol. It says that if the shooter seems active, law enforcement are supposed to storm the building. They are supposed to move toward the sound of gunfire and even disregard victims. There is one objective: neutralize the shooters.

Caldwell states that prior to Columbine, the plan was to surround and negotiate. Officers used to surround the school, contain it for a good perimeter, and then try and negotiate with the intruder and talk him out. If that did not work, police waited until SWAT went in. That is what happened at Columbine and because of it, the thinking has now changed.

Now, says Caldwell, there are active shooter programs where a team goes into the school with the sole purpose of stopping the offender. They strive to locate the person and pin him down so that he cannot harm more victims. It is a whole new tactical training that is now taught in every police department. Even if there is only one officer on the scene, that officer is now trained to go in and search for the suspect.

Officers face a second decision point when they reach the shooters. If the shooters hold up in a classroom, holding kids, but not firing, responders may need to stop there and use traditional hostage techniques. Storming the classroom could provoke the gunmen. But if the shooter is firing, even just periodically, officers are told to move in.

As will be detailed in chapter 3, collaboration and cooperation between schools and law enforcement are essential from the planning stage of a school emergency plan to any necessary execution of an emergency plan.

PARENTS AND COMMUNITY APPROACHES

We know there is a gap between the youth culture and the adult culture. As we shall see throughout this book, students do not go to teachers or parents with concerns about violence. Either they do not take threats seriously or they do not know what to do about them. Building more trusting relationships with young people is one way to improve threat assessment measures.

There is also the pervasive presence of guns, the lack of difficulty in obtaining them, as well as the glorification of guns and violence in television, movies, video games, and other media. According to a 2000 joint statement of the American Medical Association, APA, the AAP, and the American Academy of Child and Adolescent Psychiatry, more than one thousand studies—including reports from the Surgeon General's office, the National Institute of Mental Health, and numerous studies conducted by public health organizations—point overwhelmingly to a causal connection between media violence and aggressive behavior in some children.

Their conclusion, based on more than thirty years of research, is that viewing entertainment violence can lead to increases in aggressive attitudes, values, and behavior, particularly in children. Its effects are measurable and long-lasting. Prolonged viewing of media violence can lead to emotional desensitization toward violence in real life. These include the following:

- Children who see a lot of violence are more likely to view violence as an effective way of settling conflicts
- Children exposed to violence are more likely to assume that acts of violence are acceptable behavior
- Viewing violence can lead to emotional desensitization toward violence in real life and can decrease the likelihood that one will take action on behalf of a victim when violence occurs
- Entertainment violence feeds a perception that the world is a violent and mean place
- Viewing violence increases fear of becoming a victim of violence, with a resultant increase in self-protective behaviors and a mistrust of others
- Viewing violence may lead to real-life violence. Children exposed to violent programming at a young age have a higher tendency for violent and aggressive behavior later in life than children who are not so exposed.

The most immediate step parents can take to reduce the effects of entertainment violence is to limit their children's exposure to it. Media coverage of violent events is believed to motivate copycats.

Millions of students are unsupervised after school. Community-based programs are ways to build bridges with youth. Mentoring can make a difference: a student with a mentor is more likely to graduate from high school and less likely to hurt someone. Supervised recreation programs, parent education, boys and girls clubs, and big brother/big sister programs all provide the opportunity for students to connect to and be connected with caring and supportive adults. If those adults are also knowledgeable and informed about warning signs, they can potentially save lives.

PROMISING PROGRAM: STRAIGHT TALK ABOUT RISKS

The Center to Prevent Handgun Violence in Washington, D.C., developed the Straight Talk about Risks (STAR) curriculum in response to the escalating number of gun-related deaths of children and teens. STAR is a prekindergarten through grade-12 curriculum that educates students about the risks of handling guns. It teaches them to recognize situations that may lead to gun-related injuries, identify trusted adults, make safe choices, combat negative peer pressure, and resolve conflicts nonviolently.

According to the U.S. Office of Juvenile Justice and Delinquency Prevention website, the activities presented in the STAR curriculum include (1) learning and practicing gun safety skills that can be used outside the classroom; (2) self-reflection and role-playing using typical coping mechanisms for anger and fear; (3) setting personal and societal goals for change; and (4) developing competency and leadership skills to address gun safety issues with peers and the community. The STAR program teaches younger children how to behave safely when a gun is encountered, how to resist peer pressure to play with or carry guns, and how to distinguish real-life violence from television violence.

For older children, the program offers activities that teach coping skills, decision-making skills, refusal skills for resisting peer pressure, and conflict management skills. In addition, STAR provides information to parents to ensure that guns and other weapons are not accessible to their children. Parents are encouraged to talk to their children about the dangers of guns and the consequences of gun violence. Currently, STAR is being used in more than ninety school districts nationwide as part of police-led crime prevention efforts and in conjunction with recreation and health education programs.

An independent research firm conducted an evaluation of STAR to examine STAR implementation and student outcomes. It included participant self-reports, direct observation, teacher interviews, and student group interviews. STAR was found to be developmentally and culturally sensitive, and the program has been well received and generally rated positively by younger students. STAR was found to be most effective for increasing gun safety knowledge, attitudes, and behavior of students in grades 3 to 5.

LESSONS LEARNED ABOUT SCHOOL SHOOTINGS

Rocque (2012) reminds us that school rampage shootings remain very rare occurrences. With such small numbers, it is difficult to determine whether the policies have had an impact on school shootings. Roque says that exaggerations about school violence distort our understanding of the problems, create a climate of fear, and lead to misguided policies. There are simply no policy solutions that reduce the risk of a school shooting to zero.

Things that do not work include zero tolerance, profiling, correctional boot camps, suspensions and expulsions, and scared straight programs. Things that do work include quality of school-based violence prevention programs, staff and resources to respond to student mental health needs, limiting student access to guns, avoiding sensational news coverage of school violence, and public health initiatives that provide parent education and early childhood education. Early childhood programs have delivered remarkable effectiveness, says the U.S. Department of Health and Human Services, decreasing crime and violence when children reach adulthood.

Though schools and communities must be prepared and plan for such tragedies with the hope that they never need to activate those plans, it is also important to be prepared for myriad other types of school violence, including intruder violence, which will be covered next. It is one thing when a student or students is the perpetrator. There are the warning signs and resources inside the school for referring troubled students and their families.

Intruder violence is a completely different situation. The perpetrator is completely unknown and unknowable. The intruder usually does share one similarity with the student school shooter, however: he (because usually it is a male) does not care what happens to him.

REFERENCES

Caldwell, M. (2012, December 12). Does your child's school teach "violent intruder defense strategies"? *Mother Jones*.

Cornell, D. (2006). *School violence: Fears versus facts*. Mahwah, NJ: Lawrence Erlbaum.

Cullen, D. (2009). *Columbine*. New York: Twelve Hatchett Book Group Publishers.

Harris, E. (Journal Entry, n.d.). Retrieved from http://www.acolumbinesite.com/eric/writing/journal/jindex.html

Joint Statement on the Impact of Entertainment Violence on Children. (2000, July 26). Retrieved from http://public.psych.iastate.edu/caa/VGVpolicyDocs/00AAP%20-20Joint%20Statement.pdf

Klebold, D. (Journal Entry, n.d.). Retrieved from http://crimeandcolumbine.tumblr.com/post/78973886035/quotes-and-excerpts-from-dylans-journal-i-was

Langman, P. (2009a). Rampage school shooters: A typology. *Aggression and Violent Behavior*, *14*(1), 79–86. doi:10.1016/j.avb.2008.10.003.

Langman, P. F. (2009b). *Why kids kill: Inside the minds of school shooters*. New York: Palgrave Macmillan.

Newman, K. S. (2004). *Rampage: The social roots of school shootings*. New York: Basic Books.

O'Toole, M. E. (2000). *The school shooter: A threat assessment perspective*. Quantico, VA: U.S. Department of Justice, Federal Bureau of Investigation.

Preventing School Shootings: A Summary of a U.S. Secret Service Safe School Initiative Report NIJ Journal no. 248, 2002.

Rocque, M. (2012). Exploring school rampage shootings: Research, theory, and policy. *Social Science Journal*, *49*(3), 304–313.

Straight Talk about Risks Program (STAR), Center to Prevent Handgun Violence, Washington, DC. Retrieved from http://www.ojjdp.gov/pubs/gun_violence/profile54.html

Sugai, G. (2007, December). Responsiveness-to-intervention: Lessons learned and to be learned. Keynote presentation at and paper for the RTI Summit, U.S. Department of Education, Washington, D.C.

Wiese, J. (Journal Entry, 2005). Retrieved from http://www.nytimes.com/2005/03/24/us/signs-of-danger-were-missed-in-a-troubled-teenagers-life.html?_r=0

Chapter Two

Intruder Violence

It was December 14, 2012. Twenty-year-old Adam Lanza, dressed in black fatigues and wearing a military vest, shot his way into an elementary school in Newtown, Connecticut, and killed twenty beautiful children, who were between the ages of six and seven years, and six staff members. He shot and killed his mother in their home before arriving at the school. He shot himself in the head as police approached him. No shots were ever fired by those officers.

The police arrived at the scene at about 9:45 a.m., which was about ten minutes after the first 911 call and evidently about fifteen minutes after the shooting had started.

Lanza at 112 pounds despite a height of 6 feet, was anorexic and malnourished. He was described as an isolated loner and had been diagnosed as a child with Asperger syndrome and obsessive-compulsive disorder. His father later stated that the family might have missed signs of undiagnosed schizophrenia due to mistakenly attributing his bizarre behavior and isolation to Asperger syndrome.

RECENT HISTORY ON INTRUDER VIOLENCE

Sadly, as of October 2015, there have been 186 shootings on school campuses in the United States since twenty children and six adults were killed at Sandy Hook Elementary school in Newtown, Connecticut, according to Everytown For Gun Safety, an advocacy organization. These numbers include incidents when a firearm was discharged inside a school building or on campus, as documented in news accounts, and includes situations that did not target students or teachers, like suicides, misfires, and other activity. According to the

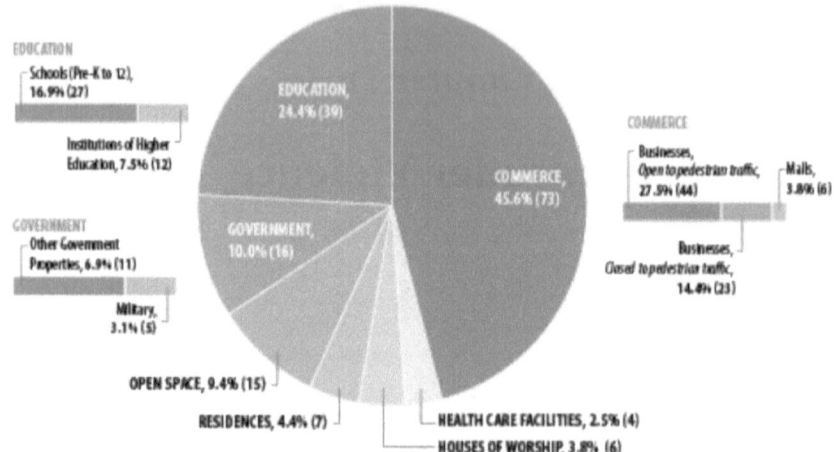

Figure 2.1 Active Shooter Incidents. A study of 160 active shooter incidents in the United States between 2000 and 2013, by location.

FBI (2014), schools are the second most likely target for active shooter incidents after the workplace (see figure 2.1).

It must be emphasized that such attacks on schools are extremely rare. Still, no school can afford to be unprepared for such an emergency. And it is not always about guns, though they tend to be the most lethal and result in the most injury and death. In the years since Columbine, and now Sandy Hook, many schools and communities have realized that it is crucial to prepare for such attacks. As previously stated, more and more resources have been spent on security measures: in 2012, $2.7 billion was spent on school security, and by 2018, $4.9 billion will be spent on a variety of security measures (figure 2.2).

When it comes to intruder violence, what do we mean? The FBI describes an armed assailant as an armed person who attempts to use deadly force on others, typically in a confined and populated area, as was the case in Newtown, Connecticut.

The fear from these incidents continues to resonate. According to a 2006 Harris poll, when asked about the likelihood of an intruder entering their child's school, two-thirds (65 percent) of youth and three-quarters (77 percent) of parents said it was "extremely" or "very" likely. Three-in-ten (29 percent) parents indicated that they were not satisfied that the school their child attends could prevent intruders from entering the school grounds. And just over half of the parents were unsure whether there was a policy to notify parents or caregivers that an intruder was identified on their child's school grounds.

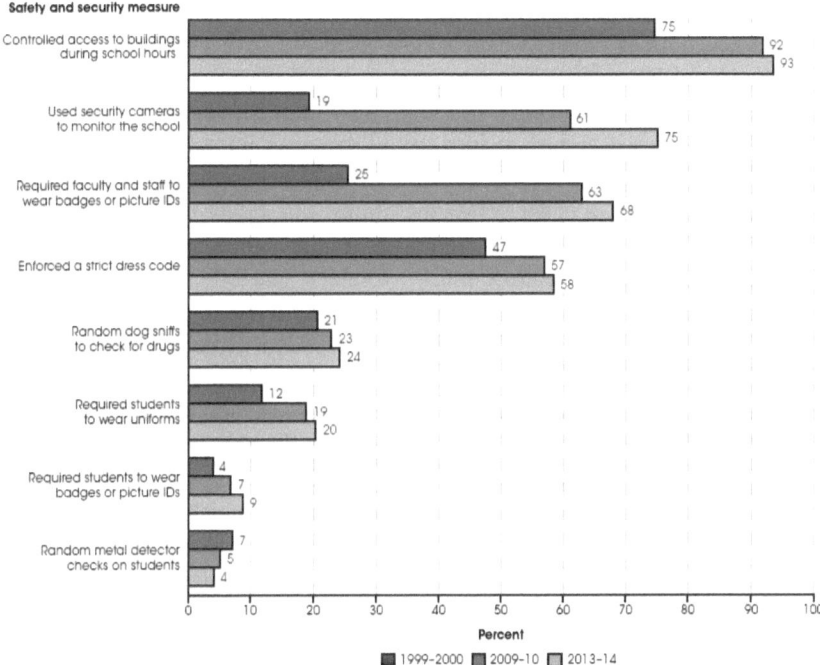

Figure 2.2 Percentage of Public Schools That Used Selected Safety and Security Measures: 1999–2000, 2009–2010, and 2013–2014. *Source*: Kena et al. (2016).

Given these findings, it is important not only for schools to develop comprehensive plans for that rare possibility of intruder violence, but it is also vitally important to make sure parents and community members are fully aware of what those plans are.

Most schools have security and surveillance designed to keep intruders out and to prevent weapons from coming into the schools. In 2011, 88.2 percent of surveyed schools had strict access control measures for buildings, up from 81.5 percent in 2003. The National Center for Education Statistics (NCES) found that in 1999, 19 percent of schools were using security cameras. By 2013, that number was 75 percent. Other approaches include controlled entry and identification systems, metal detectors, security personnel or volunteers who challenge intruders, or doors fitted with electromagnetic locks, police, and school resource officers.

Students reported in that 2006 Harris poll that their school had created rules about who is allowed to enter school grounds or buildings in an effort to prevent intruders from entering the school (64 percent), followed by ID cards for students and teachers (48 percent), surveillance cameras (42 percent), guards (32 percent), gates (21 percent), student hall monitors (21 percent), and metal detectors (5 percent). A greater percentage of students (those aged thirteen to eighteen) than tweens (those aged ten to twelve) reported their school's use of ID cards (63 percent versus 38 percent), surveillance cameras (51 percent versus 33 percent), and guards (44 percent versus 22 percent).

The goal when it comes to intruder violence is impeding the intruder's access and/or movement in the school to prevent access to staff and students and minimize injury. It is suggested that things like bullet-resistant doors and windows can slow down or prevent access to allow time for help to arrive.

What about metal detectors, many wonder? The effectiveness of metal detectors is highly contested, with studies producing conflicting findings. Some studies find them effective, others ineffective. Others have concluded that metal detectors actually *increase* problems in schools, while still others say that, though they may decrease violence, they also add to a culture of fear. Metal detectors would have made no difference in either the Columbine or Sandy Hook cases, as the offenders simply shot their way into the buildings.

One study of school superintendents in Georgia, which focused on their strategies for school security (Ballard & Brady, 2007), found that 97 percent of respondents reported the use of security cameras in their schools. While anecdotal evidence suggests that video cameras in schools have decreased the level of vandalism in particular, their effect on violence is unknown.

Studies of video cameras in schools have concluded that in schools without a history of violence, video surveillance can actually have a detrimental effect on both students' and teachers' perceptions of their personal safety (http://criminal-justice.iresearchnet.com/). Yet, there were cameras at Columbine and Sandy Hook, and it turned out that they were not enough, either.

Other technological responses to violence in schools include motion detectors, intruder alarm monitoring systems, two-way radios and walkie-talkies, lapel microphones, locked doors linked to the fire alarm system to restrict entry to and exit from buildings, and ID card machines (which register attendance, lateness, and discipline records).

THE NEED FOR COMPREHENSIVE PLANNING

So, comprehensive plans are a necessity today. Yet, how should schools develop such plans? Guidance to do so has come from a variety of sources. This chapter highlights findings and recommendations on preventing, responding to, and recovering from intruder violence from three valuable resources for school districts:

1. *Guide for Developing High Quality School Emergency Operation Plans* (2013) developed by the Departments of Education, Health and Human Services, Homeland Security, Justice, FBI, and Federal Emergency Management Agency (FEMA)

2. *Safe and Sound: A Sandy Hook Initiative*—From the Sandy Hook parents themselves who formed an organization and foundation, called the *Safe and Sound Schools*, and have developed publications to assist in the planning of such comprehensive plans
3. *Best Practice Considerations for Schools in Active Shooter and Other Armed Assailant Drills by* the National Association of School Psychologists (NASP) and the National Association of School Resource Officers (NASRO). These two organizations collaborated with input from Safe and Sound: A Sandy Hook Initiative and the ALICE Training Institute.

Guide for Developing High-Quality School Emergency Operations Plans

The *Guide for Developing High Quality School Emergency Operations Plans* (2013) is a joint publication of the U.S. DOE, Health and Human Services, Homeland Security, Justice, FEMA, and the FBI. This section includes a summary of their recommendations.

Preventing

While there is no profile of an active shooter, we now know that there may be warning signs or other indicators that school staff, students, parents, and community members should be trained to be aware of. The FBI behavioral analysis unit suggests that there are observable behaviors that, if recognized, could lead to the disruption of a planned attack. These behaviors include:

1. development of a personal grievance;
2. contextually inappropriate and recent acquisition of multiple weapons;
3. contextually inappropriate and recent escalation in target practice and weapons training;
4. contextually inappropriate and recent interests in explosives;
5. contextually inappropriate and intense interest and fascination with previous shootings or massive attacks;
6. experience of a significant real or perceived loss in the week and/or months leading up to an attack, such as a death, breakup, divorce, or loss of a job.

Planning

Schools should have emergency plans well developed relating to goals, objectives, and courses for action in case of emergency—things like how to evacuate, how to communicate in case of an emergency, and how staff and students will know when the emergency is over. This information should be shared with local first responders and police and fire personnel and kept up-to-date. Plans of the building and photos with information on access are important, as are strong partnerships with these professionals so that they know the systems in place in a building if they need to intervene. It is also recommended that there be practice drills and that schools should train staff, students, and families and also include emergency personnel during this training.

Threat Assessment

The guide states that one of the most useful tools a school can develop to identify, evaluate, and address such a situation is having a multidisciplinary school threat assessment team. Such a team should include school administrators, relevant employees, medical and mental health professionals, and law enforcement personnel.

It notes that it is extremely important to rely on factual information, including observed behavior, and that the team should avoid unfair labeling or stereotyping of students. Threat assessment has to be based on what someone has done, and not on what they look like. This team would review troubling or threatening behavior and complete a holistic assessment and management strategy.

The team, once it identifies an individual who may pose a threat, then identifies a course of action for addressing the situation. It is thought that recognizing preattack warning signs and indicators might help disrupt such an active shooter situation.

Responding

In the unlikely event of an active shooter situation, an emergency plan of action can be helpful regarding evacuations, safe alternative locations, and communication. Because each situation is different, there is no one blueprint.

The guide also notes that there are three basic options: to run, hide, or fight. If possible, individuals should run away from the shooter as quickly as possible to a designated safe place. If that is not possible, staff and students need to find a place of safety, which will prevent the shooter from access to them. It also recommends hiding where there are thick walls and few windows, locking the doors and barricading them with heavy furniture, turning off all lights and electronic devices, and remaining in place until given the all clear by officials.

A last resort is for adults to try to incapacitate the shooter by force. In one study of forty-one active shooter events (Blair & Schweit, 2014), researchers found that before law enforcement officers arrived, the potential victims stopped the attacker themselves in sixteen instances. In thirteen of those cases they physically subdued the attacker.

Afterward

After the incident, the school's emergency plan should indicate who will provide assistance to victims, family, and community members. The guide further recommends establishing an incident response team, including local first responders and other community partners trained to appropriately triage the situation and provide emergency intervention in victim services. This should begin immediately after the incident and run throughout the recovery.

It is also important to provide family members with timely, accurate, and relevant information as much as possible during and afterward the incident. This includes periodic updates, being prepared to explain what to expect, and addressing any communication barriers such as language or disability. Counselors should be available immediately to assist all persons involved. The plan should also include strategies for working with the media and protecting the privacy of those involved.

Safe and Sound Schools

The *Safe and Sound Schools* approach recommends a three-pronged approach to planning: (1) critically assessing the current situation in a school, and (2) acting to develop comprehensive approaches as a result of this analysis, and (3) auditing that plan, making adjustments as the audit suggests improvements. They say that school stakeholders should conduct a school-wide assessment and consider the following items as they relate to a specific school community:

Assess: Facilities

- Operations (school use and after-hours/nonschool use)
- Access (e.g., fencing, lighting, doors, windows, parking, perimeter security)
- Building systems (power, HVAC [heating, ventilation, and air conditioning], security equipment [alarms, cameras, mirrors, buzzers, etc.])
- Review of key control and accountability
- Emergency communications systems (phones, cell phones, radios, public address systems, reverse 911, backup power)
- Evacuation locations
- Reunification locations.

Assess: Policies and Practices

- Emergency response manual
- Emergency response procedures (weather, environmental, fire, bomb, insider and intruder threat, bus and site evacuations, reunification, etc.)

- Security and safety policies and protocols (threat assessment management and crime and violence prevention)
- Involvement and consideration of the community in planning and practice
- Definitive assignment of responsible person(s) to actively update plans/policies.

Assess: Security Awareness and Training

- Emergency drills, exercises, education, and training
- School/district interaction and relationships with police, fire department, and emergency medical service (EMS)
- Support staff roles in security and planning (food services, transportation, physical and mental health, etc.)
- Personnel and internal security (e.g., fingerprinting, background checks, badge systems, and visitor management).

They strongly recommend the posting and teaching of safety alerts to all school community members and visitors, which gives everyone a sense of empowerment and preparation in the event of an emergency. Each alert scenario requires practice and direct instruction to ensure familiarity and increase success.

According to the *Safe and Sound Schools* program, the following are common safety oversights that need to be considered by schools:

Building Access: Most schools are not designed to limit access.
Poor Planning: Many schools are unprepared for a variety of emergencies.
Inadequate Practice: Only with practice can success be achieved.
Faulty Equipment: Doors that do not lock, disabled cameras, inactive intercoms.
Complacency: Unworn IDs, unmonitored visitor check-ins, propped doors, poor key control.
Little or No After-Hours Security: Access control is a twenty-four-hour-a-day priority.
Lack of Community: The entire school community (e.g., students, staff, volunteers, local and state PD, FD, EMS, etc.) must be involved in school security.
A Checklist Mentality: School security is not accomplished by checklist alone.
No Safety "Go-To": No designated personnel to address ongoing and evolving issues.
Poor Communication: All community members need to know emergency commands and alerts and how to communicate in an emergency.
Poor Coordination: Individual schools require individualized plans; however, district-wide coordination helps schools better maintain and adjust plans, and take advantage of district-level resources and support.

Best Practice Considerations for Schools in Active Shooter and Other Armed Assailant Drills

The NASP/NASRO Best Practices guide says that critical elements to effective crisis preparedness and response of any kind are: (1) a common understanding of purpose and procedures among all participants, (2) a respect for each other's roles and perspectives, and (3) a shared commitment to ensure the safety and well-being of all members of the school community.

And while lockdowns have been the standard approach for the school response to threatening situations for nearly two decades, they are not enough, it says. Lockdowns should continue to be included in any options-based approach to active assailant training. An options-based drill provides students and staff with a range of alternative strategies to save lives and the permission to use them, depending on the situation.

In 2009, the International Association of Chiefs of Police published a guide for preventing and responding to school violence. This organization also concluded, that lockdown and evacuation were insufficient ways to prepare for such violence and advocated for the training of teachers to know how to defend themselves. This is because, as was seen in the Sandy Hook tragedy, almost half of such events are over before the police ever arrive. The shooter either committed suicide, as Adam Lanza did, or someone else stopped him.

Recognizing the limitations of many school safety approaches and technologies, many schools are turning to staff training and armed intruder drills. The percentage of schools engaging in active shooter drills with students increased from 51.9 percent in 2009 to 70 percent in 2013.

The NASP/NASRO report on drills simulating school shootings called the rising practice uncharted territory. It urges districts to proceed cautiously, especially when young children are involved, but that practicing disaster response procedures has been found to increase the probability of adaptive behavior during a crisis. Specifically, lockdown drills implemented according to best practices have been suggested to increase knowledge and skills of how to respond appropriately without elevating anxiety or perceived safety risk.

The primary purposes of an armed assailant drill are to provide law enforcement and relevant school leadership and staff the opportunity to practice skills and protocols, and to identify and correct areas of weakness in knowledge, communication, coordination, and decision-making.

The premise of options-based drills is to allow participants to make independent decisions including when and whether to evacuate, barricade classroom doors, or as a last resort, counter the attack of the armed assailant. They emphasize that, as with other safety drills (e.g., fire or tornado), it is important that options-based drills take into account the developmental levels of students as well as the physical layout of the school campus (e.g., ease of access to outside doors and proximity of places to hide other than classrooms).

It is critical that participation in such drills be appropriate to individual development levels of the students involved, and take into consideration prior traumatic experiences, special needs, and personalities. It is essential to include parents in discussions about their child's developmental level, education, and readiness for armed assailant drills. The report also recommends that school-employed mental health professionals should be involved in every stage of preparation. Prior to the drill, staff should be trained to recognize common trauma reactions. Further, participation should never be mandatory, and parental consent should be required for all students.

Finally, safety and security professionals (e.g., SROs, police officers) have expertise and can play leadership roles in conducting drills. Like any endeavor, they need to work collaboratively with school administration and school-employed mental health professionals in joint planning to ensure best practice guidelines are followed.

The following are the recommended NASP/NASRO steps for conducting safe, effective, and appropriate drills:

1. Create a school safety team (including an administrator, a school mental health professional, a school nurse, security personnel, teachers, and parents) that also coordinates with local law enforcement and emergency responders
2. Conduct a needs assessment of the school community
3. Implement a cost–benefit analysis that considers all emergency preparedness needs and options
4. Tailor drills to the context of the school environment
5. Create a plan of progression that builds from simplest, lowest-cost training; identifies obstacles and goals; and establishes a timeline
6. Prepare for drill logistics that ensure physical and psychological safety as well as skills and knowledge acquisition
7. Develop a communications plan that gives all participants advance warning and the ability to opt out and/or provide feedback
8. Establish a long-term follow-up plan to support sustainability that includes assessing ongoing and/or changing preparedness training needs (Best Practices Considerations for Schools in Active Shooter and Other Armed Assailant Drills, 2014, p. 7).

The ultimate point of such drills, says Montgomery (2015), is to present human targets with options beyond the traditional response of locking doors, switching off lights, and hoping the shooter does not spot them. The basic tenets of these drills are usually organized around the Run, Hide, Fight concept endorsed by the U.S. Departments of Justice, Education, and Homeland Security and described earlier.

PROMISING PROGRAM

ALICE: Alert, Lockdown, Inform, Counter, Evacuate

According to its website, the ALICE program was authored by a police officer to keep his wife, an elementary school principal, safe after the tragic events at Columbine. Since then, ALICE continues to be a leading active shooter response program in the United States. ALICE training helps prepare individuals to handle the threat of an active shooter. ALICE teaches individuals to participate in their own survival, while leading others to safety.

Though no one can guarantee success in this type of situation, this new set of skills, developers say, will greatly increase the odds of survival should anyone face this form of disaster. ALICE is endorsed by law enforcement across the country and is in line with recommendations from the Department of Homeland Security (DHS); Federal Emergency Management Agency (FEMA); U.S. Department of Education; along with many state agencies across the United States.

In 2013, the U.S. Department of Education issued new guidance for active shooters response. ALICE protocols are used almost exclusively in all new guidance. ALICE has a free active shooter security self-assessment available on its website.

The ALICE program also has ten key questions parents and staff should ask school administrators as to whether their schools are prepared to respond to an active shooter or violent intruder. Communicating well thought out responses to each question will help ensure that everyone is on the same page when it comes to readiness. They are:

1. *What is the school's training/policy when it comes to active shooter or violent intruders?*
2. *What does research show that supports the school's plan for active shooter or violent intruder?*
3. *Is the school's plan supported by the recommendations from the Department of Education or DHS?*
4. *If the school has a lockdown-only response, what are teachers telling my child to do if the attacker gets in the room?*
5. *How is the school training students for violent intruder or active shooter events?*
6. *Does the school run drills?*

7. *What steps are taken to ensure that my child knows the layout of the building?*
8. *Who is authorized to make an alert announcement during an emergency?*
9. *Are codes used to indicate there is violence in the building?*
10. *What options do students and teachers have in an active shooter or violent intruder event?*

LESSONS LEARNED ABOUT INTRUDER VIOLENCE

It is impossible to anticipate when someone with mental illness and/or intent to harm will choose to invade a school. It is possible, however, to be informed and prepared for such emergencies. Once again, there are challenges society must address when it comes to recognizing, preventing, stigmatizing, and treating mental illness. There are other issues to grapple with as well: easy access to powerful guns like assault rifles, the glorification of violence in the media, and even our culture's definition of maleness. But this work is about what schools can do.

As we have seen, the thinking about school responses to intruders and armed attacks has changed even since 2007 when the U.S. DOE issued its previous guidelines. We now understand that lockdowns and passive responses are not enough. We know that the average arrival time for help is roughly five minutes, enough time for an incident to be over. We now have more guidance for examining our facilities, protocols and policies, training of staff and even students, and communication with families and the community.

Fortunately, lessons have been gleaned from these tragedies. This chapter has presented key highlights and recommendations from three vitally important resources, which have been developed in response to those lessons. The critical importance of having emergency operation plans, doing audits and evaluations of those plans, providing training to school personnel, and ensuring information and support for parents and families has been emphasized.

While there is no way to ensure 100 percent safety, if thoughtfully and carefully implemented, these recommendations and suggestions will:

1. enhance the ability of school personnel to respond if necessary;
2. increase our students' sense of safety while they are in school; and
3. inspire the confidence of parents and community members that, if the unthinkable happens, knowledgeable, informed, and trained professionals will take care of their children.

There were incredible stories of unbelievable bravery at Sandy Hook on December 14, 2012. Teachers, staff, and even substitute teachers made every effort to protect their charges, even if it meant injury—or death—to themselves. As the Sandy Hook mothers who founded the Safe and Sound Schools initiative have done, making the safety of school children our highest priority is the best possible tribute we can make to the children and staff who lost their lives that day.

REFERENCES

ALICE Training. (2013–2016). Retrieved from http://www.alicetraining.com/our-program/

Ballard, C., & Brady, L. (2007). Violence prevention in Georgia's rural public school system. *Journal of School Violence*, 6(4), 105–129.

Best Practices Considerations for Schools in Active Shooter and Other Armed Assailant Drills. (2014). Retrieved from http://www.nasponline.org/Documents/Research%20and%20Policy/Advocacy%20Resources/BPArmed_Assailant_Drills.pdf

Blair, J. P., & Schweit, K. W. (2014). *A study of active shooter incidents, 2000–2013*. Washington, DC: Texas State University and Federal Bureau of Investigation, U.S. Department of Justice.

Guide for Developing High Quality School Emergency Operations Plans. (2013). U.S. Department of Education, U.S. Department of Health and Human Services, U.S. Department of Homeland Security, U.S. Department of Justice, Federal Bureau of Investigation, Federal Emergency Management Agency.

Harris Interactive Intruders in Our Public Schools. (2006). www.prnewswire.com/news-releases/intruders-in-our-public-schools-two-thirds-of-youth-and-three-quarters-of-parents-find-it-likely-that-and-intruder-could-enter-a-school-56176692.html

Kena, G., Hussar, W., McFarland, J., de Brey, C., Musu-Gillette, L., Wang, X., ... Dunlop Velez, E. (2016). *The condition of education, 2016* (NCES 2016-144). Washington, DC: U.S. Department of Education, National Center for Education Statistics. http://nces.ed.gov/pubsearch

Montgomery, R. (March 9, 2015). Controversial lessons show schools how to thwart an armed intruder. *Kansas City Star*. Retrieved from http://www.emergencymgmt.com/training/Controversial-Lessons-Show-How-Thwart-Armed-Intruder.html

Safe and Sound Schools. (2013–2016). Retrieved from http://www.safeandsoundschools.org

Technological Responses to Violence in High School. (n.d). Retrieved from http://criminal-justice.iresearchnet.com/crime/school-violence/technological-responses-to-violence-in-high-school/

U.S. Department of Education Guide for Developing High Quality School Emergency Operations Plans. (2013). Retrieved from http://rems.ed.gov/docs/rems_k-12_guide_508.pdf

Chapter Three

Aggression and Intimidation

She was ten years old. They said it was a fight over a boy. They said that classmates possibly encouraged the girls to fight. It is estimated that at least a half-dozen students watched the fight, which occurred near the Willard elementary school in Long Beach, California. Fifth-grader Joanna Ramos died after the fight that supposedly lasted only one minute. Witnesses said that she was kneed in the forehead during the fight. She fell ill hours afterward and died at a local hospital. Her death was ruled a homicide.

Across the country in Delaware school, officials say three students have been indefinitely suspended following the death of sixteen-year-old girl, Amy Inita Joyner-Francis, in a bathroom fight. The fight occurred on April 21, 2016, as classes started. It happened in a bathroom on the main floor of the school. The principal said later that the fight initially started between two students and then additional students joined in. Amy was badly injured during the fight and transported by helicopter to the hospital, where she died.

OVERVIEW OF ISSUES RELATED TO AGGRESSION AND INTIMIDATION

This chapter presents other types of aggression and physical violence that occur at school. It covers fighting, hazing, robbery and theft, physical assault, being threatened with a weapon, and possessing a weapon. Each of these, in addition to the threat of school shootings and the potential for intruder violence, can lead to pervasive and lasting fear of attack or harm. How significant are these types of school violence? The 2013 National Crime Victimization Survey results show that 7.4 percent of students are victims of robbery (one out of every thirteen), 8.6 percent of aggravated assault (one out of every twelve), and 2.1 percent rape or sexual assault, or one in forty-seven.

There are a variety of different and conflicting national reports detailing the extent of crime and violence in our schools. They have widely differing numbers depending on definitions used and data collection methods (e.g., telephone interviews or anonymous surveys versus face-to-face interviews). The *Indicators of School Crime and Safety Report: 2015* found that there were 850,000 nonfatal victimizations at schools in 2014. These included 363,700 thefts and 486,400 violent victimizations (either assaults or serious violent victimization).

Schools reported 1.3 million serious disciplinary incidents (including alcohol and drug possession, violence and weapons possession), which resulted in at least one day of out-of-school suspension. The indicators report also stated that such violence is greatest in rural schools, with a ratio of fifty-three incidents per every one thousand students (or one out of every nineteen students). This compares with twenty-eight per one thousand in suburban schools (one out of every thirty-six students) and thirty-two per one thousand in urban schools (one out of every thirty-one students).

Another national report, the *Youth Risk Behavior Surveillance System* (YRBSS), reported that in 2013, 5.2 percent of students responded that they had carried a weapon on school property, 6.9 percent reported being threatened or injured with a weapon on school property, and 8.1 percent were in a fight on school property. Additionally, 7.1 percent reported not going to school on a least one day in the previous month because they felt unsafe at school or on their way to and from school.

Most reports conclude that crime at schools has gone down in the last twenty years, reflecting a general decline in violence in the general population and an overall decline in youth violence (see figure 3.1). Some researchers

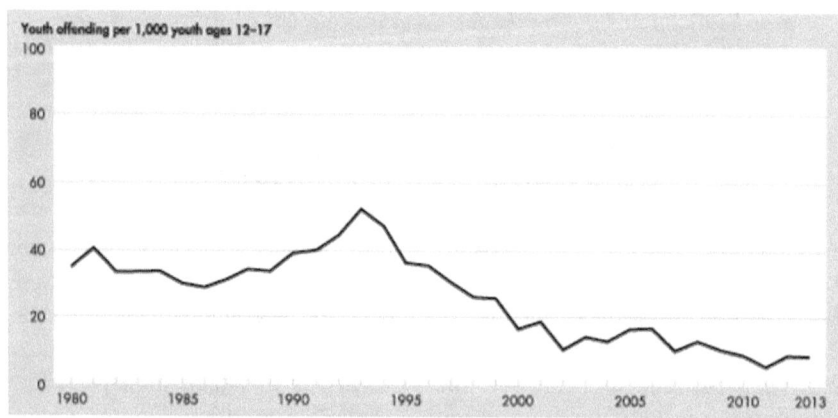

Figure 3.1 Trends in Youth Violence 1980–2013. *Source*: **America's Children: Key Indicators of Well Being (2015).**

say that these same reports reflect voluntary reporting of school crime and do not reflect the true picture. Dinkes et al. (2009), for example, show that many crimes, even violent crimes, committed at school are not reported to the police. They point to the 2003–04 school year report, when fully 81 percent of public schools experienced one or more violent crimes, but just 44 percent reported violent crimes to the police.

These violent incidents included physical attacks, fights with or without weapons, threats of physical violence with or without weapons, rape, sexual battery (other than rape), and robbery with or without weapons. Low-reporting trends also occurred with thefts, they assert, even though 46 percent of public schools experienced one or more thefts.

Even some serious violent crimes were not reported. In that same school year, 18 percent of public schools experienced one or more serious violent crimes, and only 13 percent reported any serious violent crimes to the police. The rate of violent incidents reported by principals is much higher for middle schools than either elementary or high schools, somewhat higher for city schools than those in suburban or rural communities, and higher in predominantly minority schools than those with less than half minority.

According to the Centers for Disease Control and Prevention (CDC), youth violence can include verbal and physical aggression, threatening, and intimidating behaviors that are associated with short- and long-term adverse academic and psychological outcomes for perpetrators and victims. Less serious forms of violence are generally classified as aggressive behavior, which include targeted verbal, physical, or gestural behavior that is intended to cause minor physical harm, psychological distress, intimidation, or to induce fear, say Espelage et al. (2013).

Espelage et al. also say that generally, aggressive and less serious forms of violent behavior invariably precede more serious forms of violence. This dynamic can be seen in event sequences (e.g., inadvertent bumps or verbal slights, which can escalate into more serious forms of violence), as well as a progression from childhood to adolescence (the pushes and shoves of elementary school children turn into vicious fights during adolescence).

Among the various changes that the 2002 No Child Left Behind Act (NCLB) required was a provision mandating that states work on making schools safer. U.S. DOE notes:

> Under Title IV of ESEA as reauthorized by the No Child Left Behind Act, states are required to establish a uniform management and reporting system to collect information on school safety and drug use among young people. The states must include incident reports by school officials and anonymous student and teacher surveys in the data they collect. This information is to be publicly reported so that parents, school officials and others who are interested have information

about any violence and drug use at their schools. They can then assess the problems at their schools and work toward finding solutions. Continual monitoring and reports will track progress over time.

To hold schools accountable for ensuring student safety, the NCLB requires states to create a definition of persistently dangerous schools. States must permit students to attend an alternate public school choice if their school consistently falls into this category. In addition, student victims of violent crime are also allowed public school choice even if the school is not considered persistently dangerous. If deemed persistently dangerous, a school will need to show significant improvements to regain its place on the safe school list.

The National Association of School Resource Officers (NASRO) believes that schools will be even more hesitant to report crimes so that they will not be labeled as persistently dangerous, however. They suggest that by falling into this designation, such schools will undoubtedly lose enrollment and school funds. As such, schools may begin to underreport such crimes so that they maintain a clean rating.

Georgia, for example, has developed specific requirements that such schools must follow, which include taking corrective measures. After a year of showing that it is no longer dangerous, a school can reapply to the GDOE. When it filed its report in 2003, the GDOE indicated that no Georgia schools were deemed persistently dangerous. Is that possible? Or just a reflection of the fear and pressure on school officials in fear of their schools being labeled as persistently dangerous?

The NASRO asked its members what impact the NCLB (2004) would have on school administrators reporting school-based crimes. Most of those surveyed (54 percent) believed it would result in decreased reporting of crimes at schools. The vast majority (86 percent) said that the number of crimes on school property was underreported to law enforcement.

FIGHTING AND ASSAULT

Fighting is a problem that occurs frequently at schools. While 25 percent of students grades 9 to 12 reported being in a fight during the past twelve months, 8 percent of those occurred at school. The CDC reports the number of fights at school to be 13.6 percent, with 3.6 percent of those resulting in injury requiring medical treatment one to three times in the previous twelve months.

While most fights do not result in serious injury, fighting *can* lead to serious injury—and even death—as seen in the chapter's opening vignettes. There are other effects as well. Injuries incurred in physical fighting during adolescence can result in significant losses in verbal intelligence, notes the Childtrends Data Bank. Childtrends "Physical Fighting by Youth Study" (2014) identified the following risk factors that predict youth violence: substance abuse, conflict and abuse at home, harsh or inattentive parenting, antisocial and delinquent peers, and neighborhoods where crime and drug use are prevalent. Youth who are involved in physical fighting are also often engaged in other high-risk activities, such as bullying, cigarette smoking, and alcohol use, this study notes (figure 3.2).

This study also found that the students attending schools where fighting is common may be unable to maintain the focus necessary for academic success. Adolescents who are victims of violence are also more likely to be victims or perpetrators of violence during adulthood. The likelihood of drug use, property offenses, and stress during adulthood also all increase in association with youth violence.

Other findings offer direction for approaches to deal with such fighting and aggression. Garafalo et al. studied school-related victimizations among adolescents and found most fights to be scuffles, threats, and disagreements, rather than calculated assaults or violence. Almost 80 percent of the incidents were committed by offenders well known to the victim. Forty percent of the weapons used in such conflicts were available items grabbed on the spur of the moment such as rocks, baseball bats, scissors, or screwdrivers, and the resulting injuries were relatively minor.

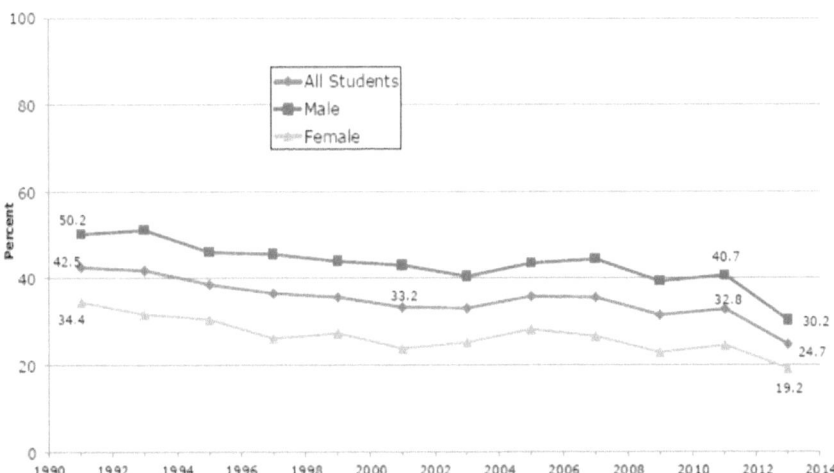

Figure 3.2 Trends in Reported Fighting 1991–2013. Percent of students in grades 9 through 12 who reported they were in a physical fight in the past year. *Source*: ChildTrends Data Bank.

Johnson and Johnson (1995) found that while students were involved in conflicts daily, the conflicts primarily consisted of putdowns and teasing, playground conflicts, access or possession conflicts, and physical aggression in fights. Targeting these issues (which will be discussed later in the chapter) has been found to produce some significant results.

HAZING

According to the Minnesota High School League, hazing refers to "any activity expected of someone joining a group (or to maintain full status in a group) that humiliates, degrades, or risks emotional and/or physical harm, regardless of the person's willingness to participate. Hazing is an activity that a high-status member orders other members to engage in or suggests that they engage in that in some way humbles a newcomer who lacks the power to resist, because he or she wants to gain admission to a group."

Like bullying, hazing involves humiliating someone into doing something that he or she would not do normally. Parents and educators have become concerned that hazings are getting more and more aggressive and violent, says Doak (2009). Hazings, which often occur as initiations to a school or social club, are considered a rite of passage to some, just horseplay to others, and degrading and devastating to various victims. Some athletic teams claim that hazing is done to toughen up younger players—to help them bond with the team. And unlike bullying, Doak notes, hazing is often done with the consent of its victims.

For example, succumbing to peer pressure and wanting to be part of the group or clique, many students actually allow themselves to be subjected to humiliating acts that they do not report. Hazing can go too far and the victims can be seriously harmed. A few victims have even died. Hazings usually involve older students (veterans) initiating young classmates (newcomers) into a group. The situation can quickly turn violent when the older group gangs up on the younger group, which has no idea what has been planned or what they should expect. Researchers have consistently found that students will do things in a mob situation that they would never do on their own.

Hazing activities are generally considered to be subtle, harassing, and/or violent. The specific behaviors or activities within these categories vary widely among participants, groups, and settings. Alcohol use is common in many types of hazing. Other examples of typical hazing practices include personal servitude, sleep deprivation, and restrictions on personal hygiene; yelling, swearing, and insulting new members/rookies; being forced to wear embarrassing or humiliating attire in public; consumption of vile substances or smearing of such on one's skin; brandings; physical beatings; and binge drinking and drinking games.

Doak contends that hazing incidents are underreported. This occurs for several reasons: (1) the victim believes that hazing is an unpleasant, but a necessary part of joining an organization; (2) the victim is threatened into remaining silent; (3) the victim is ashamed and wants to forget the incident occurred; (4) the victim assumes everyone has to endure such acts; or (5) the victim does not want to involve parents, school officials, or police because that would bring more trouble from the hazers.

THEFT

A theft occurs any time there in an unauthorized taking of property from another with the intent to permanently deprive that person of the property. Robbery is essentially theft accomplished through the use of physical force or fear. According to the National Center for Educational Statistics, between 1992 and 2014, the rate of theft against students aged twelve to eighteen at school declined (from 114 to 14 thefts per 1,000 students), as did the rate away from school (from 79 to 11 thefts per 1,000 students). See figure 3.3.

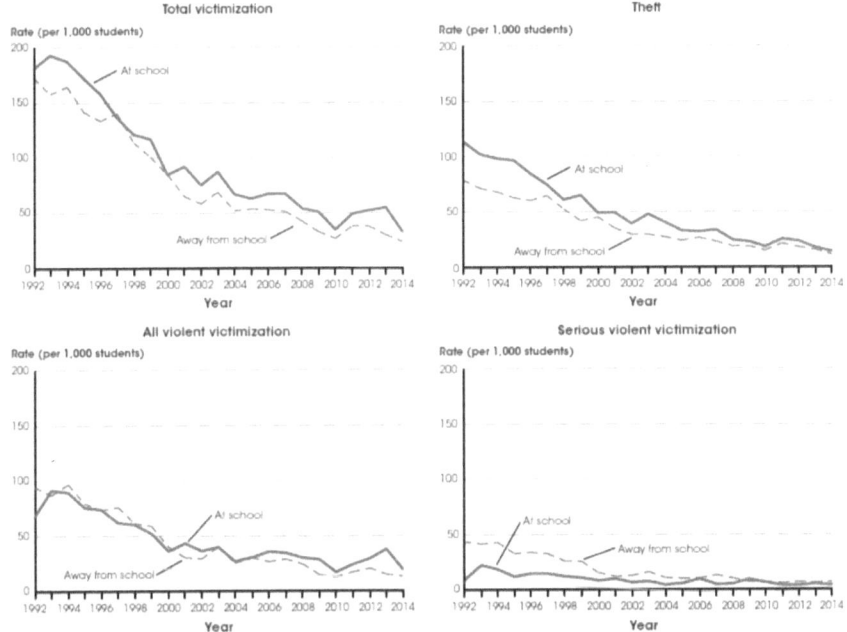

Figure 3.3 Rate of Nonfatal Victimization per 1,000 Students Aged Twelve to Eighteen, by Type of Victimization and Location: 1992 through 2014. *Source*: NCES.

In 2006, high-school students were more likely to experience property crime than fights at school, says the National Crime Prevention Council, and by the age of seventeen, 43 percent of youth in the United States have stolen property worth $50 or less. Any theft—or fear of theft—diminishes the school climate and culture and students' sense of safety there.

POSSESSION OF/INTIMIDATION WITH WEAPONS

As of 2011, the percentage of high-school students reporting being threatened or injured with a weapon at school at least once in the last year was 7, or one in thirteen students. The figure peaked in 2003 at 9.2 percent. In the same time period, however, a lower percentage of students reported bringing weapons to school. In 2011, 5.4 percent of students said they carried a weapon on school property, down from 11.8 percent in 1993. In 2013 it was 6.9 percent (figure 3.4).

Alarmingly, a disproportionately large number of *bullied* high-school students in the United States brought weapons—including guns, knives, and clubs—to school, according to a study of CDC 2011 data. In one study, the researchers examined data from a nationally representative survey of fifteen thousand U.S. high-school students. It found that 9 percent of high-school students who had been bullied in the past year had carried a weapon to school, while 5 percent of kids who had not been bullied carried a weapon. It also found that the rate rose sharply among those who were bullied the worst, with 63 percent saying they had brought a gun to school in the past month.

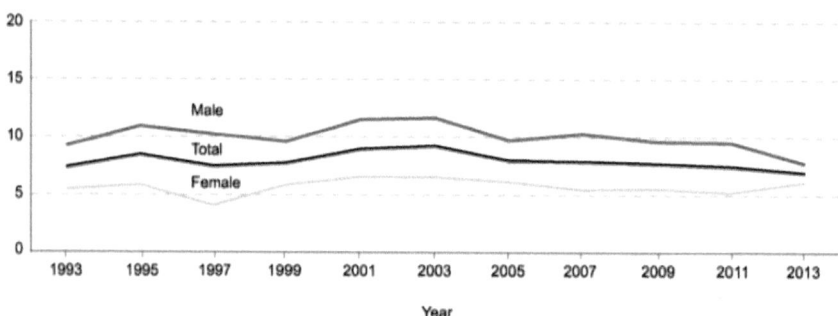

Figure 3.4 Percentage of Students Threatened by a Weapon. *Source*: **National Youth Risk Behavior Survey 2013.**

"The figures are staggering," said study author Dr. Andrew Adesman, chief of developmental and behavioral pediatrics at Steven and Alexandra Cohen Children's Medical Center of New York. "What we are finding is exceptionally high rates of high-school students carrying weapons to school if they have previously been a victim of bullying, and they have otherwise had threats to their safety and property," said Adesman (Blaszczak-Boxe, 2004).

The percentage of students who report being threatened with or injured by a weapon while at school has remained fairly steady according to CDC data. About 8 percent of students in grades 9 to 12 reported being threatened or injured with a weapon on school property within the past twelve months in 2013. This figure was a slight increase from 1993, when 7.3 percent of students reported being threatened or injured by a weapon. Figure 3.5 depicts weapon carrying by gender and race. Between 1993 and 2013, the percentage remained in the range of 7 to 9—no clear pattern of improvement or worsening was seen. It continues at that worrying level today.

CDC figures also show that male students received considerably more weapon threats and injuries in all years surveyed in 2011 than did female students (10 percent for males versus 5 for females). Among students from different ethnic and racial backgrounds, the victimization rate was the highest among the Pacific Islanders in 2005, at 14.5 percent, down from a high of 24.8 percent in 2001. Native American students (9.8 percent) and Hispanic

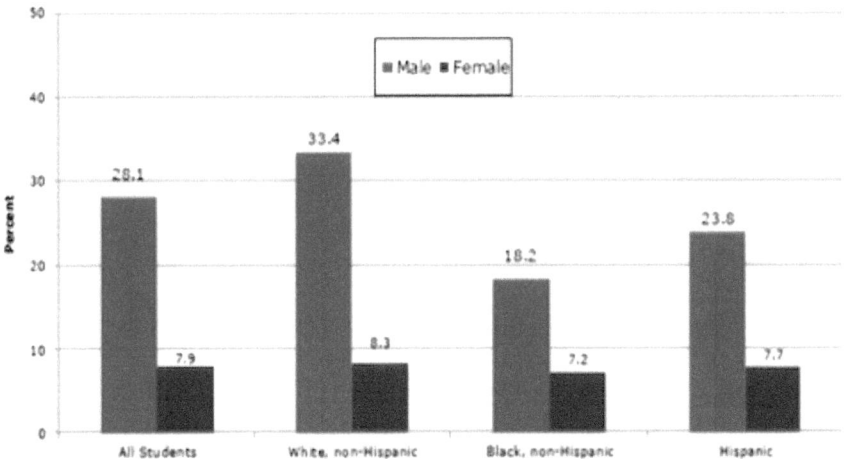

Figure 3.5 Percentage of High School Students Who Report Carrying Weapons, by Gender, Race, and Hispanic Origin, 2013. *Source*: Childtrends.

students (9.8 percent) also had fairly high victimization rates. Asian students were the least likely to be threatened by or injured with a weapon in 2005 (4.6 percent) as shown in figure 3.5.

The youngest students were the most likely to report being threatened by or injured with a weapon. More than one out of ten (10.5 percent) ninth graders reported being threatened or injured with a weapon in 2005, compared with 8.8 percent of tenth graders, 5.5 percent of eleventh graders, and 5.8 percent of twelfth graders. Similar patterns were observed in other years as well. Doak speculates that younger students are viewed as more vulnerable to intimidation and are, therefore, more likely to be targets of students carrying weapons.

IMPACT OF AGGRESSION AND INTIMIDATION

Many students worry about their safety at school. In 2011, 6 percent of students reported missing one or more days of school in the last month because they believed it was too unsafe at school or going to and from school. More female students (5 percent) than male students (4 percent) reported this experience. This response to their fear was much higher among Hispanic students (10.2 percent) and African American students (8.7 percent) than it was among white students (4.4 percent).

Younger children reported not going to school because of safety concerns more than did older children: 7.7 percent of ninth graders, 6.3 percent of tenth graders, 4.7 percent of eleventh graders, and 4.9 percent of twelfth graders reported skipping school because of safety concerns in the previous month.

The issue of fear of attack or harm at school or en route to and from school has also been studied. Dinkes et al. reported that in 2005, 6.2 percent of students aged twelve to eighteen reported being afraid of attack or harm at school during the previous six months, down dramatically from 11.8 percent of students in 1995. By 2013, it was down to 3 percent. In 2005, females were slightly more likely to be afraid of harm (6.6 percent) than were males (5.9 percent). Hispanic (10.1 percent) and African American (9 percent) students were more likely than white students (4.5 percent) to feel afraid of attack at school.

Younger students were more likely than older students to fear attack or harm at school. Urban students (10.2 percent) were far more likely than suburban (4.7 percent) or rural (5.1 percent) students to report being afraid of attack or harm. Fewer students were afraid of attack or harm away from school than they were at school (5.1 and 6.2 percent, respectively).

The percentage of youth, aged twelve to eighteen, that feared attack at school, or on the way to and from school, fell by half between 1995 and 2001, from 12 percent in 1995 to 6 percent in 2001. The proportion remained steady through 2005, before decreasing to 4 percent in 2013 (see figure 3.6).

When students have fears about personal safety at school, or on the way to and from school, they may miss days of class, states the *Child Trends Safety at School Report* (2015). It notes that perpetrators and victims of school violence are more likely to experience health problems, social and emotional difficulties, and/or poorer academic performance. Additionally, the report found that fear at school can contribute to an unhealthy school climate and can lead to negative student behaviors.

One study found, for example, that students who witnessed violence at school were more likely to perpetrate violent behavior. Students who are fearful may also feel they need to protect themselves through actions that can actually increase the likelihood of violence, such as carrying weapons at school, as seen in the disproportionate numbers of students who have been bullied bringing weapons to school.

Green (2005) reminds us that the consequences of school violence that subvert the academic purposes of schooling include school avoidance, diminished ability to focus on academic pursuits, internalizing psychological problems such as depression, social anxiety, and fearfulness among

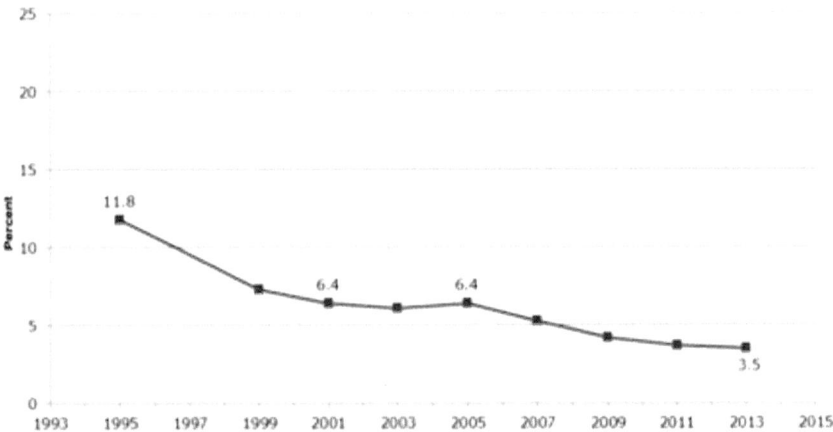

Figure 3.6 Percentage of Students Ages 12 to 18 Who Feared Attack at School or on the Way to and From School: Selected Years, 1995–2013. *Source*: Childtrends.

teachers and other school personnel, increased aggression and weapon carrying in the guise of self-defense, and the acceptance of violence as a reasonable form of conflict resolution. The consequences of high levels of aggression can be extremely damaging to perpetrators as well as their victims.

MENTAL HEALTH/INDIVIDUAL CONSIDERATIONS

Research findings on aggression in childhood are startling and unsettling:

> Children who display high rates of aggression are at substantial risk because of the developmental continuity in patterns of aggressive behavior (Feshbach & Fraczek, 1979, p. 2). Excessive levels of aggressive behavior in childhood are extremely stable over time (Kazdin, 1987; Olweus, 1979) and are often followed by a host of negative developmental outcomes. Longitudinal data have described a linear pattern of behavioral development that may lead from high rates of problem behaviors in the early years (e.g., pushing others in toddlerhood) to violence in adolescence (e.g., assault with an object) (Patterson, 1992). For example, children who are highly aggressive in school settings, males in particular, are more likely than less aggressive children to engage in significantly higher rates of juvenile delinquency as they grow older (Loeber & Stouthamer-Loeber, 1987). These boys are also more likely to experience poor overall school adjustment, peer rejection, greater than average rates of school dropout, and higher than average rates of referral for clinical mental health interventions (Kupersmidt & Coie, 1990). Hudley et al. (1998, p. 271)

Johnson and Johnson (1995) assert that there are three factors in play for children and adolescents at risk for using violence. They are poor academic performance, alienation from schoolmates, and psychological pathology.

Children and adolescents who fail academically are more at risk for violent and destructive behavior than students who achieve academically. Unable to secure self-esteem and positive ways, some students seek status or antisocial behavior. Children and adolescents who are disliked are alienated from their schoolmates and are also at more risk for violence and destructive behavior than are students who are integrated into strong, caring, and supportive relationships at school.

The most powerful constraints on violence and antisocial behavior, assert Johnson and Johnson, are healthy human attachments. Usually these originate in early relationships of parental affection and guidance where parents teach children trust, competent self-management, and prosocial behavior. Peer relations, however, are very powerful influences. Bonding with a set of constructive peers is one of the most powerful influences on a person's behavior.

Children and adolescents who have high levels of psychological pathology are also more at risk for violent and destructive behavior, they have found, than are students who are psychologically well adjusted.

Gottfredson (2011) tells us that individual factors which have links to crime include early problem behavior, impulsiveness or low levels of self-control, rebellious attitudes, beliefs favoring law violation, and low levels of social competency skills such as identifying likely consequences of actions and alternative solutions to problems, taking the perspective of others, and correctly interpreting social cues.

The individual factors predictive of school behavior problems can be seen in figure 3.7. They include attachment to school, commitment to education, academic performance, exposure to and association with negative peers, impulsiveness and low self-control, attitudes toward law violation and drug use, early problem behavior, peer rejection, and social competency skills.

Hudley et al. (1998) discuss attribution theory and how this theory provides important insights into the display of high levels of aggression in childhood. In social situations, they explain, individuals try to understand how their own and others' behavior may cause the outcomes they experience in a situation. An attribution occurs when an individual assigns a cause to the behavior of others in a social interaction.

Highly aggressive children, say Hudley et al., often incorrectly attribute deliberately hostile intentions to peers. For example, if asked to imagine being bumped by a peer while walking in the hallway at school, excessively aggressive children stated that the bump was on purpose more than twice as

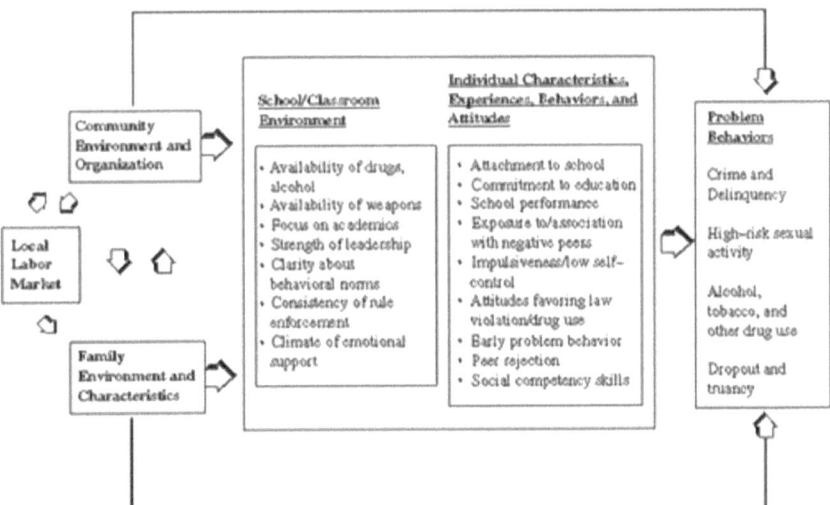

Figure 3.7 Gottfredson's (2011) School-Related Predictors of Problem-Related Behavior.

often as a less aggressive peer in the absence of any information regarding the cause of the bump.

Biased attributions may explain why these children are more likely to retaliate aggressively in inappropriate circumstances, they explain. They also cite prior research, which finds that children with a reputation for extreme aggression among peers were more likely to receive hostile attributions themselves from peers and to be the objects of retaliatory aggression.

A hostile attributional bias may, therefore, follow logically from aggressive students' actual experiences with peers because children with reputations as aggressive actually contribute to a more hostile environment in which they must interact. This creates a vicious cycle of aggression, aggression responses, and repeated aggression, thus confirming the child's attributions and belief system.

Stage et al. (2007) studied risk factors that would best predict borderline/clinical levels of problem behavior of kindergarten and first-grade children at risk for emotional and behavioral disorders. Results showed that among the risk factor domains considered, five were most predictive of borderline/clinical levels of problem behavior: externalizing behavior patterns, internalizing behavior patterns, early childhood child maladjustment, family functioning, and maternal depression. Within these five areas, they found that the strongest set of individual risk factors were difficult child (i.e., temperament, parent management skills, interaction between temperament and parent management skills), destroys own toys, and maternal depression.

As discussed earlier, many children have problematic coping strategies that can lead to aggression and other behavioral problems. Interventions to improve social behavior and decision-making have been shown to decrease aggression. Such programs address negative affect work to reduce children's feelings of anger. Programs to improve social skills generally focus on developing cognitive problem solving, conflict resolution, and friendship skills based on the assumption that these skills need to be explicitly taught.

One research study conducted on the Brain Power Program, an attribution retraining intervention (Hudley et al.), collected measures of children's behavior and self-reports of attributions for twelve months following intervention to assess changes in social cognition and social behavior. Results suggest that improvements in behavior were related to changes in subjects' attributions. The intervention effects were moderate-to-strong for many students, but not evident at all for some students. Further, they found that treatment effects diminished over time.

Such programs seek to develop students' skills in recognizing situations in which they are likely to get into trouble, controlling or managing their impulses, anticipating the consequences of their actions, perceiving accurately the feelings or intentions of others, and coping with peer influence that may lead to trouble. These interventions use instructional methods that explicitly teach principles for self-regulation and recognizing antecedents of problem behavior.

Yet, individual approaches are simply not enough. Table 3.1 presents a useful overall picture of the multitude of factors and predictors of problem

Table 3.1 Summary of Evidence on School Climate and Problem Behaviors

Tagiriuri (1968) Classification	Feature of School Environment	Evidence from Observational Studies
Ecology	School size	School size generally unrelated to levels of problem behavior (weak evidence)
Milieu	Demographic characteristics. of students in the school	Demographic composition of the school matters for level of problem behavior: net of individual demographics Important compositional characteristics include grade levels included in the school or average age of the students in the school: the percentage male students, and the social class composition of the school (strong evidence)
Social System	Organizational structure: Number of different students taught by teacher/number of classroom changes	Teaching more students and allowing more classroom changes promotes higher levels. of problem behavior (moderate evidence)
	Administration/ management: Discipline management	Schools that establish and maintain rules, effectively communicate clear expectations for behavior, monitor student behavior, consistently enforce rules: experience lower levels of problem behaviors (strong evidence)
	Student involvement	Giving students a meaningful role in establishing mechanisms for reducing misbehavior reduces problem behaviors (moderate evidence)
	General school management	Effective management of the school reduces problem behaviors (moderate evidence)
Culture	School norms related to problem behaviors	The attitudes, beliefs, and behaviors of students in the school predict the level of problem behavior (strong evidence)
	Students affective bonds/ communal social organization (CSO)	Average student attachment to school and CSO more generally do inhibit student problem behaviors (strong evidence)

Source: Cook et al. (2010, p. 104).

behavior. This clearly indicates that there are a variety of considerations, in addition to individual factors discussed in this section, that need to be explored if we are to take a comprehensive view of both the problem and the potential solutions. We turn to those considerations next.

SCHOOL CONSIDERATIONS

The school factors that impact levels of school violence include the following considerations: (1) school organization (structure, size, class size); (2) school climate and culture; and (3) school policies (e.g., retention, suspension) and norms (and their consistent and fair enforcement). The Cook et al. School Climate and Problem Behaviors chart (see table 3.1) summarizes key findings.

School Organization and Structure

Studies are largely consistent in showing that the grade levels included in the school, or average age of the students in the school, the percentage male students, the social class composition, and the racial and ethnic composition of the schools are related to measures of problem behavior. Cook, MacCoun, Muschkin, and Vigdor (2008) found schools that moved to a middle-school model for sixth grade, for example, experienced a sharp increase in disciplinary infractions relative to those who stayed with an elementary school (K–8) model. More interesting, perhaps, is that the higher infraction rate persisted through ninth grade.

The little available research that exists in this area suggests, however, that it may be fruitful to reorganize schools by creating smaller groups of students who stay together for an extended period during the school day and who are taught by a small group of teachers. The research on these efforts suggests that this approach might be effective for increasing students' sense of connection, which serves to hold aggressive and potential criminal behavior in check.

School organizational features that promote more cohesive teacher–student relationships promote learning (Lee, Smerdon, Alfred-Liro, & Brown, 2000). Schools in which the typical teacher interacts on a regular basis with fewer different students can facilitate more cohesive student–teacher relationships.

Organizational arrangements that can be expected to reduce the number of different students taught include reducing class size and organizing instruction so that smaller groups of students remain together for an extended period during the school day and are taught by a small group of teachers. Some schools accomplish such reorganizations by breaking into smaller "schools-within-schools", and others through creative use of block scheduling.

Class size can also make a difference. A recent review of research on class size (Finn, Pannozzo, & Achilles, 2004) summarizes results from nineteen studies, including five large-scale class-size reduction initiatives conducted in Indiana, Tennessee, North Carolina, Wisconsin, and California.

The research clearly demonstrates positive effects of reduced classroom size in the early elementary grades on both academic achievement and negative or antisocial behaviors. Lasting effects on academic outcomes of having attended smaller classes were also observed. Finn, Gerber, and Boyd-Zaharias (2005), reporting on long-term effects from a Tennessee class size study, found that high-school graduation was more likely for students who had attended smaller classes for three or more years.

Analyses of possible mechanisms linking class size to these outcomes conclude that the positive effects are—at least in part—due to teachers getting to know students better in smaller classes, which increases students' sense of belonging in the classroom. Also, teachers in smaller classes are better able to prevent discipline problems, therefore reducing time that must be spent on behavior management.

Although these reports suggest that reducing class size is likely to reduce student misbehavior by increasing teachers' attention to students, increasing student engagement and sense of belonging in the school, and facilitating more effective management of classroom behavior, only one study to date relates class size to actual crime. The authors attribute this to the fact that most of the research on class size is conducted at the elementary school level.

School Policies

School-wide Discipline

There are alternatives to the get tough zero tolerance approach with its reliance on deterrence and exclusion. Some schools do a much better job than others in controlling the behavior of their students. These schools are close knit communities where rules of acceptable behavior are clearly communicated and consistently enforced. In addition to good organization and management practices, there is much that can be done in the classroom that has demonstrated effectiveness in improving behavior.

Cook et al. say that research consistently shows that in schools where students report that the rules are clearly stated, fair, and consistently enforced, and where students have participated in establishing mechanisms for reducing misbehavior, students are less likely to engage in problem behaviors. They highlight evaluations of specific school-based programs using behavioral strategies, such as the promising program described in this chapter, to monitor and reinforce student behavior, which were proven effective both for controlling behavior in school and for reducing subsequent crime.

Altering school-wide discipline management policies and practices to incorporate behavioral principles, clarifying expectations for behavior, and consistently enforcing rules reduce problem behavior, they say. Their research suggests that behavioral principles can be incorporated into normal school disciplinary practices, and that an emphasis on consistency of rule enforcement—as opposed to severity of punishment—provides an effective deterrent.

When schools monitor students and control access to the campus, and when students perceive that school rules are fair and consistently enforced, schools experience lower levels of problem behavior. Inclusion of students in establishing school rules and policies for dealing with problem can be effective, say Cook et al. On the other hand, severity of sanctions is not related to a reduction in problem behaviors. They say that these findings are consistent with findings from deterrence research that the certainty of punishment has greater deterrent effect than the severity of punishment.

Among the most effective school-based strategies for reducing youth violence, aggression, and problem behavior are behavioral interventions that target specific behaviors, systematically remove rewards for undesirable behavior, and apply contingent rewards for desired behavior or punishment for undesired behavior.

Retention

The effect of retention on behavior of the retained students has been extensively studied. Most studies have focused on academic outcomes: a meta-analysis (i.e., a study of studies) of this literature concludes that the long-term effect on academic achievement is null or negative, with a greatly elevated risk of dropping out (Jimerson et al., 2006). Students with academic difficulties are more prone to misbehavior (Nagin, Pagani, Tremblay, & Vitaro, 2003), and it is not surprising that being held back a grade would contribute to behavior problems. In fact, when a student is already struggling, being held back behind peers could exacerbate them.

Muschkin, Glennie, and Beck (2008) conducted a cross-sectional analysis of infraction rates by seventh graders, finding that the prevalence and incidence of infractions increase with the prevalence of retained students (students who were retained at least once in the previous three years) and the prevalence of old-for-grade students who were not retained during that three-year period.

Truancy

The rate of unexcused absence determines not only the number of students in the school building, but also the behavioral propensities of those students. Chronic truants are not a representative sample of the student body, but rather tend to come from dysfunctional families and be at risk for delinquency, violence, and substance abuse (McCluskey et al. cited in Cook et al.). If at-risk youths are encouraged to attend school regularly, the long-term result may be to improve their chances of bonding with school staff, observing positive peer role models, of graduation and subsequent life success and satisfaction.

Several studies demonstrate that it is possible to increase school attendance among delinquency-prone youths, and that doing so also reduces delinquency, school dropout rates, and subsequent crime rates.

School Culture and Climate

The National School Climate Center defines school climate as the quality and character of school life. School climate is based on the patterns of students', parents', and school personnel's experience of school life and reflects norms, goals, values, interpersonal relationships, teaching and learning practices, and organizational structures. An organization's culture includes the prevailing beliefs, values, norms, and attitudes of the people in the organization and pertains more to the quality of human relationships than to the formal social organization of the organization.

Two important aspects of organization culture in the school context are the peer culture and the extent to which the organization is communally organized. As school culture refers to the quality of human relationships in the school and includes both peer culture, these dimensions influence youth behavior and propensity toward crime and can be successfully manipulated to reduce it.

Gottfredson says that an increase in delinquent behavior is also likely to be encouraged during the school day by the presence of social norms that support (or at least appear to youth to support) delinquent behavior, and by peer reinforcement for the expression of deviant attitudes, beliefs, and behaviors. Dishion and Dodge (2006) even suggest that peer reinforcement of deviant behavior may be particularly strong in school cultures that fail to reinforce nondeviant behavior. These considerations are important ones for developing strategies to reduce such aggression.

Cook et al. (2010) discuss informal controls, which bond youths to the social order through emotional attachments, investments in the future, and beliefs about what is right and wrong. These controls drive behavior to the extent that young people believe that by engaging in proscribed behaviors, they risk losing the respect of loved ones, gambling with a good future, or suffering a bad conscience. This basic understanding of the mechanism underlying crime and other forms of misbehavior implies that schools can reduce these behaviors in the following ways:

- Reducing availability of opportunities to engage in problem behaviors
- Reducing positive reinforcement of problem behaviors
- Increasing formal controls (e.g., increasing the probability of formal sanction as a consequence for problem behavior as well as the perceived legitimacy of sanctioning process)
- Increasing informal controls (e.g., increasing emotional attachments, investments in goals inconsistent with engaging in crime, and beliefs about right and wrong behavior)
- Increasing self-control. (Cook et al., 2010, p. 31)

School-wide Prevention Program

The three-tiered public health model can be useful in developing approaches for dealing with behavioral problems. Universal school-based prevention and intervention programs for aggressive and disruptive behavior target elementary-, middle-, and high-school students with the intention of preventing or reducing violent, aggressive, or disruptive behaviors. Students can be taught different skills and coping mechanisms to reduce misbehavior and promote positive behavior.

There are a number of school-based interventions that focus specifically on reducing aggressive or disruptive behavior of students, including cognitively oriented strategies, social skills training, behavioral strategies, counseling (group, individual, and family), anger management programs, and social problem-solving programs.

Other universal school-based programs teach students topics and skills such as emotional self-awareness, emotional control, self-esteem, positive social skills, social problem solving, conflict resolution, and teamwork (Hahn et al., 2007). In addition to the classroom components, many also have support materials for parents—and even peers—to reinforce classroom lessons.

Cook et al. report that secondary intervention programs targeting higher-risk youths rather than entire classrooms also have produced positive effects on measures of antisocial behavior and aggression. They cite numerous studies that have concluded that school-based interventions targeting more at-risk populations produced larger effect sizes on measures of delinquent, disruptive, and aggressive behaviors than even those targeting the general population.

There were also increases in social bonds—attachment and commitment to school—resulting from these interventions. These were by far the largest correlates of reductions in problem behaviors, say Cook et al.

Increases in academic performance resulting from the interventions were also modestly related to changes in problem behaviors. They conclude that multiple research reviews suggest that interventions aimed at increasing academic performance also reduce crime, especially if these interventions are also successful in increasing attachment and commitment to school.

Najaka, Gottfredson, and Wilson (2001) concur. They provide evidence from experimental and quasi-experimental studies of school-based interventions, which find that improving academic performance reduces problem behavior, increases in social bonds, attachment, and commitment to school.

So a key to reduce such behaviors and increase school attachment is helping those students academically. Schools need to do even more in this area.

PROMISING PROGRAM: STUDENTS MANAGING ANGER AND RESOLUTION TOGETHER

According to the U.S. Department of Education's website, the Students Managing Anger and Resolution Together (SMART) program is a multimedia computer-based program for students in grades five to nine. It is a universal violence prevention program. The program's goals are to increase students' repertoire of nonviolent conflict resolution strategies and anger management strategies, to decrease the incidents of violent behavior, and to increase acts of prosocial behavior.

Skills taught through the program increase in difficulty level from novice to expert. The authors consulted with a panel of ten teenage advisers throughout the development of the program. The input of this panel shaped the composite four characters that appear throughout the modules as advisers. SMART Team's computer instruction program uses the four teenage characters to give advice and feedback to students as they interact with scenarios and questions. Interactive interviews, cartoons, game shows, and animation are used to teach anger management, dispute resolution, and perspective taking.

The modules can be used in sequence or independently, because key concepts are reinforced throughout each module of the program. The software accommodates students' learning needs at various stages of mastery. The content of SMART Team can be integrated with other violence prevention strategies a school may implement.

The U.S. DOE reports that the evaluation of the program involved a survey, assessing student self-reports of use of aggressive and violence-related behaviors. Evidence from the matched control group study showed that the program diminished sixth-, seventh-, and eighth-grade students' beliefs supportive of violence and increased their awareness of how to handle anger situations to a statistically significant degree for the intervention group. The program increased middle-school students' intentions to use nonviolent strategies to a statistically significant degree for the intervention group.

An intervention-only pilot test also yielded statistically significant evidence of decreased student self-reports of incidents of getting into trouble; and increased student declarative knowledge about conflict management terms and principles, self-reports of altruistic behavior, and self-knowledge of how certain behaviors could contribute to the escalation of a conflict situation. Reviewers concluded there were overall statistically significant effects in the long-term control group study on targeted risk and protective factors, but not on violence, although there was evidence of short-term reduction in getting into trouble in the intervention-only pilot test. (SMART, 2002)

LESSONS LEARNED ABOUT AGGRESSION

Aggression and intimidation have extremely negative effects on victims, the bystanders, and, we now know, on the perpetrators themselves. They have a poisonous impact on school and classroom climate and culture and on the very purpose of school, on learning, and development. Left unchecked, they erode the confidence and safety and respect of students and staff.

The good news is that early intervention can make a difference. The good news is that there are research-based strategies at every level, from the individual to the family to the school and community to address and reduce these negative impacts.

The universal prevention model can serve as a guide for schools to use in the analyses and audits recommended by the Newtown parents in the *Safe and Sound* approach. As each school and its needs are unique, that analysis and critique of the existing situation is the starting point for developing a comprehensive school-wide approach. This must include a focus on misbehavior and aggressive behaviors before they spiral and escalate into more serious and dangerous behavior that can be harmful and—as we saw in the cases of Joanna Ramos and Amy Inita Joiner-Frances—even lethal.

But it is not only aggression and intimidation that can result in serious harm, and even death, if left unchecked, but also bullying, which has become pervasive. What was once considered—even accepted—as just "kids being kids" has also resulted in life-long problems and even death for some. What is being done about it? That is the focus of the next chapter.

REFERENCES

America's Children: Key Indicators of Well Being. (2015). Forum on Child and Family Statistics. p. 45. Retrieved from http://www.childstats.gov/americaschildren/beh5.asp

Blaszczak-Boxe, A. (2004). Bullied high-school kids carry weapons to school. Live Science. Retrieved from http://www.livescience.com/45345-bullying-weapons.html

Child Trends, (n.d.). Physical fighting by youth. *PsycEXTRA Dataset.* doi:10.1037/e303162005-001

Cook, P., Gottfredson, D., & Na, C. (2010). School crime control and prevention. *Crime and Justice, 39*(1), 313–440. doi:10.1086/652387

Cook, P. J., MacCoun, R., Muschkin, C., & Vigdor, J. (2008). The negative impacts of starting middle school in sixth grade. *Journal of Policy Analysis and Management, 27*(1), 104–121.

Dinkes, R., Kemp, J., & Baum, K. (2009). Indicators of school crime and safety: 2008 (NCES 2009–022/NCJ 226343). Statistics, Office of Justice Programs, U.S. Department of Justice. Institute of Educational Sciences, U.S. Department of Education, and Bureau of Justice, Washington, D.C.: National Center for Educational Statistics.

Dishion, T. J., & Dodge, K. A. (2006). Deviant peer contagion in interventions and programs: An ecological framework for understanding influence mechanisms. In K. A. Dodge, T. J. Dishion, & J. E. Lansford (Eds.), *Deviant peer influences in programs for youth: Problems and solutions* (pp. 14–43). New York: The Guilford Press.

Doak, M. J. (2009). Issues affecting America's youth. Chapter 9, hazing, cengage learning. Retrieved from http://www.encyclopedia.com/social-sciences-and-law/law/crime-and-law-enforcement/crime-and-violence-schools

Espelage, D. L. (2013). Annual meeting, San Diego, CA. Program to reduce aggression, victimization, and sexual violence. *Journal of Health, 53*(2), 180–186.

Finn, J. D., Gerber, S. B., & Boyd-Zaharias, J. (2005). Small classes in the early grades, academic achievement, and graduating from high school. *Journal of Educational Psychology, 97*(2), 214–223. doi:10.1037/0022-0663.97.2.214

Finn, J. D., Pannozzo, G. M., & Achilles, C. M. (2004). The "why's" of class size: Student behavior in small classes. *Review of Educational Research, 73*, 321–368.

Gottfredson, D. C. (2011). Chapter 5, *School-based crime prevention, preventing crime: What works, what doesn't, what's promising.* A Report to the United States Congress, National Institute of Justice. Retrieved from https://www.ncjrs.gov/works/wholedoc.htm

Greene, M. B. (2005). Reducing violence and aggression in schools. *Trauma, Violence, & Abuse, 6*(3), 236–253. doi:10.1177/1524838005277406

Hudley, C., Britsch, B., Wakefield, W. D., Smith, T., Demorat, M., & Cho, S. (1998). An attribution retraining program to reduce aggression in elementary school students. *Psychology in the Schools, 35*(3), 271–282. doi:10.1002/(sici)1520-6807(199807)35:33.;.co;2-a

Jimerson, S. R., Pletcher, S. M. W., Graydon, K., Schnurr, B. L., Nickerson, A. B., & Kundert, D. K. (2006). Beyond grade retention and social promotion: Promoting the social and academic competence of students. *Psychology in the Schools, 43*, 85–97.

Johnson, D. W., & Johnson, R. (1995). Teaching students to be peacemakers: Results of five years of research. *Peace and Conflict: Journal of Peace Psychology, 1*(4), 417–438.

Lee, V. E., Smerdon, B., Alfed-Liro, C., & Brown, S. L. (2000). Inside large and small high schools: Curriculum and social relations. *Educational Evaluation and Policy Analysis, 22*(2), 147–171.

Muschkin, C., Glennie, B., & Beck, A. (2008). Effects of school peers on student behavior: Age, grade retention, and disciplinary infractions in middle school. *Journal of Policy Analysis and Management, 27*, 104–121.

Nagin, D. S., Pagani, L., Tremblay, R. E., & Vitaro, F. (2003). Life course turning points: The effect of grade retention on physical aggression. *Development and Psychopathology, 15*, 345.

Najaka, S. S., Gottfredson, D. C., & Wilson, D. B. (2001). A meta-analytic inquiry into the relationship between selected risk factors and problem behavior. *Prevention Science, 2*, 257–271.

National Association of School Resource Officers. (2004). Survey of members. Retrieved from http://www.schoolsecurity.org/resources/bak/nasro_survey_2004.html

Nelson, J. R., Stage, S., Duppong-Hurley, K., Synhorst, L., & Epstein, M. H. (2007). Risk factors predictive of the problem behavior of children at risk for emotional and behavioral disorders. *Special Education and Communication Disorders Faculty Publications*. Paper 32. Retrieved from http://digitalcommons.unl.edu/specedfacpub/32

Physical Fighting by Youth Study. (2014). ChildTrends. Retrieved from http://www.childtrends.org/?indicators=physical-fighting-by-youth

School Crime and Safety, NCES (National Center for Education Statistics). Retrieved from https://nces.ed.gov/programs/coe/pdf/coe_cld.pdf

SMART Program. U.S. Department of Education, Office of Safe and Drug-Free Schools. (2002).

"Youth Risk Behavior Surveillance System (YRBSS)." (2016, August 11). Centers for Disease Control and Prevention. Web August 25, 2016.

Chapter Four

Bullying and Cyberbullying

Rebecca Sedgwick was twelve years old and jumped to her death in Florida in 2013. She had been taunted by students at her middle school in both face-to-face and online bullying. It was so bad that her mother filed a formal complaint against the school and homeschooled her for the rest of that year. It was estimated that Rebecca endured bullying for up to a year prior to her death. Students allegedly told her to drink bleach and die and that no one would miss her if she died. Rebecca's family also captured screenshots of anonymous messages on various text message apps telling her to kill herself. Rebecca had told a boy she met online that she was planning on committing suicide, but he did not take her seriously.

Several girls were arrested and charged with stalking due to Florida's strict laws regarding bullying, which is prohibited in schools and other public settings. Those charges were later dropped, and the girls only received counseling.

DEFINITIONS, PREVALENCE, AND RISK FACTORS

Definitions and Types

According to Espelage and Holt (2013), bullying is a subtype of aggressive behavior among students that is repetitive and occurs among students of unequal power. These two features, repetition and unequal power, characterize this particular form of peer aggression. Researchers have found that the most common forms of bullying include insults, name-calling, hitting, threats, and social exclusion, or isolation.

Renowned bullying researcher Olweus (1993) distinguishes bullying from other forms of peer victimization due to this power imbalance. The target of the bullying has difficulty defending himself or herself and feels helpless against the aggressor. This imbalance, he notes, is typically considered a defining feature of bullying.

Many victims have reported that due to the repetitive nature and fear associated with bullying, it feels like a form of torture. The final report of the *Safe Schools Initiative* (2012) emphasized that if such behaviors occurred in the workplace, they would likely meet legal definitions of harassment and/or assault.

Bullying behavior was first identified in the literature more than one hundred years ago and has only recently been recognized as something far more serious than a normal part of childhood or "boys will be boys." Given what has happened to Rebecca Sedwick, and others, it is now considered a very serious public health problem.

According to the CDC, bullying is any unwanted aggressive behavior(s) by another youth or group of youths who are not siblings or current dating partners that involves an observed or perceived power imbalance and is repeated multiple times or is highly likely to be repeated. Bullying may inflict real harm on the targeted youth, including physical, psychological, social, or educational harm.

It is important to note that not all bullying involves physical violence, as can be seen in the Rebecca Sedwick case. There are four different types of bullying and these include physical, verbal, relational, and damage to property. The physical, of course, involves the use of physical force (e.g., hitting and pushing). Verbal abuse includes taunting and name-calling. Relational bullying includes things like social isolation and rumor spreading.

A subtype of bullying is cyber bullying, which can overlap with face-to-face bullying. About 75 percent of teenagers have access to cell phones and one report found 94 percent of teens reporting daily online usage. Approximately 25 percent of teens surveyed describe themselves as constantly connected to the Internet (Lenhart et al., 2015). Given the cell phone and Internet usage among the overwhelming majority of today's youth, this subtype of bullying has increased exponentially. Some have described it as an epidemic.

There are some controversies over whether cyber bullying is more or less harmful than in-person bullying and whether it is a distinct type or simply an extension of the concept. Olweus has challenged the more sensationalized accounts of cyber bullying and takes the position that it is simply an extension of in-person victimization. He believes that in-person victimization has more negative impact.

A major report called *Preventing Bullying Through Science-Practice and Policy Report* (Rivara & Le Menestrel, 2016) is the work of the national committee, which analyzed all of the research to date on bullying prevention. It addresses the issue of cyber bullying within a shared bullying framework rather than as a separate entity. This was because of shared risk factors, shared negative consequences, and interventions that work on both, though the committee recognized that there were differences between the two.

Prevalence

According to the 2011 National Crime Victimization survey, 28 percent of students between the ages of twelve and eighteen reported being bullied at school during the previous school year. It appears to be a common experience for students of all ages, cultures, and ethnic groups. Because these estimates are based on self-reports and observations, there is great uncertainty as to the accuracy of these estimates, but making it difficult to determine trends over time (figure 4.1).

The *Preventing Bullying* report found estimates of bullying and cyber bullying prevalence, as reported by national surveys to vary greatly, ranging

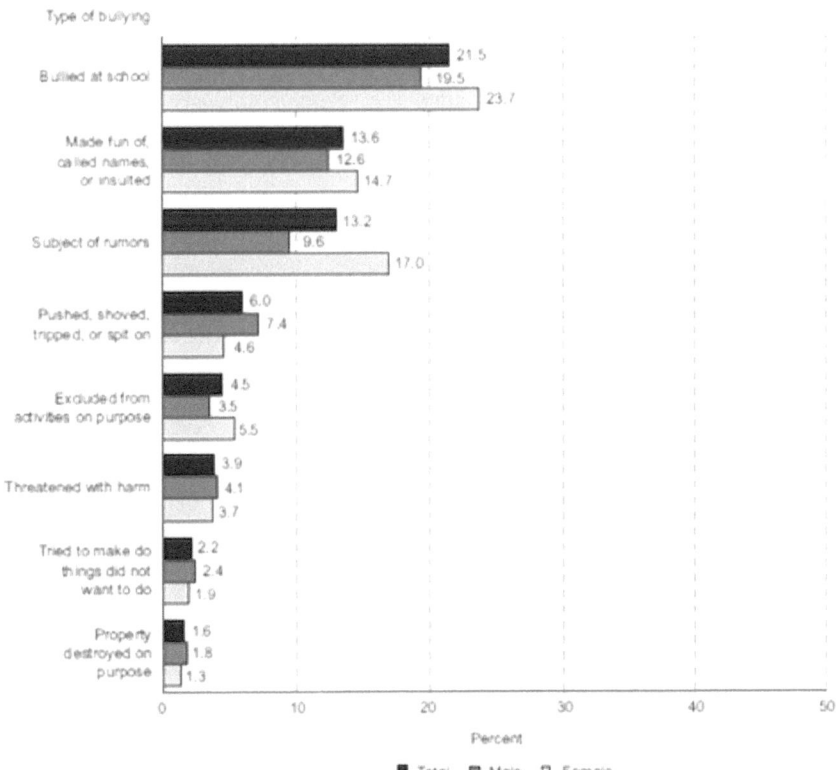

Figure 4.1 Students Reporting Being Bullied at School by Type of Bullying 2013. *Source*: School Crime Supplement to National Crime Victimization Survey, 2013.

from 17.9 percent to 30.9 percent of school-age children for bullying at school, and from 6.9 percent to 14.8 percent for cyber bullying. It also found that the prevalence of bullying of lesbian, gay, bisexual, and transgender (LGBT) youth to be approximately double that of heterosexual youth. Prevalence rates seem to be the lowest for both heterosexual boys and girls (18.3 percent and 19.9 percent) and the highest among gay boys (43.1 percent and 25.7 percent) and bisexual boys (35.2 percent and 33.2 percent), according to Olson et al. (2014).

Regarding gender, Cook et al. (2010) found that although boys and girls experienced relatively similar rates of being bullied, boys were more likely to bully others, or to bully others and be bullied, then girls. Other studies have found gender differences in the frequency with which students report bullying. Most find that girls are more likely to report being bullied than boys. Gendered forms of bullying are said to be common because physical aggression has been regularly associated with boys, whereas relational aggression has been associated with girls.

Among boys, bullying others increased from grades 3 to 12, but among girls, rates of bullying others peaked in eighth grade (Limber et al., as cited in Rivara and Le Menestrel). The likelihood of both being bullied and perpetrating bullying behavior peaked in the early adolescent years before decreasing slightly in later adolescence. Percentages for cyberbullying are shown in figure 4.2.

At-Risk Groups

The *Preventing Bullying* report concluded that there are disparities in the rates of bullying by a variety of characteristics including sexual orientation,

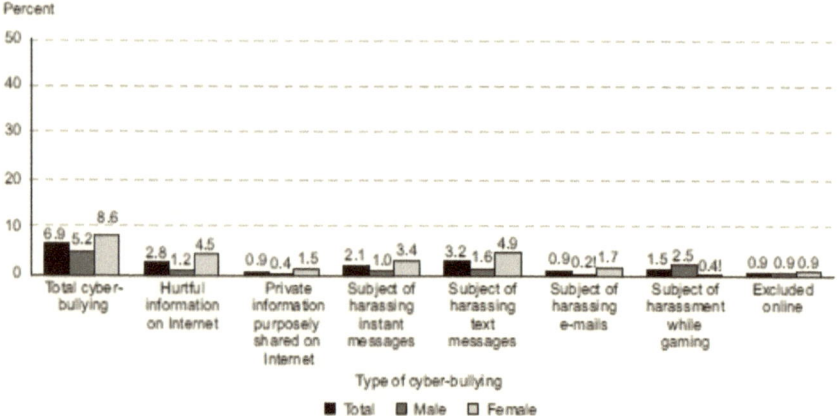

Figure 4.2 Percentage of Students Reporting Cyber bullying 2013. *Source*: School Crime Supplement to National Crime Victimization Survey, 2013.

disability, and obesity. It also noted that there is a lack of data on these and other vulnerable groups. Research reveals that students who are targeted due to bias-based bullying and harassment report more adverse psychological outcomes, however, compared to those whose bullying is not related to such bias.

Students with special needs are also at greater risk for bullying. Swearer and Hymel (2015) found that students with specific learning disabilities and autism spectrum disorders in inclusive classrooms and students with emotional and behavioral disorders and intellectual disabilities in restrictive or self-contained classrooms were more likely than their demographically matched peers without disabilities to experience higher rates of fighting and victimization.

Several studies have found that students with disabilities are overrepresented among children who have been bullied or children who have both bullied and have been bullied. Blake et al. (2012) analyzed bullying data and concluded that students with disabilities are up to 1.5 times more likely to be bullied than youth without disabilities.

One study of over fourteen thousand students in middle and high school (Rose, Simpson, Moss, 2015) found that 35.3 percent of students with emotional and behavior disorders, 33.9 percent of students with autism spectrum disorders, 24.3 percent of students with intellectual disabilities, 20.8 percent of students with other health impairment, and 19.0 percent of students with specific learning disabilities experienced high levels of victimization.

They also found that 15.3 percent of youth with emotional and behavior disorders, 19.4 percent of youth with autism spectrum disorders, 21 percent of youth with intellectual disabilities, 16.9 percent of youth with other health impairment, and 14.4 percent of youth with specific learning disabilities perpetrated bullying behavior. These numbers are in contrast to 14.5 percent of youth without disabilities who experienced high rates of being bullied and 13.5 percent who reported perpetrating bullying behaviors.

As noted, being LGBT is a risk factor. The prevalence of bullying of lesbian, gay, and bisexual (LGB) males and females ranges from 25.6 percent to 43.6 percent.

Obesity is yet another risk factor. In 2012, 31.8 percent of U.S. children and youth six to nineteen years of age were overweight and obese. Puhl and Latner (2001) found that weight was positively associated with being the perpetrator of bullying behavior compared with weight among average-weight children. They also found that girls face an increasing likelihood of being bullied and being a perpetrator of bullying. Other studies have found that overweight girls were more likely to be targets of bullying behavior than their peers.

Bullying and School Shootings

Many media reports about school shootings reported the perpetrator as having been bullied by peers. Both Langman and Newman found that a large majority of school shooters were victims of bullying. Leary et al. (2003) as cited in Rivara and Le Menestrel's report, found that social rejection, including bullying, was a key in thirteen school shooting incidents they studied. Yet, as was seen with the Columbine shooters, at times they were bullies themselves and they also had many friends. Leary also reported on case studies reviewing fifteen school shootings between 1995 and 2001, and found that acute or chronic rejection—in the form of ostracism, bullying, and/or romantic rejection—was present in all but two of the incidents.

The *Preventing Bullying through Science* report states that most investigations have concluded that bullying may play a role in many school shootings, but not all; that it is a factor, and perhaps an important one, but it does not appear to be the main influencing factor in a decision to carry out these violent acts.

THE IMPACT OF BULLYING

The *Preventing Bullying* report highlights the fact that bullying has long-term effects, not only on the bullied child, but also on the child who bullies and on bystanders. Existing evidence suggests that the children and youth who are bullied experience a range of somatic disturbances, including sleep disturbances, gastrointestinal concerns, and headaches.

The committee also found research that suggests that bullying can result in biological changes. It concluded that, although the effects of being bullied on the brain are not yet fully understood, there are changes in the stress response systems and in the brain that are associated with increased risk for mental health problems, cognitive function, self-regulation, and other physical health problems.

The report also points to studies that suggest that individuals who bully and who are also bullied by others are especially at risk for suicidal behavior, due to increased mental health problems. Individuals who are involved in bullying in any capacity (as perpetrators, targets, or both) are statistically significantly more likely to contemplate or attempt suicide, compared to children who are not involved in bullying.

Other consequences for those who are bullied, for the perpetrators of bullying, and for the bystanders present during a bullying event, include poor school performance, anxiety, depression, and future delinquent and aggressive behavior. Being bullied also seems to carry over into mental health functioning during adulthood.

Kretschmer and colleagues (2015) found that bullied children experienced a variety of mental health outcomes including problems with withdrawal and depression, anxiety, somatic complaints, delinquency, and aggression. Further, when these outcomes were considered together, internalizing problems (e.g., withdrawal and anxiety) were the most common.

Children who bully are more likely to be depressed, engage in high-risk activities such as theft and vandalism, and have adverse outcomes later in life compared to those who do not bully. Also, according to the *Preventing Bullying* report, those who both bully others and are themselves bullied appear to be at the greatest risk for poor psychosocial outcomes compared to those who only bully or are only bullied and to those who are not bullied.

How do students cope with bullying? How students cope with bullying seems to relate to the impact of the bullying. According to Donoghue, Almeida, Brandwein, Rocha, and Callahan (2014), coping strategies include avoidance or approach. Approach strategies include relying upon themselves to solve a problem or to asking for help from either friends, family, or teachers.

On the other hand, avoidance includes acting as if nothing happened, internalizing or keeping emotions to themselves, or externalizing, for example, taking their emotions out on others. Based on numerous studies, they say approach strategies are considered adaptive and have been linked to more positive functioning, whereas avoidance strategies are considered maladaptive and have been associated with poor social adjustment.

Unfortunately, many students avoid asking for help from adults due to low expectations of receiving help or possibly being blamed for their problems. Donohue et al. report that students have favorable attitudes toward the idea of seeking support, telling an adult, and reporting to school staff when they are victimized, but they also perceive real and difficult challenges facing them when they do. They say that students may expect that adults will not know how to respond, that coming forward will make them look weak, or that they will be victimized more in retaliation for speaking up.

They also found that distancing, that is, avoidance, was more common than internalizing, and that internalizing was more common than externalizing. In their surveys of students, they found that those who expected to engage in more adaptive coping strategies were more willing to report bullying at school as well.

THE CONTEXT OF BULLYING

The Classroom

The Preventing Bullying through Science report notes that students are embedded in contexts that moderate the effect of their individual characteristics on developmental social and health outcomes. This, it states, is the key to understanding how different social contexts affect the extent to which those characteristics are associated with bullying and perpetration, or with being bullied (figure 4.3).

The report notes that bullying can be seen as a group phenomenon with multiple peers taking on roles other than perpetrator or target. This makes peers a critical social context that affects many aspects of bullying because peers influence group norms, attitudes, and behaviors.

Thus, attitudes and behaviors can vary, depending on variables such as age, gender, social status, and even classroom norms. What happens in the classroom can reduce bullying and its effects—or exacerbate them. For example, it has been found that in classrooms where aggression is more common, children become more aggressive (Mercer et al., 2009).

Peets, Pöyhönen, Juvonen, and Salmivalli (2015) concluded that student decisions about behavior are likely to be influenced by what other classmates do in similar situations, as well as by whether they, or their peers, have previously been rewarded or punished by engaging in similar behaviors.

The bullying report cites both contemporary theory and research, which suggest that individuals who bully others are motivated to gain or maintain high status among their peers. To do that, they need others to witness their exercise of power. It notes that witnesses to bullying actually take on various roles and cites the work of Salmivalli et al., which found at least four major participant roles in typical bullying episodes in addition to the perpetrator-target roles.

These roles include assistants, or henchman, who get involved to help the bully, and reinforcers who encourage the bully. Defenders actively help the victim, though research shows that few bullying episodes are intervened by such defenders. Interestingly, the presence of defenders and classrooms is associated with fewer instances of bullying.

The final participant role is that of bystanders who are present but do not help either the bully or the bullied. By doing nothing, bystanders send a message that bullying is acceptable. Bystanders might be afraid of speaking up for fear of their own social status or possibly becoming a victim of the bully themselves.

The bottom line in the classroom is the consequence for the offender. When there are norms against bullying and swift and sure consequences for engaging in such behavior, there is less bullying. The *Preventing Bullying* report committee concluded that classroom climates that foster respect, cooperation, and support have students who are free to seek help from others.

This means that teachers are vitally important in addressing this issue. If students are reluctant to seek help from their teachers, then their teachers must be alert and aware of the potential for such problems. Bradshaw (2009) found a difference between student and teacher perceptions of bullying behavior. They also found that educators underestimated the impact and

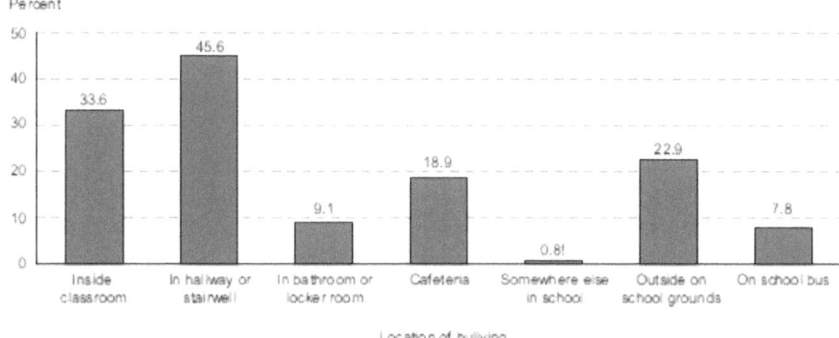

Figure 4.3 Students Aged Twelve to Eighteen Reporting Bullying in Various School Locations, 2013. *Source*: School Crime Supplement to National Crime Victimization Survey, 2013.

prevalence. This, they say, contributes to the reluctance of students to report bullying to adults at school.

The School

School climate impacts the level of bullying as well. A meta-analysis of 153 studies on the predictors of bullying and victimization found that school climate produced one of the largest effect sizes for victimization (Cook et al., 2010).

Cornell, Shukla, and Konold (2015) found a correlation between strict but fair enforcement of school rules and positive student–teacher relationships which were associated with measures of peer victimization. Students in a more positive school climate reported less teasing and bullying, fewer personal experiences of being bullied, and generally less victimization.

Gerlinger and Wo (2014) also found that authoritative schools, schools with high discipline structure and high student support, had lower levels of bullying victimization, but that school security measures (such as the use of security guards, metal detectors, and locked entrances) had little or no association with bullying. They found that it was the consistency and fairness of school discipline, rather than high levels of supervision and enforcement of rules, that affected student behavior.

Cornell et al. reported on a study of 39,364 seventh- and eighth-grade students attending 423 schools. It found meaningful associations at both the student and school levels of analysis. Higher disciplinary structure was associated with lower levels of prevalence of teasing and bullying, bullying victimization, and general victimization. Higher student support was associated with lower prevalence of teasing and bullying and general victimization.

Thus, school leaders need to ensure that a school climate, with high disciplinary structure and positive student–teacher relationships, is a top priority. How to do that will be discussed further in chapter 10.

The Family

Family involvement and support are also extremely vital for the students involved. Interventions that involve parents are essential. Informing parents about bullying and parent training were important family factors. Parents also play a key role when it comes to cyber bullying since this often occurs when students are away from school.

Parents can advocate for their children, as Rebecca Sedwick's mother tried to do. They can monitor their children's access to the Internet. They can provide support and encouragement by listening to their children and helping them problem solve when they face such challenges.

The Community

Just as school and classroom norms pertain to bullying, so do community norms. Whether bullying behavior is recognized, tolerated, or even condoned in a neighborhood or community contributes to either its reduction or escalation.

There is no federal law on bullying, but all fifty states and the District of Columbia now have laws to address bullying. All but one of these addresses cyber bullying. At the federal level there are certain protections. Civil rights and discrimination laws have been used because of the legal responsibility that schools have for providing safe and nondiscriminatory environments.

The U.S. DOE provided eleven recommended components that state and local laws and policies should include. They are:

- a purpose statement;
- a statement of scope;
- a specification of the prohibited conduct;
- enumeration of specific characteristics—actual or perceived—of students who have historically been targets of bullying;
- development and implementation of local education area policies;
- essential components of local education area policies;
- provision for regular review of local policies;
- a communication plan for notifying students, families, and staff of policies related to bullying;
- training and prevention education;
- transparency and monitoring; and
- a statement that the policy does not preclude those who are bullied from seeking other legal remedies. (U.S. Department of Education, Office of Civil Rights, 2010; as cited in Rivara and Le Menestrel, 2016, pp. 5–6)

Rivara and Le Menestrel describe Holben and Zirkel's review of twenty years of cases of litigation. They found 166 bullying claims, 89 percent of which were filed in federal court and 84 percent filed as members of a protected class. Holben and Zirkel note that litigation on bullying is an especially difficult process. The plaintiff must prove that the school district should have known about the bullying or that its response was ineffective. They found that claims under the Individuals with Disabilities Education Act and Title IX had the best success rates, but that court decisions consistently favored the defendant.

Hatzenbuehler, Schwab-Reese, Ranapurwala, Hertz, and Ramirez (2015) compared the laws of twenty-five states with at least one DOE-recommended component in their law. They found that those recommended components had a 24 percent reduced odds of reported bullying and 20 percent reduced odds of reported cyber bullying. They also found that inclusive antibullying policies were significantly associated with lower risk of suicide attempts among lesbian and gay youth, even after controlling for sociodemographic characteristics and exposure to peer harassment and victimization.

RESEARCH ON BULLYING PREVENTION

Bradshaw, Pas, Debnam, and Johnson (2015) says the most effective bullying prevention programs are whole-school, multicomponent programs that combine elements of universal and targeted strategies. Most studies show moderate effect sizes and that when they are positive, they are more likely to be effects on attitudes and knowledge.

The *Preventing Bullying* report found that the vast majority of research on bullying prevention focused on universal school-based programs. It concluded that multicomponent, school-wide programs appear to be the most effective at reducing bullying. It recommends that these should be the types of programs implemented and disseminated, despite the relatively modest results that have been found to date. Many school-wide violence prevention programs have been shown to be effective at reducing aggressive behavior and violence in general. It is hypothesized that these programs would also reduce bullying.

Ttofi and Farrington (2012) did a review of antibullying interventions and estimated that the average reduction in bullying victimization was approximately 17 to 20 percent across forty-four rigorous program evaluations. Yeager et al. (2015) did a meta-analysis and found that the positive effects of bullying prevention programs were limited to students below eighth grade and that programs had no demonstrable effect for students above seventh grade.

Just as we see with violence prevention in general, the three-tiered public health model of universal, selective, and indicated (primary, secondary, and tertiary) preventive measures is also recommended for bullying prevention. Universal, whole-school interventions show that lessons targeted at reducing aggression and violence can be useful, as bullying often co-occurs with other behaviors and mental health problems.

Lessons used in the classroom can teach skills and behavioral expectations. These can include strategies for responding to bullying, and discussing emotionally relevant issues related to bullying and equity. Other effective components include parent training, improved playground supervision, and classroom management, as these are associated with a decrease in students being bullied. Caution about using students as peer mediators is strongly advised, however. Using peers to engage in conflict resolution approaches is not recommended for bullying due to the unequal power status and the possibility of retraumatizing the victim.

While there are few selective or indicated (secondary or tertiary) interventions at schools, resources in this area need to be provided to students and families involved as well. They need to be integrated into a multitiered system of supports for students at risk of engaging in or being victimized by bullying.

The following approaches are not recommended:

1. Suspension and exclusion
2. Encouraging students to fight back
3. Grouping bullies together because of the contagion process
4. One-day awareness sessions or one-shot programs.

PROMISING PROGRAMS: THE OLWEUS BULLYING PREVENTION PROGRAM

The Blueprints for Healthy Youth Development website provides a registry of evidence-based positive youth development programs designed to promote the health and well-being of children and teens. Blueprints has identified the Olweus Bullying Prevention Program as a promising program. It is a multilevel, multicomponent program designed to reduce and prevent school bullying in elementary and middle schools.

The Olweus Bullying Prevention Program is the most extensively studied bullying prevention program. It aims to reduce bullying through components at multiple levels including school-wide components, classroom activities and meetings, targeted intervention for individuals identified as perpetrators or targets, and activities designed to increase involvement by parents, mental health workers, and others. According to the program's website, studies of this program have reported significant reduction in students' reports of bullying and antisocial behaviors and improvements in school climate.

Other goals include increased awareness and knowledge about bullying, involvement of teachers and parents in bullying prevention, development of clear rules against bullying, and providing support and protection to victims.

The program includes school-level, classroom-level, and individual-level components. The school-level components consist of an assessment of the nature and prevalence of bullying in the school, the formation of a committee to coordinate the prevention program, and development of a system ensuring adult supervision of students outside of the classroom. Classroom components include defining and enforcing rules against bullying, discussions and activities to reinforce antibullying values and norms, and active parental involvement in the program. Individual components intervene with students with a history of bullying and/or victimization.

Outcomes from the program include the following:

- Reductions in self-reported bullying are mixed across multiple evaluations, but generally positive
- Reductions in self-reported victimization are mixed across multiple evaluations
- Decreases in other forms of delinquency and antisocial behavior, such as theft, vandalism, and truancy found in the original Norway study and South Carolina replication
- Improvements in positive social relationships found in a study conducted in Norway.

LESSONS LEARNED ABOUT BULLYING

A key finding in the study of reducing bullying is that connectedness to others is a significant buffer for the development of adjustment problems among bullied youth. Schools can play essential roles in building that connectedness.

The *Preventing Bullying through Science* report recommends that schools consider implementing a multicomponent program that focuses on school climate, positive behavior supports, social and emotional learning, or violence prevention. Rather than implementing a bullying-specific prevention intervention, more inclusive programs may reach a broader set of outcomes for students in the school environment. Tiered preventive interventions appear to be promising for schools, though the report concludes that there is a lack of research on selective, and indicated prevention interventions, which focus specifically on bullying.

Such school-wide programs should not simply be add-ons, but thoughtfully integrated with an overall approach to improving culture and climate. Schools use a multitude of different programs to address varying issues. These need to be integrated—not disjointed efforts with no overall vision of how they fit together to advance a school's goals.

No matter what the intervention, the quality of the implementation of school-based programs is what matters most. This takes real leadership, responsible use of resources, sustained training, and supervision. It also entails the use of data to monitor and evaluate the effectiveness of the implementation and to guide any modifications to ensure results.

Fidelity of administration of any research-based program means that, if school leaders want to achieve similar results in their schools, they have to be relentless about ensuring that program guidelines are implemented as recommended. The very foundation of success, however, is the belief of everyone involved that bullying is not normal child's play. This means a commitment to create school and classroom cultures where it cannot flourish and grow. As we saw in the case of Rebecca Sedwick, this can mean the difference between life and death.

We now turn to another type of violence that impacts our schools, that of suicide, the fifth leading cause of death for children aged five to fourteen, and the third leading cause of death for adolescents.

REFERENCES

Blake, J. J., Lund, E. M., Zhou, Q., Kwok, O.-m., & Benz, M. R. (2012). National prevalence rates of bully victimization among students with disabilities in the United States. *School Psychology Quarterly, 27*(4), 210.

Bradshaw, C. P., Waasdorp, T. E. (2009). Measuring and changing a "culture of bullying." *School Psychology Review, 38*(3), 356–361.

Cook, P., Gottfredson, D., & Na, C. (2010). School Crime Control and Prevention. *Crime and Justice, 39*(1), 313–440. doi:10.1086/652387.

Cornell, D., & Bradshaw, C. P. (2015). From a culture of bullying to a climate of support: The evolution of bullying prevention and research. *School Psychology Review, 44*(4), 499–503.

Cornell, D., Shukla, K., & Konold, T. (2015). Peer victimization and authoritative school climate: A multilevel approach. *Journal of Educational Psychology, 107*(4), 1186–1201.

Donoghue, C., Almeida, A., Brandwein, D., Rocha, G., & Callahan, I. (2014). Coping with verbal and social bullying in middle school. *International Journal of Emotional Education, 6*(2), 40–53.

Espelage, D. L., & Holt, M. K. (2013). Suicidal ideation and school bullying experiences after controlling for depression and delinquency. *Journal of Adolescent Health*, *53*(1). doi:10.1016/j.jadohealth.2012.09.017

Gerlinger, J., & Wo, J. (2014). Preventing school bullying: Should schools prioritize an authoritative school discipline approach over security measures? *Journal of School Violence*. Advance online publication. Retrieved from http://dx.doi.org/10.1080/15388220.2014.956321

Hatzenbuehler, M. L., Schwab-Reese, L., Ranapurwala, S. I., Hertz, M. F., & Ramirez, M. R. (2015). Associations between antibullying policies and bullying in 25 states. *JAMA Pediatrics*, *169*(10). doi:10.1001/jamapediatrics.2015.2411

Kretschmer, T., Barker, E. D., Dijkstra, J. K., Oldehinkel, A. J., & Veenstra, R. (2015). Multifinality of peer victimization: Maladjustment patterns and transitions from early to mid-adolescence. *European Child and Adolescent Psychiatry*, *24*(10), 1, 169–1, 179.

Mercer, S. H., Mcmillen, J. S., & Derosier, M. E. (2009). Predicting change in children's aggression and victimization using classroom-level descriptive norms of aggression and pro-social behavior. *Journal of School Psychology*, *47*(4), 267–289. doi:10.1016/j.jsp.2009.04.001

Olsen, E. O., Kann, L., Vivolo-Kantor, A., Kinchen, S., & Mcmanus, T. (2014). School violence and bullying among sexual minority high school students, 2009–2011. *Journal of Adolescent Health*, *55*(3), 432–438. doi:10.1016/j.jadohealth.2014.03.002

Olweus Bullying Prevention Program, Blueprints for Healthy Youth Development. University of Colorado-Boulder Center for the Study and Prevention of Violence. http://www.blueprintsprograms.com/evaluation-abstract/olweus-bullying-prevention-program

Olweus, D. (1993). *Bullying at school: What we know and what we can do*. Oxford, England: Blackwell.

Peets, K., Pöyhönen, V., Juvonen, J., & Salmivalli, C. (2015). Classroom norms of bullying alter the degree to which children defend in response to their affective empathy and power. *Developmental Psychology*, *51*(7), 913–920. doi:10.1037/a0039287

Puhl, R. M., & Latner, J. D. (2001). Stigma, obesity, and the health of the nation's children. *Psychological Bulletin*, *133*, 557–580. doi:10.1037/0033-2909.133.4.557

Rivara, F., & Le Menestrel, S. (Eds.). (2016). *Preventing bullying through science, policy, and practice*. National Academies of Sciences, Engineering, and Medicine. Washington, DC: The National Academies Press. doi:10.17226/23482

Rose, C. A., Simpson, C. G., & Moss, A. (2015). The bullying dynamic: Prevalence of involvement among a large-scale sample of middle and high school youth with and without disabilities. *Psychology in the Schools*, *52*(5), 515–531. doi:10.1002/pits.21840

Swearer, S., & Hymel, S. (2015). Bullying and discrimination in schools: Exploring variations across student subgroups. *School Psychology Review*, *44*(4), 504–509.

Ttofi, M. M., & Farrington, D. P. (2012). Risk and protective factors, longitudinal research, and bullying prevention. *New Directions for Youth Development, 2012*(133), 85–98.

U.S. Secret Service Safe School Initiative. (n.d.). *PsycEXTRA Dataset.* doi:10.1037/e684902012-001

Yeager, D. S., Fong, C. J., Lee, H. Y., & Espelage, D. L. (2015). Declines in efficacy of antibullying programs among older adolescents: Theory and a three-level meta-analysis. *Journal of Applied Developmental Psychology* (2015), http://dx.doi.org/10.1016/j.appdev.2014.11.005

Chapter Five

Suicide and Suicidal Behaviors

The murder–suicide happened at Independence High School in Glendale, Arizona, in February 2016. Dorothy Dutiel was a fifteen-year-old sophomore who had been depressed over a cooling off of the two-year relationship she had had with a fifteen-year-old sophomore Mary Kieu. Dorothy had been depressed over the previous week, describing it as the worst in her life. She had made comments to her friends about whether she should continue living, but they did not take them seriously. She had asked a boy to loan her a gun for protection. He had taken a handgun from his home without telling his family. Dorothy shot Mary and then herself. There were no witnesses to this event and both girls died from a single gunshot wound.

The night before this tragedy, Dorothy tweeted that she felt rejected and told the world goodbye. She left a suicide note for the first responders and for her family members, indicating that she acted alone, and was of sound mind. She even included emergency numbers in the note.

DEFINITIONS AND PREVALENCE

Definitions

Suicide is the third leading cause of death for among adolescents and young adults and the fifth leading cause of death among children aged five to fourteen in the United States, according to the CDC (2013). Despite a previous decline, that there has been a notable increase in the rate of youth suicide over time. In various reports, youth suicidal behavior has been described as an enormous societal problem, an astonishing national problem, a global public health problem, and a major public health crisis.

In 1999, the U.S. Surgeon General put out a call to action to prevent suicide. The Surgeon General called for strategies to prevent suicide, including increasing public awareness of suicide and risk factors, and enhancing research to understand risk and protective factors. In 2001, the U.S. Public Health Service released its strategy for suicide prevention. In 2004, the Garrett Lee Smith Memorial act was signed into law. This was the very first youth suicide prevention bill and in it, the U.S. Congress noted that youth suicide was a public health tragedy, and that early intervention and prevention activities should be national priorities.

Suicide itself is only one behavior along a continuum. According to Mazza and Reynolds (2008), there is suicidal ideation, which includes thoughts of suicide often seen as previewing more serious forms of suicidal behavior; suicidal intent, which includes the intentions of an individual at the time of the attempt in regard to his or her wish to die; and finally, suicide attempts themselves, described as self-injurious behaviors conducted with the intent of causing death. Suicide ideation is a prerequisite of suicide. Not everyone who attempts suicide should be viewed in the same way as those who commit suicide.

Mazza and Reynolds state that suicidal behavior includes a much larger set of behaviors than suicide alone. They note that behaviors along this continuum vary and are not mutually exclusive, nor do all suicidal individuals advance sequentially through them. They also note that although the frequency of each behavior decreases as individuals move along the continuum, the level of lethality and probability of death increases.

Mazza and Reynolds also state that because the suicide attempts of most children and adolescents tend to be of low lethality, there is a possibility that many of them may be ambivalent about taking their lives. Common methods of suicide include drug overdose and wrist cutting, with the use of firearms, the most frequently used method among males between the ages of ten and nineteen who die by suicide.

Prevalence

The CDC states that every year, countless adolescents require medical attention for self-inflicted injuries. According to Miller and Eckert (2009), the 2007 data indicated that approximately one out of every seven high-school students engaged in serious suicidal ideation, one in every ten made a suicide plan, and one in fourteen made a suicide attempt, some to a degree that required medical treatment or hospitalization.

It is estimated that these incidents are drastically underreported. The National Center for Health Statistics estimates are that for every one suicide completion, there are approximately 100 to 200 who have attempted suicide

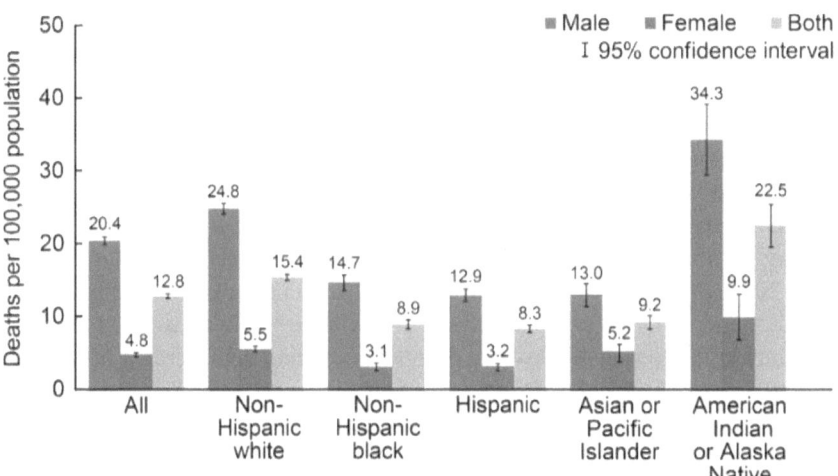

Figure 5.1 Suicide Rates by Young Adults by Race and Gender 2012–13. *Source*: CDC/NCHS National Vital Statistics 2012–13.

and thousands more who engage in suicide-related communication and suicidal ideation (Mazza, 2006). Oregon is one state that requires hospitals to report attempts to the State Department of Health. In 2004, for example, 920 youth there attempted suicide, a year in which 10 successfully took their own lives.

The suicide rate has fluctuated over the last several decades, but Berman, Jobes, and Silverman (2006) note that the overall suicide rate for children and adolescents has increased over 300 percent since the 1950s (see figure 5.1). Again, the CDC notes that more teenagers and young adults die from suicide than cancer, heart disease, AIDS, birth defects, stroke, pneumonia, influenza, and chronic lung disease combined.

Gender, Race, Age

Whetstone, Morrissey, and Cummings (2007) found that suicide risk varies by gender, race, and age. While adolescent males are more likely to die from suicide, females are more likely to plan and attempt it. Studies indicate that more females than males report thinking, planning, or trying suicide. Miller and Eckert concur, stating that gender appears to have a stronger influence on youth suicidal behavior than race or ethnicity.

Girls seem to be more likely to engage in self-harm behavior, but boys are more likely to succeed in killing themselves. According to Berman et al. (2006), although more females report suicidal ideation than males and attempt suicide at rates two to three times the rate of males, males commit suicide at a rate five times that of females. They describe the typical individual who attempts suicide as an adolescent female who ingests drugs, as opposed to the typical youth who commit suicide as an adolescent male using a firearm.

Maris, Berman, and Silverman (2000) attributed this difference to the higher rates of significant suicide risk factors among males (e.g., access to firearms) as well as their being less likely than females to engage in a number of protective behaviors, such as seeking help, being aware of warning signs, having flexible coping skills, and building effective social support systems.

In 2008, the CDC reported on a survey of students in grades 9 through 12, which found that 14.5 percent of those students seriously considered attempting suicide in the previous twelve months, including 18.7 percent of females and 10.3 percent of males. During this same one-year period, 11.3 percent of students made a plan about how they would attempt suicide (13.4 percent of females and 9.2 percent of males), 6.9 percent reported making at least one suicide attempt (9.3 percent of females and 4.6 percent of males), and 2 percent reported making at least one attempt that resulted in an injury, poisoning, or an overdose that had to be treated by a doctor or nurse.

Berman states that the probability of suicide increases in both males and females as children grow older, with adolescents aged fifteen to nineteen being at higher risk than younger youth. The CDC also states that the number of children aged ten to fourteen committing suicide is a growing concern, with suicide rates increasing among that group. According to Yang, Burrola, and Bryan (2009), younger suicide ideators are more likely to be female, concerned about depression, and vulnerable to cumulative stress.

Regarding race, whereas suicide is the third leading cause of death among all children and youth in the United States, it is the second leading cause of death among Caucasian youth and the third leading cause of death among African Americans. Mazza (2006) found the highest rates of youth suicide to be among Native Americans and the lowest rates among Asian Pacific Islanders.

Berman notes that the highest suicide rate is among Caucasians, followed by African Americans and Latinos, and that the rate of suicide among African American males has had the greatest increase in recent decades. It more than tripled in males between fifteen and nineteen years of age, increasing by 234 percent during that period. African Americans have been found to be less likely than whites to report suicidal ideation, whereas Native American and Alaska native females were more likely than white females to report both suicidal ideation and plans. Hispanic and Latina females were also more likely than white females to make a suicide attempt, according to Nickerson and Slater (2009).

Both socioeconomic status (SES) and location are also related to suicide and suicidal behaviors. Stack (2000) says that although suicide occurs across all economic classes, there seems to be an inverse relationship between SES and suicide rates. And compared to cities, rural communities have higher suicide rates, which, Walker, Ashby, Hoskins, and Greene (2009) say, are compounded by poor access to mental health care.

Several studies have also found associations between academic achievement and suicidal behavior. Adolescents reading below grade level were found to experience suicidal ideation or attempts and to drop out of school more than students reading at grade level, even when controlling for psychiatric and demographic variables (Daniel et al., 2006).

Another study found that perceptions of failing academic performance were associated with an increased probability of a suicide attempt among adolescents, even when controlling for self-esteem, locus of control, and depressive symptoms (Richardson et al., 2005). These studies provide additional areas of needed support (e.g., remediation of academic deficits) and the rationale for resources addressing the academic needs of students.

RISK FACTORS AND WARNING SIGNS

Risk Factors

Joiner (2005) believes the root cause of most suicidal behavior is the pain, which is a combination of perceived burdensomeness (i.e., the sense that one is ineffective and/or expendable) and thwarted belongingness (i.e., the sense that one is disconnected and isolated from others). Such individuals are in incredible psychic pain. Suicide experts believe that individuals contemplating or attempting suicide often do not want to die as much as they want their pain to end. They see death as their only viable option.

Miller and Eckert state that although numerous risk factors for suicidal behavior have been identified, the most reliable of which is the presence of psychopathology. Estimates are that approximately 90 percent of youth who die by suicide experienced at least one mental disorder at the time of their death, the most common of which are mood disorders (e.g., major depressive disorder, bipolar disorder), followed by substance-related disorders and disruptive behavior disorders. They cite Fleischmann et al. (2005), who say that approximately 42 percent to 66 percent of youth who die by suicide appear to have been experiencing some type of depressive disorder at the time of their death.

Miller and Taylor (2005) also found that most youth who commit suicide have multiple psychiatric disorders and/or psychological problems. Mazza notes that this finding indicates that suicide does not occur in isolation, but rather is the byproduct of other mental health problems. Joiner also points out that another prominent risk factor for suicide is previous suicidal behavior.

Miller and Eckert list a number of studies, which identify other risk factors, including biological deficits in serotonin functioning, social isolation, low self-esteem, dysfunctional family environments, exposure to violence, and access to weapons. Joiner says that childhood physical abuse is also related to risk factors for suicide.

Kalafat (2006) describes additional risk factors for suicide including anxiety, conduct disorders, characteristics such as cognitive rigidity and problem-solving deficits, and stressful life events such as social rejection. Whetstone et al. (2007) added even more: parental psychopathology, parental divorce, access to fatal methods of suicide, barriers to treatment, feelings of hopelessness, impulsive or aggressive tendencies, and physical illness.

Berman et al. note that the risk of suicidal behavior is a function of intention. In general, they say the stronger the intention to commit suicide, the greater the potential lethality of the method selected to carry it out. Choice of method is influenced by things like accessibility, knowledge and experience, the cultural significance of suicide, as well as the state of mind of the individual.

Warning Signs

Warning signs, on the other hand, according to Miller and Eckert, are more dynamic factors that include rage, anger, seeking revenge; acting reckless or engaging in risky activities, seemingly without thinking; feeling trapped, as if there is no way out; increasing alcohol or drug use; withdrawing from friends, family, or society; and experiencing anxiety and/or agitation; being unable to sleep or sleeping excessively; dramatic mood changes; and perceiving no reason for living or no sense of purpose in life.

While many of these warning signs may appear to be typical behaviors for adolescents, experts strongly advise that multiple warning signs need immediate attention.

Suicide and Other Types of Violence

There seem to be links between suicidal behavior and other types of violence. The U.S. Secret Service and DOE report on school shootings, for example, found that almost eight of ten shooters had experienced suicidal ideation and over 60 percent had a history of depression. The majority were found to have either bullied or have been victims of bullies as well, though the relationship between bullying and suicide is mixed.

One study (Nickerson & Slater, 2009) looked at the extent to which violent behavior and peer victimization were associated with suicidal ideation, plans, and attempts. They looked at a nationally representative sample of over 11,000 adolescents who completed the 2005 Youth Risk Behavior Survey. Boys were more likely to be involved in physical fighting and weapon carrying, and girls more likely to report suicidal behavior and feeling unsafe at school. Predictors for suicidal behavior for both male and female adolescents included carrying a weapon, being threatened or injured at school, having property stolen or damaged at school, and getting in a fight.

As Joiner has emphasized, child abuse is related to suicide attempts. One longitudinal study cited by Nickerson and Slater found that abused children were more likely to have significant problems at ages fifteen and twenty-one, including depression, suicidal ideation, and suicide attempts. Being a victim of violence, and even being a witness to violence, can lead to suicidal behavior.

The American Association of Suicidology (AAS) held a conference in 1998 in collaboration with youth suicide researchers, firearms safety groups, and firearms advocacy groups in attendance. They worked to reach a consensus on a statement regarding youth suicide by firearms and then recommended strategies (*Consensus Statement on Youth Suicide by Firearms*, 1998). The areas of consensus included the following:

- Firearms are the most common method of suicide by youth
- The increase in the rate of youth suicide from the 1960s to the early 1990s was largely related to the use of firearms as a method
- The most common location of firearms suicides by youth is in the home
- There is a positive association between the accessibility of firearms in the home and the risk for youth suicide
- The risk conferred by guns in the home is proportional to the presence of loaded and unsecured firearms and the number of guns in the home
- If a gun is used to attempt suicide, a fatal outcome will result 78% to 90% of the time. (pp. 89, 90)

Even though very little has been done regarding gun control in the wake of the school tragedies that have been discussed, such initiatives that would restrict access to guns are associated with a reduction in suicide, particularly among youth (figure 5.2).

Berman et al. note that the risk of harm by guns is proportional to their accessibility and the number of them available. They say that if a gun is used in a suicide attempt, as we saw in the case Mary Kieu and Dorothy Dutiel, a fatal outcome will occur 80 to 90 percent of the time. They also suggest that potentially one of the most powerful youth suicide prevention strategies is the removal of guns from the home or, at the very least, restricting children's access to them.

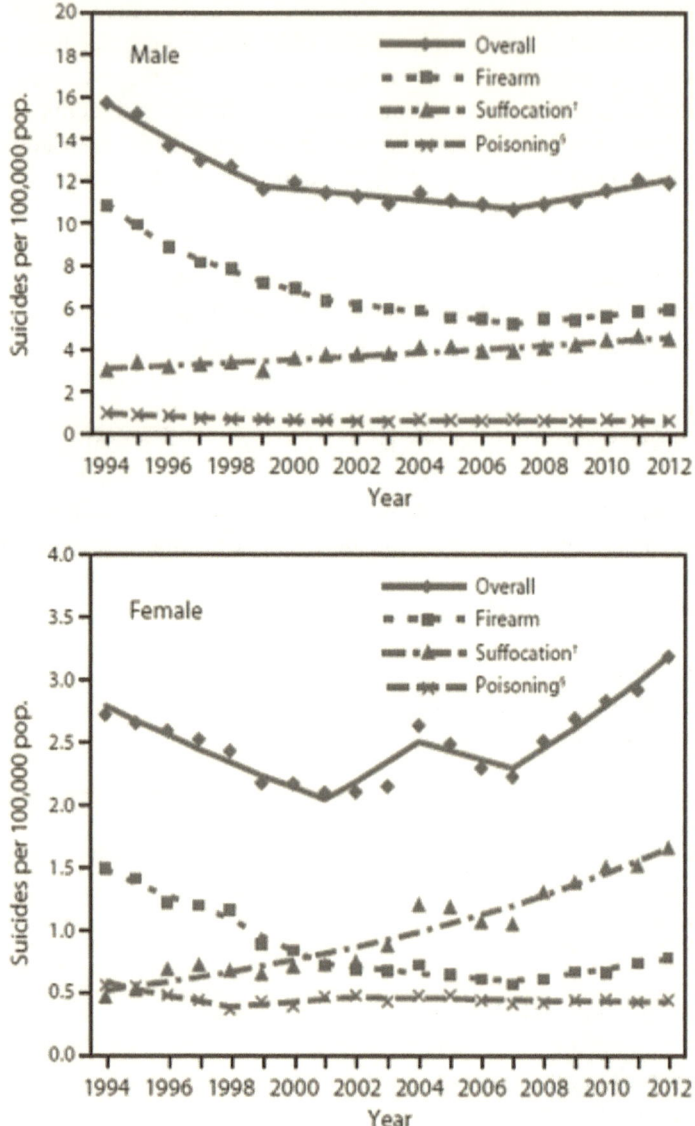

Figure 5.2 CDC Age-Adjusted Suicide Rates for Youth Aged Ten to Twenty-Four by Gender/Means.

Suicide and Specific At-Risk Populations

As stated, suicide is the third leading cause of death among U.S. youth. Sadly, suicide attempts are nearly two-and-a-half times more likely to occur among lesbian, gay, and bisexual (LGB) youth. Adolescence and young adulthood are the periods when suicide among this population is most frequent. Meyer (2003) describes the minority stress model, which applies to this population and this issue.

Being a member of a disparaged or stigmatized group evokes stress. Minority stress influences mental health for sexual minority people. Stress factors include the experience of prejudice events, expectation of rejection or discrimination, concealment of one's sexual orientation, and internalized homophobia. It reflects society's negative reactions and attitudes, and the experience of these stressors is related to lower well-being, higher levels of depression, and suicidal ideation.

Sadly, the 2011 National School Climate Survey reported that over 80 percent of LGB and over 60 percent of transgender students reported being verbally harassed, and almost 40 percent reported having experienced physical violence at the school during the previous year.

One survey of 876 students who self-identified as LGBT youth showed an association of sexual orientation victimization with depression and suicidal ideation, which was mediated by perceived burdensomeness (Baams, Grossman, & Russell, 2015). Feeling like a burden to others is a critical mechanism in explaining higher levels of depression and suicidal ideation among these youth.

They suggest that, because a sense of belonging is often impacted, the interventions should address youth's beliefs of burdensomeness as well as focusing on decreasing their social isolation. Such a lack of belonging has been correlated with suicidal behavior. In fact, they state that their results strongly indicate that it is the notion of being a burden to others that is underlying the adverse effects of minority stress on depression and suicidal ideation among LGBT youth.

Another risk factor to consider is the issue of perceived weight status. Whetstone et al. found that in addition to more females than males thinking, planning, and attempting suicide, those girls who thought of themselves as overweight were significantly more likely to report suicidal thoughts and actions. For males, they found that perceptions of both overweight and underweight were significantly associated with suicidal thoughts and actions. This held true, they found, even controlling for personal and family characteristics among middle-school boys and girls.

Suicide is known to be one out of the most common causes of death for those with anorexia nervosa, and suicide is more common among adolescents and young adults who are anorexic than those who are not. The Youth Risk Behavior Risk Surveillance Survey showed that high-school students who viewed themselves as overweight or underweight were more likely to report suicide ideation and attempts. Underweight boys were found to be more likely to think, plan, or try suicide.

Finally, Whetstone et al. state that the relationship between weight perception and suicidal thoughts and behaviors is complex and may also be influenced by other confounding variables such as self-esteem, social exclusion, parental neglect, and a variety of psychiatric disorders. They concluded that perceiving oneself to be overweight was associated with self-reported suicidal thinking and behavior in middle-school-aged males and females, while the perception of underweight was significant in males.

Now that we have examined the prevalence, risk factors, and warning signs, we turn to issues of addressing suicide and suicidal behavior. What are the roles and responsibilities of the various stakeholders? What should be done when a school staff member or family member notices multiple warning signs? What are research-based best practices? Three areas to be considered include prevention, intervention, and post prevention.

PREVENTION AND INTERVENTION

Universal/Primary Prevention

Kalafat (2006) tells us that prevention strategies can be grouped into three categories: (1) identifying and referring at-risk youth to treatment, (2) addressing risk factors, and (3) enhancing protective factors (e.g., social interaction, family connectedness). The three-tiered public health model, discussed earlier in regard to aggression and bullying, has prevention as its major emphasis. Prevention approaches include student awareness and response curricula, screening, and staff (gatekeeper) training programs.

Protective factors for suicide prevention include individual characteristics such as a positive outlook, self-efficacy, and effective problem-solving skills. It also includes environmental factors such as contact with caring adults, and a sense of connection and contribution to school and community. Problem behaviors, including suicide, substance abuse, interpersonal violence, and unsafe sexual behavior share common individual and environmental risk and protective factors.

Kalafat says that enhancing protective factors may be a more effective prevention strategy than addressing risk factors. There is evidence from longitudinal studies than programs that promote protective factors such as social competence, decision-making, family connections, contact with caring school, adults, and school bonding moderate a variety of risk behaviors, including substance abuse, delinquency, violent behavior, and problem sexual behavior.

And it seems that universal suicide prevention programs are the most widely used when a school does address suicide prevention. Kalafat also states that there is evidence for the effectiveness of school-based mental health services in treating children with mental health concerns. He says that the basis for such a universal approach is the fact that suicidal youth are more likely to tell a peer about their thoughts or plans, and that the majority of these peer confidants do not tell an adult about this. In fact, school-based adults are usually the last choice for them to turn to.

Thus, comprehensive school suicide prevention programs are designed to increase the likelihood that school staff and peers who come into contact with children at risk for suicide can more readily identify them, can provide an appropriate initial response to them, and will know how to obtain help for them.

Kalafat says that because schools have the primary responsibility for the education and socialization of children and adolescents, they perhaps have the greatest potential to identify risk and warning signs and get the needed assistance.

Miller et al. (2009) notes that specific aspects of the public health model that have particular relevance for schools include: (a) applying scientifically based evidence to the delivery of services; (b) strengthening positive behavior rather than focusing exclusively on decreasing problem behavior; (c) emphasizing community collaboration and linked services; and (d) using appropriate research-based strategies.

As more and more emphasis is being placed on schools as resources for mental health support, they are seen as effective places to locate such services. An informed, caring adult who works with the child all day every day (commonly called a gatekeeper in this field) has a better chance of recognizing a child who is struggling with suicide or suicide behaviors and referring them to the appropriate sources.

Mazza and Reynolds (2008) describe the need to focus on increasing awareness of suicide, providing information regarding risk factors and warning signs, dispelling myths about suicide, teaching appropriate responses to peers who may come into contact with someone who may be suicidal, and potentially identifying youth who may be suicidal or at risk for suicidal behavior. They say that an important aspect of effective suicide prevention programs is that they may reduce the severity and/or the frequency of specific risk factors for suicidal behavior as well as other mental health problems.

Miller also found that programs designed to enhance student social support and connectedness may also promote their sense of belonging, another vitally important protective factor. The focus on increasing competencies rather than simply decreasing problem areas is in line with the public health approach to prevention and intervention.

Yet, most schools do not have such programs and most school staff do not have such training. The CDC says that most schools do not appear to be actively engaged in prevention efforts, as less than half of all states require that suicide prevention be taught in at least one school grade. One study of 1,200 educators found that only 20 percent reported suicide prevention plans at their schools.

Even school psychologists, who are in an important position to provide support, say they need more training, particularly in the area of suicide risk assessment. If a school staff is uninformed, this can exacerbate a problem when a crisis like the one in Arizona happens. Valuable time can be lost when staff is scrambling at a point when time is of the essence.

Miller points to evidence that prevention programs that include providing information to students regarding suicide awareness and intervention, teaching them coping and problem-solving skills, and teaching and reinforcing strengths and protective factors, all while addressing risk-taking behaviors, may lead to improvements in students' problem-solving skills and self-efficacy as well as reductions in self-reported suicide vulnerability.

Berman et al. (2006) say that it is really important to include skill-building elements (e.g., coping skills and problem solving) as components of prevention programs. Increased knowledge alone appears insufficient to change behavior. Students need to be taught interpersonal skills with role-playing and real-life situations. They need access to mentoring programs, peer mentoring, and an expanded connection to adults.

Another approach to identifying students potentially at risk is screening. Some experts advocate for specifically targeting students as a more efficient strategy. The Columbia Team Screen Program is the most widely used screening program around. An individual deemed at risk is assessed by a clinician who determines whether the student needs to be referred for treatment or further evaluation.

Other approaches to screening include surveying all students with self-report questionnaires. A student who scores above a certain score is individually interviewed to assess the need for additional services. Even though student screening is considered by experts to be an essential component of school-based prevention, one survey of school superintendents (Scherff, Eckert, & Miller, 2005) found school-wide screening programs to be consistently rated less desirable than curricular approaches and staff training. This is a concern, given the strong recommendation by experts for screening efforts.

To be effective, Kalafat advises, prevention programs must address suicide through a systems approach. Comprehensive school programs cannot be effective in training students to get help for at-risk peers, he advises, unless they also maintain coordination and confidence among school administrators, faculty, and staff; ensure disseminated policies and procedures for responding to risk behaviors; and have ongoing, cooperative relationships with parents and community emergency, social services, and mental health providers. All of the approaches must be seen as complementary, noncompeting components of an ongoing systemic response to youth behavior problems.

Dade County Miami Youth Suicide Prevention Program

Zenere and Lazarus (2009) present an example of an effective, comprehensive, district-wide prevention program with longitudinal data collected over eighteen years. It is among the first to provide evidence that youth suicidal behavior can be reduced through school-based suicide prevention programs. The study of this program was only one among the thirteen school-based suicide prevention programs to be classified as exhibiting promising evidence of significance.

In 1988, eighteen students in the Miami-Dade County public schools in Miami, Florida, committed suicide. Because of a very high rate of suicide (5.5 per 100,000 students aged five to nineteen) during the period of 1980 to 1988, the district implemented its youth suicide prevention and intervention program based on the three-tier suicide prevention model. Since implementation of this program, a significant decrease in the suicide rate (from 5.5 per 100,000 to 1.4) was observed from 1989 to 2006. There was also a steady decline in the suicide attempt rate during this same period.

The program's curriculum focuses on the delivery of prevention education and intervention strategies across grade levels. Its goal is to both reduce student risk factors and increase protective factors. Lessons emphasize skill building in the areas of self-awareness, communication, problem solving, coping, decision-making, relationship building, stress management, and knowledge of health issues and resources.

Zenere and Lararus describe one unit of study as devoted to teaching students the possible warning signs of suicidal behavior and the development of help-seeking behavior. In this lesson, students are taught to identify signs and behaviors associated with potential suicide risks in themselves and others, and to take appropriate action in gaining adult assistance.

School mental health professionals receive training in suicide assessments, parental notification, referral to community-based resources, and post-intervention practices. Such training is vitally important as staff in general, and school psychologists in particular, consistently report needing more information in risk assessment and student support.

The district uses a student intervention profile to identify students who may potentially represent a suicide risk. At the end of each grading period, counselors receive a printout on each student that reviews seven major areas of concern, including academic performance, effort, conduct, attendance, negative report card comments, discipline violations, and involvement with school police. Classroom teachers and other school professionals rate student performance in these areas and students demonstrating three or more of these areas are referred to a school counselor.

The program was developed, implemented, and evaluated initially over a five-year period. During the first year of the program, the number of suicide attempts was eighty-eight per 100,000. There were fifty-two attempts during the second year and thirty-nine in the third year of the program. Between 1990 and 2005, the suicide rate of the Miami-Dade school system for students aged five to nine was 1.3 per 100,000 students. This compares with 3.0 per 100,000 for Florida and 3.5 for the entire United States. For students aged fifteen to nineteen, the Miami Dade system rate was 2.5 per 100,000 compared to 6.7 per 100,000 for Florida and 7.7 per 100,000 for the entire United States.

Secondary/Selected Prevention

Kalafat assures us that there is firm evidence that therapy for children and adolescents is effective, including treatments for anxiety, depression, and conduct disorders. There is also evidence for the effectiveness of family therapy, he finds, but considerably less research on selected suicide prevention programs focusing on those students deemed identified as high risk.

Possible components of a selected program may include developing and teaching decision-making skills and strategies, identifying resources in the school and community for help, emphasizing peer involvement, the role of peers, and responding to someone who may be suicidal, and developing strategies for identifying high-risk youth (Mazza & Reynolds, 2008). Screening programs would be an example of selected prevention effort leading to intervention.

Tertiary/Indicated Prevention/Intervention

Indicated suicide prevention programs target students who are already engaged in suicidal behavior. The focus of indicated programs, therefore, is to reduce the current crisis, as well as reduce the risk for further suicidal behavior.

Possible components of indicated programs may include developing and teaching adaptive decision-making strategies that focus on times of stress or emotional turmoil, accessing emergency help, providing ongoing support to students during a crisis, and identifying at least one caring adult in the school community from whom to seek help (Mazza & Reynolds, 2008).

Kalafat notes that the limited available evidence about treating suicide indicates that cognitive behavior therapy and dialectical behavior therapy show promise. He points to treatment models that incorporate rapport-building strategies, appropriate crisis intervention, cognitive and problem-solving skills development, and appropriate risk management practices as important.

Use of Medication

A controversial area in the field of suicide prevention has been use of antidepressants with children and adolescents. In the early 2000s, research suggested that one medication demonstrated a slight increase in suicidal ideation and behavior in children and adolescents with major depressive disorder. The Food and Drug Administration (FDA) and other agencies responded to public concerns over that finding. A meta-analysis (or review of studies) was then conducted on nine antidepressant medications, none of which resulted in suicide.

Yet, in 2004, the FDA issued a black box warning for *all* antidepressants, which stated that there was a potential for an increased risk of suicide in children and adolescents. Gibbons et al. (2007) state that, ironically, there is now speculation that the decreased numbers of children and adolescents taking antidepressant medication due to these fears may be at least partly responsible for a subsequent increase in youth suicide. Others have questioned the link, or concluded that if it occurs, any danger would most likely develop in the first few weeks and wear off thereafter.

POSTVENTION

Postvention is a term coined by Schneiderman, at the first American Association of Suicidality (AAS) conference. It is defined as the help that comes after such a tragic event. As mentioned, for every one suicide, there are at least six survivors. Andriessen (2009) describes it as the activities that help suicide loss survivors facilitate recovery and prevent adverse outcomes, including their own suicidal behavior.

Because survivors are at risk after such a loss, there is grief, self-blame, and guilt exacerbated by the stigma. Children respond differently than adults. Given the developmental levels and coping skills, experts recommend explaining the circumstances and responding to questions with age-appropriate answers to help them deal effectively with the situation. Younger children may act out their emotions, while older children may isolate themselves or participate in high-risk activities.

There is also the issue of contagion, described by the AAS. This occurs when individuals who are already susceptible are more influenced toward suicidal behavior through their knowledge of another person's suicidal act. There have been cases in schools, most recently in Palo Alto, CA, where between 2009 and 2010, five students or recent graduates from the school died by suicide. The deaths were designated as a suicide cluster, defined by the CDC as three or more suicides in close proximity. There have been other clusters of youth suicides in the wake of one student's suicide.

School staff should be knowledgeable about what to expect, and on alert for behaviors that other students are not coping well with the news of such a tragedy. It is also recommended that community mental health providers and organizations be part of the postvention plan of any school district.

IMPLICATIONS FOR SCHOOLS

Program Implementation Barriers

Many universal prevention programs have been of short duration. They have failed to assess program effects on more severe forms of suicidal behavior, despite research that such programs should be of longer duration, have a comprehensive mental health focus, and assess a broader spectrum of suicidal behaviors (e.g., suicide attempts, rather than simply focusing on knowledge and attitude change), say Miller et al., citing the work of Berman, Kalafat, Mazza, and others.

Miller also notes that the most prominent barriers to getting help for students themselves were: (1) an inability to discuss problems with adults, (2) the belief that one should handle their own problems without health, (3) fear of hospitalization, and (4) lack of perceived closeness to adults. These are issues that schools can and must address.

School personnel need to form closer bonds with students, says Miller (2010), so that students are more likely to perceive them as approachable and helpful, whether in regard to their own possible suicidal behavior or that of their peers. Highlighting the fact that biological factors are highly associated with depression and suicidal behavior may be helpful for some youth, particularly male students, he says, who may perceive themselves as deserving blame for them or needing to handle problems on their own.

There is also the myth that discussing suicide might lead students to do it, but experts say that has not been found to be true. Instead, Kalafat advises that presenting information to students about youth suicide can help change their attitudes about it as well.

Cultural issues, which can also be barriers if not addressed, have not been fully developed in suicide prevention programs. This is an area which is in great need of further research. Other potential barriers include parent refusal to have a student participate in a program, resistance from school staff, funding problems, and concern about ethical and legal issues. Yet, schools may be held legally responsible if they fail to act in the case of the student at risk of suicide or suicidal behavior.

Having policies for identifying and referring students and crisis intervention plans, as well as postvention and plans are imperative for schools today, as well as having a plan for student return to school after a suicide attempt.

Tompkins, Witt, and Abraibesh (2009) found that 20 percent of school personnel have had contact with at least one suicidal youth in the past month and 39 percent had such contact in the previous year. Ironically, while teachers are often identified as being in a unique position to help such at-risk students, at present they are the least likely that students turn to. Interestingly, they point to research that suggests that professionals and educators rarely recognize, or are able to provide assistance to, suicidal youth. They emphasize that improving school staff members' ability to do so also plays a vitally important role in prevention.

Training Staff

Gatekeeper training programs are described by Mann et al. (2005) as one of the most promising strategies. They prepare key stakeholders like teachers, parents, healthcare providers, first responders, and so on, to understand the risk and protective factors associated with suicide and to identify at-risk youth, to be aware of appropriate community resources, and make referrals when necessary. Gatekeeper strategies also help decrease stigma by raising awareness of effective treatment and the importance of help-seeking behaviors.

IMPLICATIONS FOR COMMUNITIES

Implementation of Prevention Programs

According to the U.S. Department of Health and Human Services (2001), the stigma associated with suicide and mental illness is a significant obstacle to community adoption of suicide prevention programs, as well as a major barrier to seeking mental health care. Gatekeeper programs, as discussed earlier, can help in addressing such stigma.

Whether community-based or school-based, Kalafat says that in order to assess far-reaching program effects, programs must be: (1) implemented with fidelity, (2) address multiple levels of school and community contexts, (3) be disseminated to enough sites to obtain large enough samples to determine impact, and (4) be sustained over a sufficient enough length of time to detect trends.

Suicide researchers' highlight have called for the development of comprehensive, integrated programs that involve multiple domains, including the individual, family, school, community, media, and healthcare systems, to address suicide prevention.

Communities must come together to talk about suicide prevention, identify their prevention weaknesses, build upon their strengths, and create plans of action. As seen with the issue of suicide contagion, media sensationalism can have an impact across the community in the wake of the suicide, especially on students.

Miller and Eckert suggest that providing guidelines to the media about the appropriate portrayal of suicide is critical. They highlight several recommended media guidelines, which include (1) avoiding sensationalistic coverage of the suicide, (2) avoiding glorification or vilification of the victim, and (3) not providing excessive details of the suicide. The message should emphasize that no one thing or person is to blame for the suicide and that help is available.

Collaboration between Agencies

For so many societal problems, the lack of cooperation and collaboration across agencies that work on problems of violence exacerbates them. Violence prevention in general, and suicide prevention programs in particular, require that concerned individuals and agencies work together, get informed, pool resources, and share information. As described, the *Connect Suicide Prevention Program* provides a template for such cross-fertilization of expertise and resources, and for the institutionalization of protocols and practices to address this issue.

Access to Guns

Given the lethality of suicide behaviors and guns, communities need to make every effort to limit access to these weapons, especially access by children and adolescents. This alone would be a huge step in suicide prevention. Back in Phoenix, Dorothy only had to ask a friend for gun who took it from his own home without asking. It was that easy for her to get her hands on a weapon with its deadly consequences. Gun violence awareness programs and safe storage programs also need to be readily available to help address this problem.

PROMISING PROGRAM: LIFELINES

Lifelines: A Comprehensive Suicide Awareness and Responsiveness Program for Teens *is the Hazelden Foundation's evidence-based program for addressing suicide among young people. According to the* Violence Prevention Works *website,* Lifelines *is a whole-school program that educates administrators, faculty and staff, parents, and students on the facts about suicide and their roles in suicide prevention, intervention, and postvention.*

The goals of Lifelines *are to increase the likelihood that:*

- *members of the school community can more readily identify potentially suicidal adolescents, know how to initially respond to them, and know how to rapidly obtain help for them;*
- *troubled adolescents are aware of and have immediate access to helping resources and seek such help as an alternative to suicidal actions.*

Lifelines *was the subject of extensive research during 2005 in twelve public schools in Maine. This outcome evaluation demonstrates that the curriculum promotes increases in students' knowledge about suicide and resources, as well as expressed intent to intervene on behalf of at-risk peers. Findings also support teacher acceptance of the program and increased student confidence in the school's ability to respond to at-risk youth.*

Lifelines *has been identified as a promising program by the Suicide Prevention Resource Center and is included in the Substance Abuse and Mental Health Services Administration's National Registry of Evidence-based Programs and Practices.*

LESSONS LEARNED ABOUT SUICIDE AND SUICIDAL BEHAVIOR

When including suicidal behavior with suicide itself, we see that this is an enormous problem. So many children and adolescents are carrying so much pain around with them every day. When even our school professionals say they do not have enough training and expertise to recognize and address these behaviors, it is past time to make providing it a priority. Programs and resources exist and children who are suffering must be connected to them. Next to family members, school personnel are in the best position to be alert for signs of trouble. Knowing what those signs are and what to do about them are the first steps.

Once again we see that school-wide universal models are recommended for prevention and intervention of this type of violence as well as the types of violence already discussed. Primary, secondary, and tertiary interventions must be made available so that everyone, especially the peers, who troubled students so often turn to, know what to do when a child has the courage to speak up about the horrendous pain they are experiencing. Lives depend on it.

We now turn to another type of violence proliferating in our school: sexual harassment, which according to some experts, affects as many as 80 percent of school children at some time in their school lives (Espelage & Holt, 2007).

REFERENCES

Andriessen, K. (2009). Can postvention be prevention? *Crisis, 30*(1), 43–47. doi:10.1027/02275910.30.1.43

Baams, L., Grossman, A. H., & Russell, S. T. (2015). Minority stress and mechanisms of risk for depression and suicidal ideation among lesbian, gay, and bisexual youth. *Developmental Psychology, 51*(5), 688–696.

Berman, A. L., Jobes, D. A., & Silverman, M. M. (2006). *Adolescent suicide: Assessment and intervention.* Washington, DC: American Psychological Association.

Centers for Disease Control and Prevention (CDC). (2013). *Youth Risk Behavior Surveillance—United States, 2013.* http://www.cdc.gov/mmwr/pdf/ss/ss6304.pdf

Daniel, S. S., Walsh, A. K., Goldston, D. B., Arnold, E. M., Reboussin, B. A., & Wood, F. B. (2006). Suicidailty, school dropout, and reading problems among adolescents. *Journal of Learning Disabilities, 39*(6), 507–514. doi:10.1177/00222194060390060301

Force, F. T. (1998). Consensus statement on youth suicide by firearms. *Archives of Suicide Research, 4*(1), 89–94. doi:10.1080/13811119808258292

Gibbons, R. D., Brown, C. H., Hur, K., Marcus, S. M., Bhaumik, D. K., Erkens, J. A., ... Mann, J. (2007). Early evidence on the effects of regulators' suicidality warnings on SSRI prescriptions and suicide in children and adolescents. *American Journal of Psychiatry, 164,* 1356–1363.

Hazelden Foundation. (n.d.). *Lifelines: A comprehensive suicide awareness and responsiveness program for teens.* Retrieved from http://www.hazelden.org/web/public/lifelines.page

Joiner, T. E. (2005). *Why people die by suicide.* Cambridge, MA: Harvard University Press.

Kalafat, J. (2006). Youth suicide prevention programs. *Prevention Researcher, 13*(3), 12–15.

Mann, J. J., Apter, A., Bertolote, J., et al. (2005). Suicide prevention strategies: A systemic review. *Journal of the American Medical Association, 294*(16), 2064–2074.

Maris, R. W., Berman, A. L., & Silverman, M. M. (2000). *Comprehensive textbook of suicidology.* New York: Guilford Press.

Mazza, J. J. (2006). Youth suicide behavior: A crisis in need of attention. In F. A. Villarruel & T. Luster (Eds.), *Adolescent mental health* (pp. 156–177). New York: Greenwood Publishing Group.

Mazza, J. J., & Reynolds, W. M. (2008). School-wide approaches to prevention of and treatment for depression and suicidal behaviors. In B. Doll & J. A. Cummings (Eds.), *Transforming school mental health services* (pp. 213–241). Thousand Oaks, CA: Corwin.

Mental health: Culture, race, and ethnicity: A supplement to mental health: A report of the Surgeon General. (2001). Rockville, MD: Department of Health and Human Services, U.S. Public health Service.

Meyer, I. H. (2003). Prejudice, social stress, and mental health in lesbian, gay, and bisexual populations: Conceptual issues and research evidence. *Psychological Bulletin, 129,* 674–697. doi:10.1037/0033-2909.129.5.674.

Miller, D. N. (2010). A centennial milestone (1910–2010): 100 years of youth suicide prevention. *Communique, 38*(5), 23–24.

Miller, D. N., Mazza, J. J., & Eckert, T. L. (2009). Suicide prevention programs in the schools: A review and public health perspective. *School Psychology Review, 38*(2), 168–188.

Miller, D. N., Nickerson, A. B., & Jimerson, S. R. (2009). Positive psychology and school-based interventions. In R. Gilman, E. S. Huebner, & M. J. Furlong (Eds.) *Handbook of positive psychology in schools* (pp. 293–304). New York: Routledge.

Miller, T. R., & Taylor, D. M. (2005). Adolescent suicidality: Who will ideate, who will act? *Suicide and Life-Threatening Behavior, 35,* 425–435. doi:10.1521/suli.2005.35.4.425.

Nickerson, A. B., & Slater, E. D. (2009). School and community violence and victimization as predictors of adolescent suicidal behavior. *School Psychology Review, 38*(2), 218–232.

Richardson, A. S., Bergen, H. A., Martin, G., Roeger, L., & Allison, S. (2005). Perceived academic performance indicators of risk of attempted suicide in young adolescents. *Archives of Suicide Research, 9*(2), 163–176. doi:10.1080/13811110590904016.

Scherff, A. R., Eckert, T. L., & Miller, D. N. (2005). Youth suicide prevention: A survey of public school superintendents' acceptability of school-based programs. *Suicide and Life-Threatening Behavior, 35*(2), 154–169.

Stack, S. (2000). Suicide: A 15-year review of the sociological literature part I: Cultural and economic factors. *Suicide & Life—Threatening Behavior, summer*(30), 2.

Tompkins, T. L., Witt, J., & Abraibesh, N. (2009). Does a gatekeeper suicide prevention program work in a school setting? Evaluating training outcome and moderators of effectiveness. *Suicide and Life-Threatening Behavior, 39*(6), 671–681.

Walker, R. L., Ashby, J., Hoskins, O. D., & Greene, F. N. (2009). Peer-support suicide prevention in a non-metropolitan U.S. community. *Adolescence, 44*(174), 335–346.

Whetstone, L. M., Morrissey, S. L., & Cummings, D. M. (2007). Children at risk: The association between perceived weight status and suicidal thoughts and attempts in middle school youth. *Journal of School Health, 77*(2), 59–66.

Yang, R. K., Burrola, K. S., & Bryan, C. H. (2009). Suicide ideation among participants in an after-school program: A convenience sample. *Child & Youth Services, 31*(1/2), 3–13. doi:10.1080/01459350903505546

Zenere, F. J., & Lazarus, P. J. (2009). The sustained reduction of youth suicidal behavior in an urban, multicultural school district. *School Psychology Review, 38*(2), 189–199.

Chapter Six

Sexual Harassment and Abuse

Michaella Henry was seventeen years old and a student at the elite Phillips Exitor Academy boarding school. In October 2015, she was groped in the basement of a school building by a fellow student who was eighteen years old. She told him repeatedly to stop. When she reported the assault to the school she was discouraged and dissuaded from going to police. Staff there insisted it was harassment, not assault, because there had been no penetration.

Instead, school staff members convinced her to agree to an act of penance by the abuser, who was to bake bread and deliver it to her every week for the rest of the year. This action subjected her to forced interaction with the abuser on a weekly basis, thus revictimizing her repeatedly. She was plagued by sleeplessness and panic attacks. After months of frustration, watching the abuser go about his life as a big athlete and senior class leader, she ended up going to police. The abuser is now facing a misdemeanor charge of sexual assault and Michaella turned out not to be his only victim. The school now admits that it mishandled this case.

SEXUAL HARASSMENT AND ABUSE: DEFINITIONS AND PREVALENCE

Terms and Definitions

The American Association of University Women (AAUW) has conducted seminal studies and reports on the issue of sexual harassment. In 1993, it produced the groundbreaking report *Hostile Hallways: Bullying, Teasing and Sexual Harassment in School*. Its 2011 report, *Crossing the Line: Sexual Harassment at School*, covers sexual harassment in grades 7 to 12.

The report cites the U.S. DOE's Office of Civil Rights' definition of sexual harassment. It is the unwelcome conduct of a sexual nature, which can include unwelcome sexual advances, requests, and sexual favors, or other verbal, nonverbal, or physical conduct of a sexual nature. It can include making sexual comments, jokes, distributing sexually explicit drawings or written materials, spreading sexual rumors, and more.

Sexual harassment is considered a form of sex discrimination and prohibited by Title IX of the Civil Rights Act of 1964. Title IX of the educational amendments of 1972 is a federal law that prohibits sex discrimination in educational institutions, programs, and activities that receive federal financial assistance.

The law applies to any academic, extracurricular, research, occupational training, and other educational programs from preschool to graduate school that receive federal funding. The entire institution falls under Title IX, even if only one program or activity receives federal funds. (Some institutions are not covered by Title IX, even if they do receive federal funding, such as certain religious organizations, military training, schools, and university fraternities and sororities.)

The report further defines sexual harassment as unwanted sexual behavior that interferes with a student's right to receive an equal education. Therefore, sexual assault, rape, stalking, dating violence, and other forms of sexual violence are considered extreme forms of sexual harassment and are subject to criminal prosecution. When race and sex are involved, sexual harassment is also subject to Title VI of the Civil Rights act, which prohibits racial discrimination.

Title IX protects students against two types of sexual harassment: the quid pro quo (when someone with power uses that power to coerce students) and hostile environment (unwanted sexual conduct that is severe, persistent, or pervasive, where the vast majority of sexual harassment at school falls).

Crossing the Line reports that sexual harassment remains an unfortunate part of school culture, affecting millions of students, especially girls. It maintains that only a fraction of students who were sexually harassed during the 2011 school year reported the incident and, sadly, most told no one about it.

Gender harassment is not necessarily sexual in intent or action, the report states, but does address the targeted student's sexuality and is used to manipulate or control someone. While it is known to be common in middle and high schools, there are reports of significant sexual harassment in elementary schools as well.

Bullying and sexual harassment are often confused. In contrast to bullying, sexual harassment is a form of sex discrimination. They have different definitions and are regulated by different laws. The AAUW report notes that bullying is usually defined as repeated unwanted behavior that involves an imbalance of power, but is not necessarily sexual in nature.

Sexual harassment and bullying also differ in the typical age of students. Bullying, they say, begins in childhood, whereas sexual harassment typically begins with adolescence. Sexual harassment is covered by federal law and, while there is no federal law on bullying, most states do have antibullying legislation.

Charmaraman et al. (2013) says that bullying perpetration and homophobic teasing were significant predictors of sexual harassment perpetration. Researchers have also found that students who sexually harass others are likely to have been harassed themselves.

Crossing the Line also found that, of the 16 percent of students who admitted to sexually harassing others, the vast majority had been sexually harassed themselves (92 percent of girls and 80 percent of boys). When asked why they did it, almost a quarter said they were retaliating for something that had been done to them.

Prevalence

Figure 6.1 depicts the trends in prevalence of sexual harassment between 2009 in 2015 and compares K–12 complaints to those at the postsecondary level.

According to Espelage and Holt (2007), fully 81 percent of students had experienced some form of sexual harassment sometime during their school lives, with 60 percent reporting it occasionally, and 25 percent often experiencing sexual harassment. Fully 70 percent reported experiencing nonphysical sexual harassment at some point in their lives, and more than 50 percent experienced that often, or occasionally. Physical sexual harassment was reported by 58 percent of students as happening at some point in their school

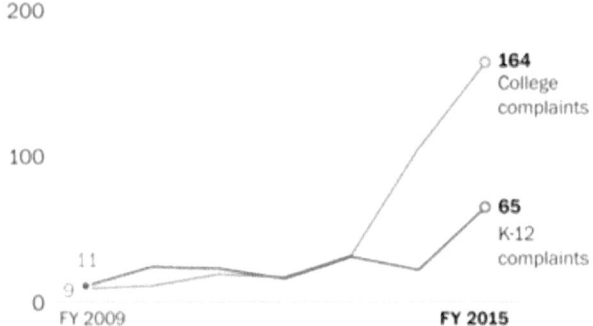

Figure 6.1 Overview of Sexual Violence Complaints in K–16 Schools. *Source*: U.S. Department of Education, Office of Civil Rights.

lives, and 32 percent experienced this form of sexual harassment often, or occasionally. Almost 90 percent of the students reported that it had a negative effect on them.

Girls report more sexual harassment than boys, although there has been a notable increase in the number of boys experiencing it. Jokes, gestures, or looks toward them were the most frequent, followed by being touched, grabbed, or pinched in a sexual way. Girls who reported any kind of sexual harassment most often reported one-on-one, male-to-female harassment, while boys were most likely to be sexually harassed by one other girl or an all-female group.

Espelage and Holt (2007) found that in terms of racial groups, African American girls were more likely than Hispanic and white girls to be touched, grabbed, or pinched in a sexual way, have someone pull at their clothing in a sexual way, or were forced to kiss someone.

Students witness sexual harassment pretty frequently as well. Espelage and Holt found that one-third of girls and about a quarter of boys said they observed sexual harassment at their school in the 2010–11 school year. More than half (56 percent) witnessed it more than once during the school year. Half of the students who were sexually harassed in the 2010–11 school year said that they did nothing afterwards in response to it. Fewer than 10 percent said they reported it to educators when they experienced it and only 24 percent reported it when they had witnessed it.

In the AAUW report, boys were more likely than girls to say they were sexually harassed by other students. Most students who admitted to sexually harassing others were also the target of sexual harassment themselves (92 percent of girls and 80 percent of boys). Of those who did admit to sexually harassing others, 44 percent did not think of it as a big deal, 39 percent were trying to be funny, or getting revenge on someone (23 percent). The study also reported that more than one quarter of the victims experienced psychological problems and many were diagnosed with anxiety, depression, PTSD, or alcohol abuse.

It also found that, of the 16 percent of students who admitted to sexually harassing others, the vast majority had been sexually harassed themselves (92 percent of girls and 80 percent of boys). When asked why they did it, almost a quarter said they were retaliating for something that had been done to them.

Grube and Lens (2003) propose possible reasons for such harassment. They identified the need for power and control, learned behavior resulting from sex-role stereotypes, expectations for male and female interactions, and gender role socialization. They say that victims, on the other hand, often isolate themselves and withdraw emotionally. They struggle with feelings of

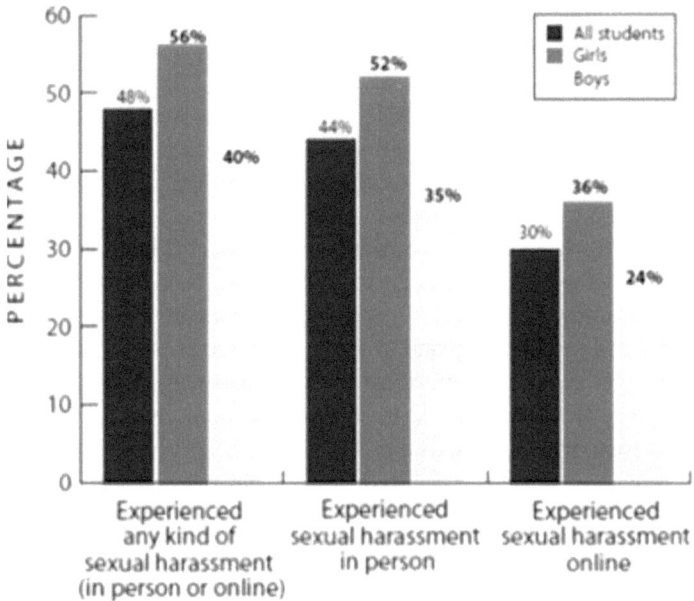

Figure 6.2 Students Who Experienced Sexual Harassment by Gender, 2010–11. *Source*: ilookbothways.com

helplessness and reduced self-confidence, and that these effects can last for some time.

As is the case with cyber bullying, there is increased proliferation of sexual harassment in cyberspace. The anonymity leads bullies and harassers to believe they will not get caught. Nearly a third of students report sexual harassment via social media and many of them report both face-to-face and online incidents. The AAUW report says sexual harassment is a big part of cyberbullying. Tokunaga (2010) found that between 20 percent and 40 percent of youths between the ages of twelve and seventeen had experienced some form of cyber bullying, and presumably, significant sexual harassment as part of it.

Figure 6.2 shows the distinctions by gender, taken from a study of prevalence during the 2010–11 school year.

Effects of Sexual Harassment

Espelage and Holt (2007) found that bully victims and victims who experienced high levels of sexual harassment victimization reported more anxiety/depression than others who had low or moderate levels of sexual harassment victimization.

Ormerad, Collinsworth, and Perry (2008) say that the psychological consequences associated with peer harassment include negative self-evaluations, such as self-consciousness, embarrassment, fear, feeling less confident, doubts about oneself and one's ability to succeed, as well as symptoms similar to PTSD. They report the negative health outcomes of adolescent sexual harassment as including a range of physical symptoms including headaches, nausea, loss of appetite, and more.

Other negative educational outcomes for adolescents include those associated with school withdrawal, such as talking less in class, receiving lower grades, not wanting to go to school, getting in trouble at school, and finding it more difficult to pay attention and to study. Ormerod et al. (2008) say students tried to manage the harassment or avoid the harassers by such things as altering routes to school, changing seats in the classroom, avoiding the harasser, getting someone else to serve as a protector, and quitting particular activities.

Gender

The AAUW reports raise the question as to whether or not sexual harassment is different for boys and girls, given the fact that girls report more negative psychological and educational consequences from it. Girls experience greater severity of harassment, and the greater the severity, the greater the negative outcomes. Ormerod et al. found that while both boys and girls are distressed by harassing behaviors, girls are far more likely to find the harassment upsetting than boys. Girls were more likely than boys to be sexually harassed, and by a significant margin (56 to 40 percent).

Girls were more likely than boys to say they had been negatively affected by sexual harassment. They perceive greater harm from harassment and report higher frequencies of physical, invasive forms. Thus, they conclude that sexual harassment does appear to be a gendered phenomenon that is directly and negatively associated with outcomes for girls. They suggest this has to do with what they call power differentials between males and females playing out in the schools as it does in the larger world.

Sexual harassment can ostracize and marginalize girls, say Rahimi and Liston (2011). They raise the question of stereotypical perceptions of sexuality, gender, race, and class and their impacts on the ways school staff address—or do not address—such harassment. They advocate for safe places in schools for girls to develop academically, psychologically, socially, and sexually.

According to the AAUW report, not only were girls more likely than boys to say it caused them to have trouble sleeping, not want to go to school, or change the way they go home from school, they were more likely in every case to say they felt that way for quite a while, compared to boys. The report also states that because sexual harassment appears to be so common for girls, they may fail to even recognize it as sexual harassment. Boys, on the other hand, were more likely to identify being called gay as the type of sexual harassment most troubling to them.

There are very long-term effects as well. Rahimi and Liston found that women impacted by sexual harassment report suffering from levels of depression and other psychological consequences that they had attributed at least partially to their experience with a sexual label as long as *twenty years* after those school experiences. Wolfe et al. (2009) refer to several longitudinal studies, which confirm that sexual harassment victimization was associated with higher risk of other forms of relationship violence 2.5 years later.

At-Risk Groups

The AAUW report concluded that students of color may be more affected than white students by sexual harassment. African American students were more likely than their white counterparts to stop doing an activity or sport, get into trouble at school, or find it hard to study because of it. Hispanic students were reported to be more likely than white students to stay home from school because of it.

Rahimi and Liston cite studies that show that women of color are less likely to be perceived as victims of sexual harassment due to stereotypical perceptions. They found that sexual harassment of girls, particularly girls of color, goes either unreported or unresolved, and that often it is viewed as warranted or even expected. They further contend that much sexual harassment of African American girls has been hugely overlooked, and instead blamed on the girls themselves, further victimizing them.

Incidence rates were high for sexual harassment based on a student's actual or perceived sexual orientation or gender expression. One study found that more than half of the LGBT students who experienced sexual harassment in the prior year did not report it to school staff. This was due to their doubts, they said, that anything would change or concern about the staff members' reactions. Another study found a relationship between a history of sexual orientation victimization and mental health symptoms, including increased trauma-related symptoms.

Stader and Graca (2007) found that homophobic remarks, verbal harassment, and physical abuse on the basis of sexual orientation to be a common experience among LGBT youth. A 2003 survey indicated that over 80 percent experienced verbal harassment and 32 percent reported more serious victimization, including physical abuse. They found that in at least one-third of the cases, verbal harassment escalated to physical harassment as well. Hillard, Love, Franks, Laris, and Coyle (2013) found that violence bullying and verbal harassment of LGBT youth may have detrimental consequences for their school attendance and academic performance as well.

Reports of harassment among LGBT subgroups range from 68 percent among straight students to 86 percent among nonwhite students. The most common forms were sexual jokes, comments or gestures, and being teased because of looks or speech. Use of homophobic language was common, and these students reported that verbal harassment was more widespread than physical harassment.

What Stader and Graca say was most concerning about their studies of sexual harassment among LGBT students was how often self-identified LGBT youth reported that teachers and administrators failed to intervene in the harassment. Hillard et al. noted findings that suggest that where students feel free to report the bullying and harassment, they were more likely to feel that their school was an accepting place and that they were happy to be there.

Coping with Sexual Harassment

de Lara (2008) found that students employ various cognitive and behavioral strategies to feel safe from their peers at school. As mentioned, they rely on friends to protect them, and change their behavior to avoid the victimizer. Coping strategies at school include problem-solving skills, seeking social support, and telling an adult.

Isolation and social exclusion are extremely painful emotions. Studies have shown that being socially excluded leads to withdrawal, avoiding activities, blaming oneself, or trying to fit in. de Lara notes that cognitive behavioral exercises such as convincing oneself that the harassing behavior is inconsequential and maintaining one's composure were helpful for victims. de Lara says that students with the greatest social-emotional intelligence had greater ability to figure out how to manage such distressing social interactions.

Other responses victims try include telling harasser to stop and trying to turn the situation into a joke, according to the AAUW report. Similar numbers of girls and boys said that they tried to defend themselves against the harasser, yelled for help, or did nothing when it occurred, because they did not know what to do. Sadly, after being sexually harassed, 50 percent of students did nothing about it. Girls were much more likely than boys to talk with someone about what happened or to report it. This was attributed to differences in gender, as boys may feel less comfortable seeking help or talking about their experiences than girls do.

Figure 6.3 depicts student reactions to sexual harassment by gender.

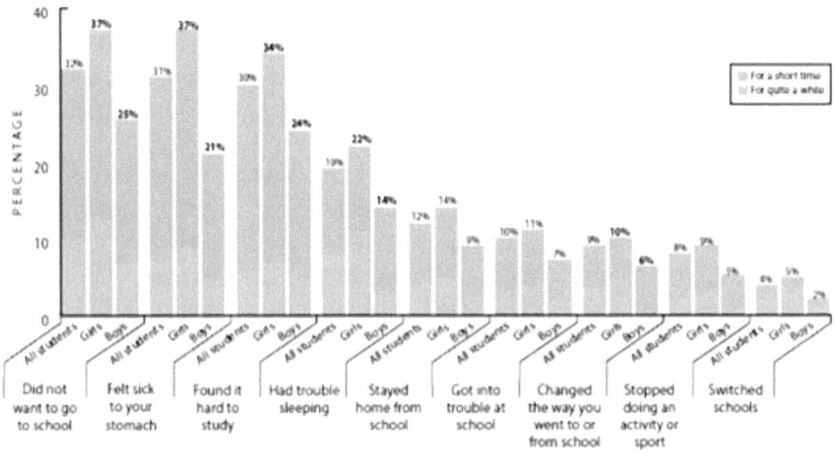

Figure 6.3   Student Reaction to Sexual Harassment by Gender, AAUW, 2011.

Witnesses to Sexual Harassment

Bystanders are affected by sexual harassment as well. When surveyed, they say that the most common reason for not intervening was not knowing what to do. Over a quarter (28 percent) of students who witnessed sexual harassment—but did nothing—said that they did not think it could make a difference. And 26 percent said they did not think of it as sexual harassment at the time.

Thirteen percent of students worried that *they* would be sexually harassed if they did something, and 9 percent of students were afraid of being physically hurt. Interestingly, students were more likely to help if they had also been sexually harassed. Among those trying to help, 60 percent told the harasser to stop.

PREVENTION OF SEXUAL HARASSMENT AND ABUSE

The AAUW report says that schools must have a clear policy regarding sexual harassment and publish procedures that automatically occur when sexual harassment is reported. Educators must respond appropriately, unlike the case at Phillips Exeter Academy, with sensitivity and patience, and must provide students with information about their rights. Schools should notify parents of the policy and help them with ways to discuss the policy with their children.

In addition to teaching students about sexual harassment, the report continues, schools must create and sustain a positive climate where harassment is not tolerated. Teachers can work to build a culture of respect in the classroom, as a prevention method, by promoting activities that encourage friendship, cooperation, and respect.

When students were surveyed, 39 percent said it would be useful if schools had a person assigned to help with sexual harassment. Most students (57 percent) also wanted a way to anonymously report sexual harassment problems. Thus, creating a reporting mechanism would increase students' willingness to report a problem. Allowing students to anonymously report problems was a top recommendation (57 percent), as was enforcing sexual harassment policies and punishing harassers (51 percent).

Since many, if not most, staff members are unfamiliar and uncomfortable with dealing with sexual harassment, schools must train their faculty and staffs to recognize and respond to it, to know how to help students, and know their obligations if they witness such behavior. Such training, says the AAUW, helps build student confidence in the ability and willingness of school staff to help them.

Charmarman concludes that when school administrators fail to provide professional development on both bullying and sexual harassment, rather than just bullying, staff members do not understand that sexual harassment occurs between students. They are unaware of policies to protect them, and not likely to understand their own role in preventing this behavior.

DeLara notes that the majority of students believe that adults do not recognize sexual harassment between students, thus reinforcing their reluctance to talk to them about it. Some students in focus groups reported that even their favorite teachers expected them to work it out themselves, rather than report problems with peers. DeLara also says that not all students are certain about the exact parameters of behavior that constitutes sexual harassment.

These focus group students believed that bullying and harassment were inevitable in high school. They felt that the ability to ignore or accept teasing, sexual harassment, bullying, or verbal intimidation was necessary to get by in high school. They reported that telling an adult did not usually result in what they consider to be positive results.

Students need to understand what sexual harassment is and be provided with support, resources, and discussions. One curriculum highlighted in the AAUW report is called *Shifting Boundaries*. It includes detailed instructions for teachers and handouts for six sessions for grades 6 and 7. This curriculum covers issues such as setting boundaries, personal space, determining appropriate and inappropriate behaviors, what sex sexual harassment is and how to respond, and the consequences for harassers.

Studies have found that students who participated in this program demonstrated an increase in knowledge about laws and consequences of sexual harassment, and dating violence. There was a reported 26 to 34 percent decrease in sexual harassment, and a reported 50 percent reduction in dating violence (an issue that will be covered in the next chapter).

Schools and parents must teach students about cyber harassment and what to do if they become aware of it. And even though cyber harassment does not necessarily take place at school, because it can affect a student's ability to learn it, too, falls under Title IX.

Hillard et al. (2013) address the negative impact of bullying and harassment on LGBT youth in schools. They found that successful districts have focused on creating healthier school environments by adopting policies, implementing training programs, increasing access to LGBT-related resources and supports, and integrating LGBT topics into classroom curricula. They say a growing body of work supports the use of a combination of these strategies to promote safer school climates.

In addition, they say, essential district programs to minimize the incidence and impact of bullying and harassment should include such things as the establishment of gay straight alliances and support groups; the creation of LGBT-related bibliographies for students and staff; the purchase of age-appropriate LGBT books and resources for schools and libraries; and the provision of administrator and staff training on such harassment and bullying.

IMPLICATIONS FOR SCHOOLS

Ormerod et al. (2008) found that school climate was associated with experiences of sexual harassment and school quality of life. For both boys and girls, climate was related to feeling unsafe while at school, withdrawal from school, and feelings of lower self-esteem. For boys, a negative climate that tolerated the harassment of girls was the only major variable associated with negative outcomes. They say that it is plausible that observing powerless individuals being victimized, while authorities tacitly sanction the behavior by ignoring it, may send a larger message about justice, with a negative influence on the well-being of bystanders.

A school environment that does not include a strong anti-harassment climate—or implicitly actually condones such harassment—makes students feel unsafe. Having policies and protocols and swift and fair enforcement of them conveys the message that harassment and abuse will not be tolerated, and increases a sense of connection to school for all. Ormerod et al. found that when students perceived that school staff tolerated sexual harassment there was a corresponding increase in peer harassment.

Grube and Lens argue that if a school ignores what it calls typical male behaviors, it normalizes such behavior. Once it is defined as appropriate and validated, accepted or minimized by a powerful and pervasive culture where little action is taken, the victim sees this type of environment as unsafe or hostile. Changing such a culture, they say, can help students understand what harassment is and empower them to do something about it. Allowing such behavior also opens the school and district up to legal challenges.

LaShonda Davis was a fifth grader in Monroe County schools in Georgia in 1993. She was repeatedly harassed over a six-month period by a boy who used offensive language and touched her breasts and genital areas. She repeatedly complained to the teacher and even asked to have her seat changed, but that request was refused. Her mother contacted the principal about the situation but still nothing was done. The boy was eventually charged with sexual battery.

LaShanda's mother then filed a lawsuit based on the antidiscrimination language of Title IX of the federal education amendments. She lost at both the federal circuit court level and the level of the court of appeals. She then appealed to the U.S. Supreme Court, which in May 1999 overruled those two lower courts' decisions and set a precedent for how future sexual harassment charges would be handled.

The Supreme Court determined that four factors are required for finding a Title IX violation: (1) school officials must have actual knowledge; (2) officials with the authority to take remedial action instead show "deliberate indifference," which makes students vulnerable to harassment; (3) the harassment must have been severe, pervasive, and objectively offensive; and (4) the harassment must have had the effect of denying the victim's participation in educational programs or activities.

Harrington (2004) clarifies that schools are not held responsible for the actual act of sexual harassment, but for neglect and lack of response to the accusation, as seen in LaShanda's case. According to the U.S. DOE Office of Civil Rights, schools must have a clear, understandable policy that prohibits any type of sexual harassment, and should include several key components:

- Definition and examples
- Requirement of all staff and students to report instances immediately
- Steps for reporting an incident
- Assurance that retaliation against alleged victims will not be tolerated
- Steps for investigating a complaint
- An explanation of due process in an appeal for the accused
- Discipline consequences for peer sexual harassment
- Assurance that all complaints will be taken seriously
- Assurance that all statements will be kept as confidential as possible
- Assurance that victims to not have to face their harassers

- Information for the victim that the schools process may be abandoned at any point and a formal criminal complaint filed
- Assignment of one person to receive and investigate complaints. (U.S. DOE, Office of Civil Rights, 33)

Under Title IX, schools are now required to have and distribute policies against sex discrimination, and these policies must specifically address sexual harassment. So schools are now required to adopt and publish grievance procedures, evaluate their current policies and practices, and appoint at least one employee to be responsible for making sure that Title IX is enforced.

Stader and Graca (2007) note that some teachers and administrators seem to be reluctant to apply these safeguards to LGBT students like they do other incidents of sexual harassment. They say there are many cases where there has been a failure on the part of school officials to take action after learning of student-on-student sexual orientation harassment. They point out, however, that equal protection requires that the government (i.e., schools) treat similarly situated persons in the same way.

An equal protection claim requires the student to show that the school officials did not abide by anti-harassment policies when dealing with sexual orientation harassment or that the student was treated differently from other similarly situated students. Stader and Graca also report that administrators are not required to purge their schools of homophobic behavior, just fairly enforce their own policies.

They recommend that school districts should take these actions specifically to protect LGBT students:

1. Review district policy and sexual harassment training practices for district personnel, making sure the training includes student-on-student sexual harassment on the basis of sexual orientation
2. Affirm that the reporting procedures for heterosexual harassment apply to harassment on the basis of real or perceived sexual orientation
3. Educate staff on the potential harmful effects of peer harassment on LGBT students and the importance of support for those students
4. Insist that staff apply the same disciplinary standards to student-on-student harassment on the basis of sexual orientation that are applied to all sexual harassment cases reported in the schools. (Stader & Graca, 2007, p. 121)

IMPLICATIONS FOR COMMUNITIES

The AAUW report highlights the fact that parents and other concerned adults can help prevent sexual harassment among children by being good role models. Since children learn as much from actions as words positive, respectful behavior instills tolerance of experts and respect for others without regard to gender presentation in sexual orientation. It advises parents and concerned adults to respond sensitively and appropriately when students tell them about a sexual harassment incident and offers guidance for handling such discussions.

The report notes that parents are in the best position to help their children deal with cyber harassment since it usually occurs outside of school hours and off school grounds on computers and cell phones owned and purchased by parents. Parents need to talk with their children about appropriate online etiquette and how to interact with others respectfully in that environment.

It also advises parents to learn as much as they can about the technology their children are using so that they can help when problems arise and make sure that their children understand the potential dangers. They should create an action plan detailing what their child should do if they become a target of sexual harassment, either by someone they know, or someone they do not know.

PROMISING PROGRAM: SECOND STEP THROUGH PREVENTION PROGRAM

Espelage, Low, Ryzin, and Polanin (2015) describe a three-year clinical trial of a program called Second Step through Prevention, a middle-school program, which covers bullying, cyber bullying, homophobic name-calling, and sexual harassment perpetration. Thirty-six schools in Kansas and Illinois were assigned to either this program, or the control group, and 3,651 sixth-grade students completed self-reported surveys at four time points across three years.

The lessons follow best instructional practices, and include direct instruction, group discussion and hands-on activities, reflection, opportunities, and more. The lessons are skill-based with homework assignments and extension activities included. Teachers are also provided with suggestions for connecting lessons to events of the day and revisiting the skills as conflicts occur.

Students in the Second Step program received a total of forty-one lessons across the three-year study. The program targets the following risk factors: inappropriate classroom behaviors, such as aggressive and impulsivity; favorable attitudes toward problem behavior; friends who engage in problem behavior; early initiation of the problem behavior; peer rejection; and impulsiveness. It targets the following protective factors: social skills, empathy, school connectedness, and norms about drug use.

After one year of implementation, students were less likely to report engaging in physical fights. After two years, they were less likely to report being a target of homophobic name-calling, and less likely to report engaging in sexual harassment perpetration. There were significant reductions in bullying perpetration for students with disabilities.

Decreases in self-reported delinquency over the first two years were significantly related to decreases in bullying, cyber bullying, and homophobic name-calling perpetration for the Second Step schools across the three-year study. Indirect effects of the program on bullying and aggressive behavior were also statistically significant through reductions of delinquency.

The idea, say Espelage et al., is that reducing engagement in deviant behavior should help buffer against engagement in other forms of problem behavior. Delinquency reductions that in turn lead to reductions in bullying and other forms of aggression were found to be explained through the strengthening of teacher–student relations, or the more prosocial interactions among classmates. These findings are consistent with other studies that report lower conduct problems for youth in schools with social emotional learning programs, compared to those who do not have such programs.

The study's authors encourage schools to reinforce these lessons outside of the classroom and outside of the lesson. They say that all school staff need to be reinforcing the content of these programs due to their finding that suggests that such behavior and homophobic name-calling may be viewed as early indicators of risk for later bullying and aggressive behavior.

LESSONS LEARNED ABOUT SEXUAL HARASSMENT AND ABUSE

The reports and studies described here document an alarming level of sexual harassment in our schools, much of which goes underreported and unreported. Many students say they are not even sure what sexual harassment is. When they have been victimized, and muster the courage to speak to someone in authority about it, their experiences are often denied or minimized, as was Michaella Henry's.

Yet, we now know how devastating the consequences of all types of sexual harassment and abuse can be to girls, but also to boys, especially those who do not conform to gender norms and stereotypes. These effects are harmful, not only to the victims of sexual harassment but also to the perpetrators, who, as we have seen, are frequently victims of sexual harassment themselves. This behavior has negative fallout on an entire school, an entire community.

A school climate of ignorance, indifference, and disregard is no longer acceptable and thanks to the Supreme Court decision on *Monroe v. Davis*, it is no longer legal. Still, the 2016 Phillips Exeter Academy scandal illustrates how institutionalized and pervasive the ignorance, indifference, and disregard can be.

We now have research-based programs that address student social emotional needs and reduce student delinquent behaviors, behaviors that can be precursors to more serious, life-long problems. With the proliferation of social media, these solutions need to go beyond the four walls of the classroom and the school.

Everyone in the community, from parents and family members, to leaders of community organizations, mental health members, leaders of organizations, churches as well as schools, must commit to taking sexual harassment and violence of our young people seriously. This means being deeply informed about it, and ensuring that the resources that our students deserve to be free from sexual harassment in their schools, and in their daily lives, are provided to them.

Left untreated we now know that perpetrators of aggression can become bullies who can also sexually harass and who incorporate violence into all of their personal relationships. Next up is another insidious type of violence often seen in school hallways and classrooms. Teen dating violence can also be lethal, if unchecked and unaddressed. Ortrella Mosley tried to leave her abusive boyfriend and was stabbed to death right in her high school one day, after her last class.

REFERENCES

48% of 7th–12th Graders Were Sexually Harassed Last School Year. (2011). ILookBothWays.Com. Retrieved from https://ilookbothways.com/tag/sexual-harassment/

Charmaraman, L., Jones, A. E., Stein, N., & Espelage, D. L. (2013). Is it bullying or sexual harassment? Knowledge, attitudes, and professional development experiences of middle school staff. *Journal of School Health*, *83*(6), 438–444. doi:10.1111/josh.12048

Crossing-the-Line-Sexual-Harassment-at-School. (2013). AAUW. Retrieved from http://www.aauw.org/files/2013/02/Crossing-the-Line-Sexual-Harassment-at-School.pdf

DeLara, E. W. (2008). Developing a philosophy about bullying and sexual harassment: Cognitive coping strategies among high school students. *Journal of School Violence*, *7*(4), 72–96. doi:10.1080/15388220801973862

Espelage, D. L., & Holt, M. K. (2007). Dating violence and sexual harassment across the bully-victim continuum among middle and high school students. *Journal of Youth and Adolescence*, *36*(6), 799–811.

Espelage, D. L., Low, S., Ryzin, M. J., & Polanin, J. R. (2015). Clinical trial of second step middle school program: Impact on bullying, cyberbullying, homophobic teasing, and sexual harassment perpetration. *School Psychology Review*, *44*(4), 464–479. doi:10.17105/spr-15-0052.1

Grube, B., & Lens, V. (2003). Student-to-student harassment: The impact of *Davis v. Monroe. Children's Schools*, *25*(3), 173–185. doi:10.1093/cs/25.3.173.

Harrington, L. (2004). Peer sexual harassment: Protect your students and yourself. *The Delta Kappa Gamma Bulletin*. Fall 2004.

Hillard, P., Love, L., Franks, H. M., Laris, B. A., & Coyle, K. K. (2013). "They were only joking": Efforts to decrease LGBTQ bullying and harassment in Seattle public schools. *Journal of School Health*, *84*(1), 1–9. doi:10.1111/josh.12120

Hostile Hallways: The AAUW Survey on Sexual Harassment in America's School. (1993). Retrieved from http://history.aauw.org/aauw-research/1993-hostile-hallways

Ormerod, A. J., Collinsworth, L. L., & Perry, L. A. (2008). Critical climate: Relations among sexual harassment, climate, and outcomes for high school girls and boys. *Psychology of Women Quarterly*, *32*(2), 113–125. doi:10.1111/j.1471-6402.2008.00417.x

Rahimi, R., & Liston, D. (2011). Race, class, and emerging sexuality: Teacher perceptions and sexual harassment in schools. *Gender and Education*, *23*(7), 799–810. doi:10.1080/09540253.2010.536143

Stader, D. L., & Graca, T. J. (2007). Student-on-student sexual orientation harassment: Legal protections for sexual minority youth. *The Clearing House*, *80*, 117–122.

Tokunaga, R. S. (2010). Following you home from school: A critical review and synthesis of research on cyberbullying victimization. *Computers in Human Behavior*, *26*, 277–287.

Wolfe, D. A., Crooks, C., Jaffe, P., Chiodo, D., Hughes, R., Ellis, W., ... Donner, A. (2009). A school-based program to prevent adolescent dating violence. *Archives of Pediatrics & Adolescent Medicine*, *163*(8). doi:10.1001/archpediatrics.2009.69.

Chapter Seven

Teen Dating Violence

It was the end of the day, the day after Ortralla Mosley had broken up with her boyfriend Marcus McTeer. Ortralla, described as a good student and a thoughtful girl, had ended their six-month relationship due to his increasing possessiveness and attempts to control her. They had been seen arguing at school that morning. There was some evidence that McTeer had behavioral problems in school. He had been abusive with his last girlfriend as well.

That afternoon, they were in a school hallway where he proceeded to viciously stab her six times. She stumbled, then collapsed, and died at the scene.

McTeer was charged for murder and got a four-year determined sentence. This means he will serve time in Texas youth commission facility until age twenty-one. If successful with that rehabilitation program, he could be eligible for parole. If not, he will serve the full forty years.

OVERVIEW OF TEEN DATING VIOLENCE: DEFINITIONS AND TERMS

Definitions

The CDC considers dating violence among adolescents and college students to be a public health problem. Dating violence is actual or threatened harm between current or former partners. It is physical, psychological/ emotional, or sexual abuse within a dating relationship. It has been described as a persistent public health problem, associated with a set of risk factors including hopelessness, suicidal ideation, and other serious problems.

Mayes (2008) states that it is alarming in its prevalence and that the silence surrounding this problem is equally alarming.

Physical violence includes mildly aggressive behavior such as scratching, pushing, and shoving, as well as more severe violent behavior, such as biting, choking, shaking, or use of a weapon. Psychological or emotional violence involves verbally abusive and coercive tactics intended to control, embarrass, humiliate, or isolate a partner from friends and family and it often precedes physical violence.

Theriot (2008) says that psychological abuse is a regular experience in adolescent dating relationships. This abuse includes things like sarcasm, derogatory remarks, emotional withholding, name-calling, being treated as an inferior, or being ignored. He cites Hickman et al., who state that dating violence is more correctly conceptualized a constellation of several abusive and violent behaviors, including homicide, physical and sexual assault, theft and property damage, threats and harassment, kidnapping, stalking, intimidation, and psychological abuse.

Cyber Dating Violence

As with other forms of victimization, cyberspace opens up whole new vistas for teen dating violence. It can include stalking, harassment, humiliation, and threats. What makes it unique with respect to teen dating violence are the opportunities for abusers to publicly degrade and/or humiliate their victims to an extent never before possible, says Zweig, Lachman, Yahner, and Dank (2013), and to gain access to victims at any time, even in absence of their physical presence.

Zweig et al. discuss ways partners use electronic communication related to violence, abuse, or controlling behaviors: (1) arguing; (2) monitoring the whereabouts of a partner or controlling their activities; (3) committing emotional aggression toward a partner; (4) distancing a partner's access to oneself by not responding to calls, text, and other contacts via technology; and (5) reestablishing contact after a violent episode.

They found that cyber dating abuse was significantly associated with a number of correlates, including being female, committing a greater and greater variety of delinquent behaviors, having had sexual activity in one's lifetime, having higher levels of depressive symptoms, and having higher levels of anger and hostility.

Stalking

Stalking occurs when behaviors are unwanted, persistent, and have a pattern; the behaviors make an implicit or explicit threat of harm to the victim; and as a result of those behaviors, the victim experiences fear. Stalking is described as a disturbance in one's attachment and is seen as a problem in identity formation where the individual defends himself against the shame of rejection by acting out in the harassing and controlling manner, says McCann (as cited in Stader, 2011). Additional risk factors for adolescent stalking of former dating partners include being unable to appropriately handle feelings of jealousy and rejection, poor social skills, difficulties in relationship formation, and mental health problems.

There is a perception that dating violence does not exist or is not a serious problem for teenagers and these perceptions contribute to a lack of focus on the issue, says Stader. He points to the relative lack of research in this area that also contributes to a lack of recognition that dating violence is a serious school safety problem.

Things have started to change in recent years. In 2010, the U.S. Congress declared February to be Teen Dating Violence Awareness and Prevention Month. Using the seventeenth anniversary of the Violence Against Women Act, Vice President Joseph Biden initiated a campaign entitled *One Is Too Many* to mobilize youth to identify strategies to prevent teen dating violence.

Teen dating violence can begin as early as middle school. One study found that more than half of U.S. adolescents reported being involved in romantic relationships within the previous eighteen months and almost three-quarters of eighth and ninth graders reportedly date by the time they are in high school (Khubchandani, Telljohann, Price, Dake, & Hendershot, 2013). Given their young age, lack of experience in relationships, and dealing with conflict in relationships, this is a very critical time for education and prevention.

Ellis, Chung-Hall, and Dumas (2012) report that positive dating relationships may provide a wide range of benefits and social development and psychological adjustment. Healthy dating relationships help teenagers develop a sense of identity, foster interpersonal skills, promote feelings of self-worth, and are a source of emotional support. It is so important that these relationships start off and remain healthy.

PREVALENCE OF TEEN DATING VIOLENCE

Just how common is teen dating violence? In a review of dating violence, the CDC found that the average prevalence of nonsexual dating violence was 22 percent among high-school students and 32 percent among college students. It also reports that, in terms of sexual dating violence, one in six women and one in thirty-three men have experienced rape or attempted rape in their lifetimes, and over half occurred before they were eighteen years old, and 22 percent before they were twelve.

Many consider these estimates to be underestimates. The ten-year trends in prevalence of the fifteen- to eighteen-year-old age group have remained stable. Prevalence estimates appear to be the lowest in grade 9 and highest in grade 11, and vary by ethnicity (Howard, Wang, & Yan, 2007), which will be discussed later in the chapter. As is the case with bullying and sexual harassment, few teens reported the situation to an adult.

Ellis et al. (2012) cite a number of research studies that indicate that 25 percent to 55 percent of dating adolescents report experiencing some form of physical or psychological abuse in their relationships. Almost half of both boys and girls reported that dating violence occurred on school property.

Theriot (2008) refers to one study where 11 percent of high-school students reported experiencing threats, abuse of language, or both, in dating relationships and 28 percent reported verbal abuse. In addition to physical and sexual violence, he cites another study that found that 76 percent to 82 percent of dating adolescents reported experiencing at least one incidence of degradation, monopolization, and isolation. The emotional and psychological aggression most often followed a relationship breakup as it was in Ortralla Mosley's case.

Howard et al. (2007) concluded that dating violence against adolescent girls was widespread. Approximately one in ten ninth- through twelfth-grade female adolescents who participated in the 2005 Youth Risk Behavior Survey reported being a victim of physical dating violence within the previous year. Estimates are much higher (up to 60 percent) when emotional abuse is included.

In a survey cited by Zweig et al. (2013), teenagers in a dating relationship reported being called by names, harassed, or put down by their partner via texting (25 percent) or via a social networking site (18 percent); having their partner share private or embarrassing pictures or videos of them (11 percent); and being physically threatened by their partner through technology (10 percent).

Stader describes a study of cyber dating abuse of nearly 4,000 teens who had been in a dating relationship in the prior year. A quarter of them said they experienced some form of cyber dating abuse victimization in the prior year, with females reporting more cyber dating abuse victimization than males. Victims of sexual cyber dating abuse were seven times more likely to have also experienced sexual coercion (55 percent versus 8 percent) than nonvictims, and perpetrators of sexual cyber dating abuse were seventeen times more likely to have also perpetrated sexual coercion (34 percent versus 2 percent) than were nonperpetrators (figure 7.1).

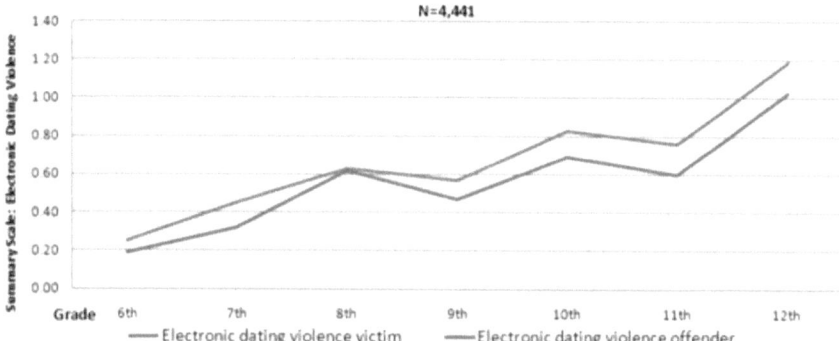

Figure 7.1 Experience with Electronic Forms of Teen Dating Violence by Grade. *Source*: Hinduja and Patchin (2010).

Gender Differences

Howard et al. state that while prevalence rates for dating violence victimization by gender are similar during adolescence, the literature on adults suggests that such intimate partner violence is largely a gender-specific issue, with victimization rates for females ranging from three to six times those for males. Between 40 and 70 percent of adolescents said that the dating violence was mutual, though many note that for girls, the responses might be self-defense.

Girls in abusive dating relationships experience more severe physical injury than boys do. Adolescent females are, however, more vulnerable to physical and sexual abuse from dating partners than males and more likely to suffer higher injury rates. Cyber dating victimization has also been found to be more common in females.

It is thought that males may be less inclined to report violent victimization. Howard et al. found that roughly one in ten adolescent males had been the victim of physical dating violence, similar to that of females. This, they say, reinforces the fact that dating violence is a public health issue for males as well as females.

Race and Cultural Differences

Adolescent dating violence does not discriminate by gender, race, or economic status (Henry & Zeytinoglu, 2012). African Americans report the most victimization and perpetuation for both community and dating violence, however. Poverty also has a relationship, especially as it relates to exposure to violence.

When the correlation between involvement in neighborhood violence and interpersonal violence is examined in African American male teens, the results show that neighborhood violence involvement, street violence involvement, involvement in gangs, and high reports of homelessness are strongly correlated with engaging in interpersonal violence.

Foshee et al. (2013) say, the differences by race may be the result of differences in attitude about violence and gender, communication skills, and exposure to family violence. They found black females were significantly more likely to report victimization than white females, and that there was an inconsistent relationship between white and Hispanic females. They cite findings from the Youth Risk Behavior Survey of 2009, which showed that African American students were more likely to be hit or hurt by a boyfriend or girlfriend than Hispanic and white students.

Howard et al. also note that the prevalence of physical dating violence was lower for Caucasian females compared to females of other ethnicities. Compared to their white peers, African American females were approximately 1.5 times as likely to report physical dating violence, though there are some inconsistencies in comparisons. Experts say that more research is required to understand how racial issues relate to teen dating violence, and to aid in the development of develop more culturally sensitive interventions.

Schnurr and Lohman (2008) found that early involvement with antisocial peers and increased involvement with antisocial peers over time were linked to perpetration of dating violence for males, females, African American females, and Hispanic males. They concluded that the lack of school safety and academic difficulties in early adolescence exacerbated the impact of parental domestic violence exposure for African American males and Hispanic males as well.

Teen Dating Violence and At-Risk Populations

Just as sexual minority students experience greater victimization and bullying than heterosexual students, research shows they experience more dating violence victimization as well.

Martin-Storey (2014) found higher prevalence of dating violence among sexual minority youth, and emphasized the importance of addressing this population specifically with interventions targeting dating violence. This elevated risk may occur as a result of rejection from both heterosexual and sexual minority communities or lowered level of protective factors like school and family support.

The minority stress model, as previously discussed, suggests that additional stressors resulting from stigmatized identities can account for disparities between sexual minority and heterosexual populations. Facing stressors like discrimination, internalized homophobia, and identity concealment are associated with increased levels of dating violence.

Martin-Storey cites research that suggests possible factors in the association between sexual minority status and dating violence. These include peer victimization, the number of sexual partners, problematic alcohol use, and aggressive behavior. They note that substantial research links sexual minority status to higher levels of peer victimization, and the fact that experiencing victimization in one context increases the likelihood of experiencing it in other contexts. The stigma surrounding sexual minority status is stronger for men than women and boys encounter higher levels of victimization than girls.

Almost all youth who reported having same-sex partners were at elevated risk. As sexual minority youth may be more vulnerable to dating violence outcomes, interventions addressing this issue need to include information on both heterosexual and nonheterosexual relationships. Adapting existing validated interventions for this population is important for better understanding the contexts in which sexual minority youth experience dating violence, as well as preventing the serious long-term ramifications of dating violence for this vulnerable population.

TEEN DATING VIOLENCE EFFECTS AND RISK FACTORS

Foshee et al. assert that dating violence can interfere with healthy and normal development of teens. It can interfere with important developmental tasks, such as the formation of identity, autonomy, and individuation, and the development of loyalty, trust, secure attachment, and more.

Espelage and Holt (2007) report on a study of high-school students that found that 56 percent of victims indicated that although the dating violence incident upset them, there were no long-term effects. Eight percent reported more long-standing emotional disturbance. They say that victims of teen dating violence are at an increased risk of a variety of academic, legal, and health-related outcomes. Regarding health-related outcomes, problems can range from minor physical ailments to severe mental health problems, including homicide and suicide, they say.

Victims of such abuse are not only at increased risk for injury, they are also more likely to engage in binge drinking, suicide attempts, physical fights, and substance abuse. Espelage and Holt cite other studies showing that adolescent victims of psychological abuse alone, as well as physical and/or sexual violence, have higher rates of major depressive disorder, PTSD, and alcohol use disorders, more frequent co-occurrence of externalizing and internalizing disorders, and more frequent negative cognitive outcomes, compared to nonvictims (figure 7.2).

Being a victim of dating violence was associated with reports of sad and hopeless feelings and engagement in high-risk sexual practices, state Howard et al., specifically recent multiple sex partners and unprotected sex. They found gender differences in this risk profile as well. Among males, attempted suicide and fighting were correlated with victimization, while among females, binge drinking and substance abuse were predictors.

Students who experience teen dating violence were four times more likely to develop major depressive episode and PTSD than students who have not suffered such violence. Girls who experienced it tended to develop PTSD and dissociation, whereas boys developed anxiety and depression as well as PTSD, report Henry and Zeytinoglu (2012), based on a variety of studies they reviewed.

Mayes (2000) documented the harms of dating violence as well. He lists the following additional negative effects: unhealthy weight control behaviors, pregnancy, truancy, social problems, dropping out of school, and school failure. Hanson (2002) also identified poor academic performance, substance abuse, and adult domestic violence as impacts. He, too, says that the impact of sexual abuse alone on victims is devastating, with both short- and long-term effects on emotional functioning, psychological functioning, physical symptoms, and behavioral and social functioning.

Henry and Zeytinoglu present additional risk factors for males. These include having no father figure, having a less than high-school-educated parents, and being in a large school. For females, they found the risk factors to include having no mother figure, not being religious, not having a high-school graduate parent, and having had more relationships.

Vagi et al. (2013) actually identified fifty-three different risk factors from a review of nineteen studies. These risk factors fit into the following general categories: health problems, aggressive thoughts, youth violence, substance use, risky sexual behavior, poor relationship and friendship quality, poor family quality, demographics, and the use of aggressive media. The factors that they found in multiple studies included depression, general aggression, prior dating violence, race, ethnicity, engagement peer violence, and parental marital conflict.

Schnurr and Lohman found that for both males and females, early involvement with antisocial peers as well as an increase in involvement with antisocial peers were the only two school factors linked to perpetration of dating violence. They cite a number of studies, which conclude that that being male, using drugs, suffering from mental health problems, experiencing sexual abuse in early adolescence, and having externalizing behavior problems were also precursors to perpetration.

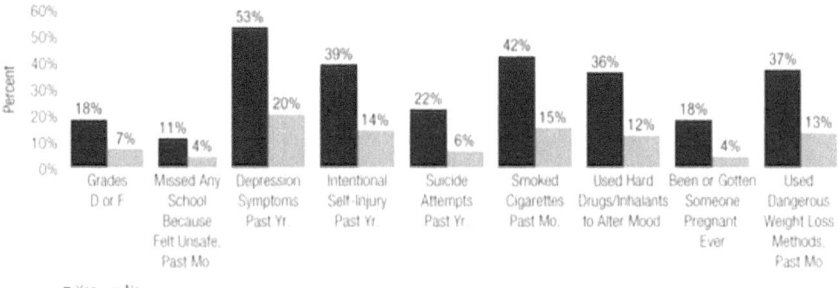

Figure 7.2 Impact and Effect of Exposure to Teen Dating Violence. *Source*: CDC Youth Risk Behavior Surveillance Survey 2007.

ISSUES RELATED TO TEEN DATING VIOLENCE

Role of Families

Families, of course, play a key role in the socialization of children and in gender role development. The family culture and belief system, closeness and support of children, quality of relationships, and monitoring of children all have a tremendous influence. Aspects of the family have been linked with both experiencing—and protecting against—dating violence, say Zweig et al. They describe a correlation between witnessing domestic violence at home and the experience of child abuse with experiencing dating violence.

Hipwell et al. state the children who experience harsh parenting learn that violence is normal, acceptable, and useful as a means of expressing feelings, releasing tension and exerting control over others. Parents may also reinforce aggressive behavior by either submitting to it or rewarding such behavior. Their review of studies on this issue concluded that punitive parenting practices, including verbal and emotional abuse, and corporal punishment, negatively impact self-regulation, and interpersonal skills.

Hipwell et al. also point to the rejection sensitivity model, which says that repeated rejection and victimization by parents and/or peers causes individuals to become hypersensitive to rejection responses such as aggression, coercion, and hostility. They cite studies, which show an association between hostility from parents, high levels of rejection sensitivity and dating violence. They also found an association between a family history of divorce, separation, and absence of a parental figure, behavior problems, and teen dating violence.

The closeness of the relationship with that parent perpetrating domestic violence has also been found to correlate with a teen's likelihood to perpetrate violence in their dating relationships, say Schnurr and Lohman (2008). This is commonly referred to as intergenerational transmission of violence based on social learning theory. Social learning theory, developed by noted psychologist Bandura in 1977, states that behavior is learned through watching others engage in behavior.

According to this theory, adolescents who are exposed to parental violence develop a cognitive pathway and view violence as less aversive. They become desensitized to the consequence of violence. This carryover effect makes the adolescent more likely to perpetrate violence in his or her personal relationships. Estimates are that about 28 percent of adolescents have witnessed domestic violence—millions of vulnerable teens.

Schnurr and Lohman discuss precursors to perpetrating dating violence. These can include having a mother with less than high school education, having low family income, having a hostile parent–child relationship, experiencing low levels of father involvement, experiencing harsh physical punishment, and receiving low parental monitoring.

Abused and neglected children are at great youth risk for interpersonal dating violence. Wolfe et al. state that abused children, as well as those who witness violence in the home, often live in a world of turmoil and extremes. This results in difficulty recognizing and regulating their internal states. They become hypervigilant and learn to relate to others in a cautious, vigilant manner, and scan their social environment for signs of anger and disapproval.

Such youth have a 3.5 times greater risk of involvement in adult domestic violence, says Coid et al. (2001). This is due, in part, to developmental processes affected by their maltreatment that interferes with their ability to form healthy relationships with others. For maltreated children who have structured their previous relationships on the basis of the roles of victim and victimizer, they say, this view becomes familiar and they are more likely to be victimized as a result. Teasing becomes bullying, and bullying becomes harassment and dating violence, which results in abuse and other forms of control.

Coid et al. found that youths without a maltreatment background had a 3 percent likelihood of perpetuating violent delinquency, but those who had experienced three or more forms of abuse were 11.2 times as likely to have perpetrated these behaviors. They described the strength of this association as astonishing in its magnitude.

On the other hand, Ellis et al. (2012) point to studies that show that youth who share close relationships with their parents may be *less* likely to experience teen dating violence. Many prevention programs, which will be discussed later in this chapter, include components for parent involvement because of the important impact family has in either perpetuating such relationship violence or preventing it. This can be especially important as teens very rarely ever disclose abuse to a parent or other adult.

Role of Peers

Just as with the family, peers who foster aggressive behavior can reinforce aggressive behavior in others, and peer relationships are considered formative for dating relationships. Foshee et al. describe three areas of peer attributes, which are relevant to adolescent risk behaviors: friends' behaviors and beliefs; the quality of relationships with peers; and social status among peers.

They say that such things as exposure to friends, overall prosocial beliefs (such as believing in societal rules and laws), being committed to conventional activities and social institutions, and holding antideviance beliefs may have a constraining influence on adolescent behaviors. They note that friendship groups prepare adolescents for dating and can perhaps explain why adolescents who are well integrated into friendships may be at less risk for dating violence. It is through friendships that teens learn skills for developing intimacy and empathy and resolving conflict in prosocial ways.

On the other hand, those without such friendship networks miss the opportunity to explore ideas about romantic relationships with peers. This, they say, can make them more vulnerable to accept idealized notions of relationships that they pick up from other sources like the media.

Hipwell et al. say that in peer groups where the modeling of aggressive behaviors gets positive reactions, adolescents learn that using aggression against others can help them achieve goals and can gain acceptance by others. They found that affiliation with physically aggressive friends is a consistent predictor of subsequent dating violence perpetration and positive attitudes toward violence among adolescents.

Further, youth who affiliate with peers who have positive attitudes toward physical violence may also be more likely to use this type of behavior in their dating relationships. Hipwell et al. found that adolescents who were members of relationally aggressive peer groups reported lower-quality dating relationships, and more dating violence victimization and perpetration. This is in line with research that shows that peer aggressors are likely to be dating aggressors as well.

Teen Dating Violence and Aggression

Connolly and Josephson (2007) discuss two types of risk factors for teen dating violence: background factors and situation factors. Background factors can lead an adolescent to use aggression as a response to interpersonal problems generally. These include violence in the family, prior use of aggression with peers, a peer group that tolerates romantic aggression, and an attitude of accepting the use of aggression to solve romantic problems. These, they say, are the factors that form the social context in which the adolescent grows up and learns about relationships.

Situation factors are the specific features of the dating relationship that lead an adolescent to respond aggressively with a romantic partner. The most significant of these are the quality of the relationship, use of psychological or verbal aggression, and poor interpersonal skills.

Gorman-Smith (2001) studied urban minority males and street violence and found that those reporting partner violence were also likely to report involvement in street violence. Of those reporting violence toward partners, 55 percent also reported participation in street violence. However, she found that there appeared to be distinct groups of violent offenders. Of those youth who reported involvement in either type of violence, 39 percent reported participation in both, 28 percent reported participation in street violence only, and 33 percent reported involvement in partner violence only.

Of the male adolescents reporting involvement in a relationship during the last period, fully 82 percent reported some type of aggressive behavior toward their partner and 31 percent reported some type of physical violence toward a partner. Gorman-Smith concluded that these results were consistent with other research in which self-reported rates of partner violence by men under twenty-five ranged from 21 percent to 23 percent.

And although seemingly less harmful than physical aggression, Gorman-Smith states that being the victim of verbal aggression has been associated with increased risk for depression, anxiety disorders, and low self-esteem. She found that youth who participated in both types of violence (i.e., street and relationship) had consistently poorer functioning families than youth in other groups.

As we have seen, bullying has been identified as a significant risk factor for dating aggression, as those who bully frequently appear to transfer their aggression to dating relationships. Connolly and Josephson say that both sexual harassment and aggression toward a romantic partner are common behaviors of both boys and girls who bully. They also say that psychological aggression usually precedes physical aggression.

Unfortunately, some aspects of psychological aggression, including controlling behaviors and jealousy, are sometimes interpreted by the partner as love. This leads to paradoxical intensifying of commitment to the relationship following aggression. Temple, Shorey, Fite, Stuart, and Le (2012) contend that individuals who perpetrate violence in their adolescent relationships may be at heightened risk for continuing this relationship into adulthood.

Teen Dating Violence and Suicide

There is an association between suicidal ideation and physical dating violence. Silverman et al. (2001) found that adolescent girls who are victims of physical dating violence had a significantly increased risk of seriously considering or attempting suicide, as well as engaging in unhealthy weight control, substance use, and risky sexual behaviors. Howard et al. found that girls who reported considering suicide and feelings of hopelessness were more likely to experience physical dating violence compared to those who did not report suicidal thoughts. A similar association was not found for boys.

In a 2014 study of teen dating and suicide, Nahapetyan et al. (2013) found after controlling for the effects of sex, adolescents who reported physical dating violence perpetration had 1.54 times the odds of reporting suicidal ideation than adolescents who did not report physical dating violence perpetration.

Students in grades 9 to 11 have higher odds of reporting suicidal ideation compared to grade 12 in high school. This study confirmed the hypothesis that both physical dating violence perpetration and victimizations were significant predictors of suicidal ideation in adolescence. Nahapetyan et al. cite studies that show that among girls, victimization—but not perpetration—was associated with suicide ideation or attempts. Among boys, it increased the risk of suicide attempts.

PREVENTION OF TEEN DATING VIOLENCE

Gorman-Smith states that later adolescence is the period of development during which intimate partner relationships are being formed and that violence in these relationships is likely to begin. Because this is such an important time, when basic attitudes, beliefs, and practices are first formed, it is critical for targeting prevention efforts.

Mayes says that primary prevention interventions, along the lines of the three-tiered public health model, are believed to be the most effective at reducing the number of teen dating violence situations and notes that such initiatives are generally cost-effective and effective.

As these studies and articles show, dating violence affects boys and girls in significant numbers. Prevention programs are needed for both, though some recommend that primary or universal prevention programs be developed for teens prior to high school. Experts also agree that programs should consider identifying and targeting students already engaging in or at high risk for engaging in relationship violence.

Vagi et al. (2013) found that effective prevention programs were those that targeted youth who had experienced maltreatment and other adverse childhood effects, who had particular mental health problems, behaved aggressively or had aggressive attitudes, used substances, and were in hostile or unhealthy dating relationships.

Schnurr and Lohman state that prevention and intervention programs should focus on reducing adolescence drug and alcohol use, improving adolescent's relationships with their parents, and decreasing antisocial behavior to lower rates of perpetration of dating violence. They add that parents and peers should be educated on healthy communication and behavior so as to improve their overall relationships.

Targeting students who abuse substances, or have witnessed family domestic violence, or already experienced relationship violence would be the ideal targets for such secondary intervention. Experts emphasize the importance for substance use prevention, given the association with teen dating violence. This is not because one causes the other, however, but because they are factors that can be addressed congruently.

Since research tells us that many students do not even realize or recognize relationship abuse, awareness programs are key as are programs for peers, or bystanders, to whom victims usually turn. As we see repeatedly with each type of victimization, most student-victims do not turn to adults, but to their friends, and most friends do not know what to do in those circumstances.

Implications for Schools

Schools are in a unique position to offer teen dating violence prevention. In one survey of students who experienced teen dating violence, 42 percent boys and 43 percent girls reported that they experienced it at school. Yet too often this issue goes unaddressed. One report of school counselors indicated that 61 percent have helped a victim of dating violence in the previous two years (61 percent). Even though, most also said their schools did not have a protocol for responding to this issue (81 percent) (Reinburg, 2012).

School nurses were surveyed on teen dating violence by Khubchandani et al. (2013) who found that most school nurses (86.4 percent) reported that they did not have a protocol in their schools to respond to an instance of teen dating violence. Over half (55.3 percent) of the high-school nurses reported assisting victims of teen dating violence in the previous two years.

A resounding majority of nurses (81 percent) reported that in the past two years, no training had been provided to personnel in their schools on this issue. Neither did their schools conduct periodic student surveys that included questions on teen dating abuse behaviors (71.5 percent). Of those nurses who had a school protocol for responding to such an incident, they perceived significantly fewer barriers to assisting victims and they actually assisted more victims.

Khubchandani recommended a variety of strategies for schools to effectively address teen dating violence. These included providing staff, faculty, and administrators with training on teen dating violence and sexual assault; educating students about teen dating violence, sexual assault, and healthy dating relationships; having a policy that addresses teen dating violence and sexual violence; keeping teen dating violence and sexual violence complaints and investigations in a separate file from academic records; and having information posted around the campus regarding teen dating violence.

Mayes, drawing on a number of studies and reports, summarized the components necessary for schools to effectively respond to teen dating violence: staff development to educate staff about the nature, prevalence, harm, and prevention of dating violence; dating violence prevention programs directed toward students; counseling for targets, and perpetrators of teen dating violence or providing appropriate referrals to available resources; and outreach to parents and the community about teen dating violence. Mayes also says that to be effective, a school's response must be ongoing rather than a one-shot deal.

A school's overall climate of safety is also a factor when it comes to dating violence prevention. Dating violence also appears more likely to occur in schools considered unsafe by their students. Debnam, Johnson, and Bradshaw (2014) found that adolescents who had been bullied were more concerned about both physical and emotional dating violence among students at their school, and that schools that were perceived as safer had lower levels of teen dating violence.

Effective prevention programs integrate instructional curriculum with efforts to improve the school environment. McLeod, Jones, and Cramer (2015) say that prevention programs, contrary to teen dating violence awareness programs, emphasize the attitudes, knowledge, and behaviors that promote healthy relationships. They assessed the effectiveness of a school-based, peer-facilitated healthy relations program among academically at-risk students. Almost three hundred ninth graders of mixed race and gender participated in a five-session healthy relationships program that had been adapted to address concerns of cultural relevance.

Evaluation of the program found measurable improvements in participants' attitudes and knowledge. They concluded that peer-facilitated models can be effective at delivering healthy relationships content in school settings.

Health education programs have been designed to delay sexual behavior and to promote healthy dating relationships among ethnic minority middle-school youth. In a study of one such program, Peskin et al. (2014) found that control students who did not have access to this program had significantly higher odds of physical dating violence victimization, emotional and physical dating violence victimization, and emotional dating violence perpetration.

Implications for Communities

Some states actually require school districts to educate students on the issue of dating violence. For example, Georgia law, Stader tells us, requires the state Board of Education to develop rape prevention and personal safety education programs and a program for prevention of teen dating violence. Texas also requires school districts to adopt and implement a teen dating violence policy to be included in district improvement plans.

Carlson (2003) asserts that a school district may be held liable for student dating violence under a variety of legal theories. A student can claim, under Title IX, that he or she was subjected to sexual harassment that resulted in a hostile education environment, due to the abusive behavior and to the school district's failure to address the problem. A student could bring a constitutional claim alleging that the school district's failure to protect him or her deprived the student of the right to be secure in his or her own person.

Carlson also says that under state tort law a student can claim negligent infliction of emotional distress. He believes a sexual harassment claim under Title IX may be the most reasonable, though most states have adopted some form of antibullying legislation as well. Dating violence could also be considered a form of bullying in that the student could potentially claim that the school or district was deliberately indifferent to such victimization.

In addition to legal considerations, collaboration between the various systems in the community can be pivotal in dating violence prevention. Lowe, Jones, and Banks (2007) found that such collaboration can serve to educate other service providers about this problem, increase awareness of available services, and provide children and adolescents with more comprehensive services.

Broad community involvement increases the likelihood of coordinated responses by schools, law enforcement, victim advocacy and support groups, and medical professionals, states Mayes. One such program, for example, is the *Safe Relationships* program, facilitated by the Safe Relationships Network, a collaborative of community agencies.

This network joined in with a local school district to develop a program to address dating violence prevention. The program involves short-term psychoeducational dating skills provided to ninth graders, with each of the participating agencies providing one hour of curriculum to students during health class. Evaluations found significantly improved knowledge about teen dating violence, positive changes among girls, and mixed results among boys.

Such collaborative programs are said to be an effective alternative for schools to reduce the number of dating violence incidents, including sexual harassment, as well as to reduce the impact on the well-being of youth, say these authors. Vagi et al.'s recommendations for those designing programs to prevent teen dating violence perpetration are that these initiatives should target multiple factors, and address both background, risk factors, and situational ones.

PROMISING PROGRAM: SAFE DATES

According to the Blueprint program evaluation, Safe Dates is an exemplary teen dating violence prevention program. It is a ten-session program for middle-/high-school students consisting of both school and community components. The school component has a curriculum that is implemented in schools by regular classroom teachers and targets primary prevention. The community component targets secondary prevention by providing support groups and activities for youth as well as information for parents. The curriculum in the school component can also be presented by community resource people outside of the school setting.

Each session is forty-five to fifty minutes in length and includes the following topics: defining caring relationships, defining dating abuse, why people abuse, helping friends, overcoming gender stereotypes, equal power through communication, how we feel/how we deal, and preventing sexual assault. Booster sessions can also be offered after the initial administration of the curriculum.

Safe Dates has been found to be effective in preventing and reducing violence perpetration among teens already perpetrating dating violence. It also has resulted in less acceptance of dating violence, stronger communication/anger management skills, less gender stereotyping, and greater awareness of community services.

According to the Blueprint Evaluation website, at the four-year follow-up point, the following results were found among Safe Dates participants compared to the control group participants:

- *Between 56 and 92* percent *reported less physical, serious physical, and sexual dating violence perpetration and victimization*
- *Adolescents who received Safe Dates reported perpetrating significantly less psychological, moderate physical, and sexual dating violence perpetration at all four follow-up check points*
- *Safe Dates-only adolescents who reported no severe physical perpetration (or average amounts of severe physical perpetration at baseline) reported significantly less severe physical perpetration than control group adolescents at each of the four follow-up points.*

LESSONS LEARNED ABOUT TEEN DATING VIOLENCE

As this chapter has illustrated, teen dating relationship violence is widespread. When almost half of all school counselors report helping a student dealing with such an issue, we see the tip of the iceberg. Once again we see that teens will generally not report such experiences to adults. They turn to their friends and peers who simply do not know what to do or how to help them.

It is the responsibility of adults at every level, from the home to the school, to the wider community, to ensure that there are programs and resources to help teens struggling with these dating relationship challenges. This is especially important given the negative impact of teen dating violence on both the perpetrator and the victim, and the potential for untreated abuse to spiral into adult domestic violence and intergenerational transmission of such violence.

We know what the risk factors are and we know that there are certain protective factors, including relationships with one's family, academic success, and school attachment, which need to be in place to prevent such relationship violence. If our students will not come to us with their relationship problems and concerns, then we must go to them.

We must provide them with the informed adults, the family supports, the school climates, the supports for personal and academic success, and the intervention resources they need, when necessary. Helping them develop the communication and problem-solving skills, conflict resolution skills, and interpersonal relationship skills will enhance their ability to successfully face these challenges and reduce the negative—often life-long impact—of such challenges left unaddressed.

Ortralla Mosley's mother, Carolyn White-Mosley, turned her grief into action and founded Trella's Foundation in 2005. The mission of the organization is to empower teens to choose healthy relationships through education, advocacy, and support; to enable teens to become survivors of, and advocates for the prevention of teen dating violence; to mobilize community involvement through social action and outreach; to provide a safe haven for teens in abusive relationships; and, finally, to prevent the loss of life. Carolyn and the Ortralla Foundation have one vision: a world where all teens choose healthy relationships, where love is learned and lives are saved.

The next chapter explores another form of violence that has its roots in alienation, a lack of connection, a lack of hope, a lack of school bonding, and the need to belong to something—even if that something is a dangerous and criminal gang.

REFERENCES

Berman, A. L., Jobes, D. A., & Silverman, M. M. (2006). *Adolescent suicide: Assessment and intervention.* Washington, DC: American Psychological Association.

Carlson, C. N. (2003, Spring). Invisible victims: Holding the educational system liable for teen dating violence at school. *Harvard Women's Law Journal, 26*, 351–393.

Coid, J., Petruckevitch, A., Feder, G., Chung, W., Richardson, J., Moorey, S. (2001). Relation between childhood sexual and physical abuse and risk of revictimization in women: A cross-sectional survey. *The Lancet, 358*, 450–454.

Connolly, J., & Josephson, W. (2007). Aggression in adolescent dating relationships: Predictors and prevention. *PsycEXTRA Dataset.* doi:10.1037/e400292008-002

Debnam, K. J., Johnson, S. C., & Bradshaw, C. P. (2014). An evaluation of a school-based, peer-facilitated, healthy relationship program for at-risk adolescents. *Children & Schools, 37*(2).

Ellis, W. E., Chung-Hall, J., & Dumas, T. M. (2012). The role of peer group aggression in predicting adolescent dating violence and relationship quality. *Journal of Youth and Adolescence, 42*(4), 487–499. doi:10.1007/s10964-012-9797-0

Espelage, D. L., & Holt, M. (2007). Dating violence among high school students. In K. Kendall-Tackett & S. Giaccamoni (Eds.), *Intimate partner violence* (pp. 14.1–14.19). Kingston, NJ: Civic Research Institute.

Foshee, V. A., Benefield, T. S., Reyes, H. L., Ennett, S. T., Faris, R., Chang, L., ... Suchindran, C. M. (2013). The peer context and the development of the perpetration of adolescent dating violence. *Journal of Youth and Adolescence, 42*(4), 471–486. doi:10.1007/s10964-013-9915-7

Gorman-Smith, D., Tolan, P., Sheidow, A. J., Henry, D. (2001). Partner violence and street violence among urban adolescents: Do the same family factors relate? *Journal of Research on Adolescence, 11*(3), 273–295.

Hanson, R. F. (2002). Adolescent dating violence: Prevalence and psychological outcomes. *Child Abuse & Neglect, 26*(5), 449–453.

Henry, R. R., & Zeytinoglu, S. (2012). African Americans and teen dating violence. *The American Journal of Family Therapy, 40*(1), 20–32. doi:10.1080/01926187.2011.578033

Hinduja, S., & Patchin, J. W. (2010). Bullying, cyberbullying, and suicide. *Archives of Suicide Research, 14*(3), 206–221.

Howard, D. E., Wang, M. Q., & Yan, F. (2007). Psychosocial factors associated with reports of physical dating violence among U.S. adolescent females. *Adolescence, 42*(166), 311–324.

Khubchandani, J., Telljohann, S. K., Price, J. H., Dake, J. A., & Hendershot, C. (2013). Providing assistance to the victims of adolescent dating violence: A national assessment of school nurses' practices. *Journal of School Health, 83*(2), 127–136. doi:10.1111/josh.12008

Lowe, L. A., Jones, C. D., & Banks, L. (2007). Preventing dating violence in public schools: An evaluation of an interagency collaborative program for youth. *Journal of School Violence, 6*(3), 69–87.

Martin-Storey, A. (2014). Prevalence of dating violence among sexual minority youth: Variation across gender, sexual minority identity and gender of sexual partners. *Journal of Youth and Adolescence, 44*(1), 211–224. doi:10.1007/s10964-013-0089-0

Mayes, T. A. (2008). Students with no-contact orders against abusive classmates: Recommendations for educators. *Preventing School Failure: Alternative Education for Children and Youth, 52*(4), 37–44. doi:10.3200/psfl.52.4.37-44

Mcleod, D. A., Jones, R., & Cramer, E. P. (2015). An evaluation of a school-based, peer- facilitated, healthy relationship program for at-risk adolescents. *Children & Schools, 37*(2), 108–116. doi:10.1093/cs/cdv006

Nahapetyan, L., Orpinas, P., Song, X., & Holland, K. (2013). Longitudinal association of suicidal ideation and physical dating violence among high school students. *Journal of Youth and Adolescence, 43*(4), 629–640. doi:10.1007/s10964-013-0006-6

Peskin, M. F., Markham, C. M., Shegog, R., Baumler, E. R., Addy, R. C., & Tortolero, S. R. (2014). Effects of the it's your game ... keep it real program on dating violence in ethnic-minority middle school youths: A group randomized trial. *American Journal of Public Health, 104*(8), 1471–1477. doi:10.2105/ajph.2014.301902

Reinburg, S. (2012). U.S. High Schools Lax in Preventing Dating Abuse, *U.S. News and World Report.*

Safe Dates Program. Retrieved from http://www.blueprintsprograms.com/factsheet/safe-dates

Schnurr, M. P., & Lohman, B. J. (2008). *Journal of Youth Adolescence, 37,* 266. doi:10.1007/s10964-007-9246-7

Silverman, J. G., Anita, R., Mucci, L. A., & Hathaway, J. E. (2001). Dating violence against adolescent girls and associated substance use, unhealthy weight control, sexual risk behavior, pregnancy and suicidality. *Journal of the American Medical Association, 286*(5), 572–579. doi:10.1001-jama.286.5.572

Temple, J. R., Shorey, R. C., Fite, P., Stuart, G. L., & Le, V. D. (2012). Substance use as a longitudinal predictor of the perpetration of teen dating violence. *Journal of Youth and Adolescence, 42*(4), 596–606. doi:10.1007/s10964-012-9877-1

Theriot, M. T. (2008). Conceptual and methodological considerations for assessment and prevention of adolescent dating violence and stalking at school. *Children & Schools, 30*(4), 223–233. doi:10.1093/cs/30.4.223

Trella's Foundation. Retrieved from http://www.ortrallafoundation.org/home.html

Vagi, K. J., Rothman, E. F., Latzman, N. E., Tharp, A. T., Hall, D. M., & Breiding, M. J. (2013). Beyond correlates: A review of risk and protective factors for adolescent dating violence perpetration. *Journal of Youth and Adolescence, 42*(4), 633–649. doi:10.1007/s10964-013-9907-7

Youth Risk Behavior Surveillance System, Center for Disease Control, Washington, DC. Retrieved from http://www.cdc.gov/healthyyouth/data/yrbs/index.htm

Zweig, J. M., Lachman, P., Yahner, J., & Dank, M. (2013). Correlates of cyber dating abuse among teens. *Journal of Youth and Adolescence, 43*(8), 1306–1321. doi:10.1007/s10964-013-0047-x

Chapter Eight

Gang Violence

On a beautiful afternoon in September 2009, sixteen-year-old Derrion Albert was caught in an ongoing fight between two gang factions after leaving Fenger High School in Chicago. Horns blared as cars tried to get down a street flooded with dozens of students walking home from school. Most wore their school uniforms and carried backpacks—a typical afternoon after school on a tree-lined street. Shouts were exchanged, then fists and railroad ties grabbed. Groups of students clustered together screaming and yelling and egging the fighters on.

Albert, who did not belong to a gang, got caught in the crossfire of blows and stomps. A group of three to four teen boys ripped into him, hitting and stomping him lifeless. Either the crowd sensed this deadly turn of events, or heard the sound of sirens coming, because as he lay still on the curb, the throng began screaming and yelling and running on down the street. Throughout this ordeal, cars kept driving by, honking and careening past the students, just moving on down the street. After the crowd fled, a few students yelled and screamed for Derrion to get up and, when he did not, they dragged his lifeless body into a nearby building.

INTRODUCTION AND OVERVIEW OF GANG VIOLENCE ISSUES

The level of exposure to violence among many children living in poverty in U.S. cities is almost incomprehensible. One study of urban school children found that 93.6 percent of all inner city youth studied had been exposed to some type of violence and 80 percent witnessed ongoing violence in their lives (Jones, 2012). Another study of inner city sixth to twelfth graders found that 35 percent worried that they would fall victim to violence.

Bradshaw, Pas, Debnam, and Johnson (2015) note that environmental factors such as poor social cohesion, increased availability of alcohol and drugs, a gang presence, and exposure to violence have all been associated with adolescent substance abuse, and involvement in violence, including gang membership. They note that, unfortunately, youth of lower socioeconomic status were more likely to be exposed to the above negative neighborhood in school environmental risk factors, and that these youth were also more likely to be minorities and live in urban environments.

Fully 75 to 93 percent of youth in the juvenile justice system are estimated to have been exposed to violence and, as a result, experienced some type of trauma. Many experts view such exposure as leading to, or causing, post-traumatic stress symptoms or full-blown PTSD. Factors that affect whether a child develops PTSD include the child's proximity to the violence, age, severity and frequency of the violence, and the availability of adults to emotionally support the child.

Children exposed to such violence have a myriad of problems. They are more likely to be aggressive and exhibit behavior problems; have depression, suicidal behavior, and low self-esteem; have an inability to concentrate, have difficulty with school work, and be significantly lower in verbal, motor, and cognitive skills; have lower levels of problem-solving skills and empathy, possibly becoming violent themselves; and have health problems in adolescence and adulthood. When threatened or exposed to something that triggers memories of the trauma, the child's brain is activated to an alarm state. They are unable to calm themselves and often have distorted views of the world. They then develop coping strategies, which often contribute to other problems (Wolfe, Crooks, Lee, McIntyre-Smith, & Jaffe, 2003).

Laquan MacDonald was a seventeen-year-old African American gang member who was shot by Chicago police in 2014 in a very controversial shooting. While he was a known gang member, he was also a victim of post-traumatic stress, which certainly contributed to his problematic behavior from about age thirteen. The system at every level let him down. His mother and family failed him when he was taken away from her not once, but twice, once at age three and again at age five, due to accusations of neglect and abuse. From there, the educational, the social services, the juvenile justice and, finally, the law enforcement systems, all failed him, as well.

He is one of thousands of children impacted by violence. One major urban school system, for example, the Chicago Public Schools (CPS), was studied by the CDC (2011). In this study, CPS social workers reported that the majority of referrals for social work services were related to the experience of trauma or anger/aggression. The social workers said that almost a third of CPS's more than four hundred thousand students reported that they felt sad or hopeless almost every day for two weeks or more in a row and that 15.5 percent seriously considered attempting suicide.

In addition to exposure to violence, many students are victims of it as well. Studies have shown that 7 percent of students report being threatened or injured with a weapon. In 2011, 25.6 percent of males reported carrying a weapon (with 8 percent carrying the weapon on school property). Not surprisingly, due to the overall culture of violence in many urban neighborhoods, the high schools that have high levels of violence are urban, with high numbers of minority students, high levels of social disadvantage, and high mobility rates. Rates of school-associated homicides are correlated with males in urban high school.

According to Gottfredson and Gottfredson (1985), the strongest correlates of school disorder are characteristics of the population and the community context in which schools are located. Schools in urban, poor, and disorganized communities experience more disorder than other schools.

As reported in the previous chapter, Henry and Zeytinoglu (2012) found African Americans to report the most victimization and perpetration of community and dating violence. They point to research which shows that overexposure to community violence can result in individuals who become desensitized to the impact of violence. This can then lead to anger and aggression. When the correlation between such exposure and involvement is examined in African American male teens, for example, results indicate that neighborhood violence involvement, involvement in gangs, and high reports of homelessness were strongly correlated to interpersonal violence.

Twenty-three percent of urban students report gang presence in their schools. The presence of gangs in schools was more than double the likelihood of violent victimization at school, with 8 percent in schools with gangs compared to 3 percent in school without a strong gang presence, according to Naber, May, Decker, Minor, and Wells (2006). There is a high correlation between student victimization of all types and gang presence. Constant exposure to violence in one's community has an impact on every level of development of children.

Naber et al. present the most widely accepted definition of a gang. It includes the following: a group, permanence, symbols of membership, and involvement in crime. It is important to note that most students who reside in areas where gangs exist choose *not* to join those gangs. In fact less than 10 percent of urban students join gangs.

A 2011 University of California at Los Angeles (UCLA) Center report describes gangs as loosely organized associations of socially excluded, alienated, or bigoted individuals acting together in a structure of informal leadership. They are bound by a common ethnicity, race, social class, or other determinant. They employ distinct symbols including dress hand signals tattoos and graffiti. They follow a defined system of rules, rituals, and codes of behavior. It notes that gangs serve some individuals as a substitute family structure. Membership in a gang can provide a sense of empowerment, as members act together to defend territory and provide mutual protection.

Estrada et al. (2014) report that studies exploring the connection between school violence and behaviors experienced and perpetrated by gang members at school are scarce. They say that gang theory and gang literature have focused primarily on the individual, family, community, and peer domains, and practically ignore these variables in the high school context.

Though more common in urban areas, gang membership crosses all socioeconomic backgrounds and boundaries regardless of age, sex, race, economic status, and academic achievement (figure 8.1). It is different from nongang violence in a multitude of ways. Gang violence typically involves a larger number of individuals and tends to be more retaliatory. It escalates much more quickly and is usually more violent in nature and often involves the greater use of weapons, according to the National School Safety and Security Services.

Ebensen (2000) notes that traditionally the typical gang member is male, lives in the inner city, and as a member of a racial minority. He says that although these characteristics may be prevalent among gang members, it should not be assumed that all or even the overwhelming majority of gang members share these qualities. There has been a growing involvement of girls in gangs in more recent years, though more than 90 percent of gang members are male.

PREVALENCE

There has been a growth of youth gangs in urban, rural, and suburban communities in recent years. The UCLA Center report notes that, after decline in the mid-1990s to the early 2000s, there has been a steady increase in gangs and gang activity. In 2007, it was estimated that there were more than 30,000 youth gangs and 782,000 active gang members in the United States.

The 2011 UCLA report indicates that 23 to 24 percent of students reported gangs in their schools and in the community. Hispanic and African American students were more likely than white students to report gangs in their schools (38 percent and 37 percent, respectively, versus 17 percent), and this pattern held among students in both urban and suburban schools. Between 2003 and 2005, reports of gangs increased among both African American and white students, but not Hispanic students. In terms of race, recent reports indicate that about 46 percent are Hispanic or Latino, 35 percent are African American, 11 percent are white, and 7 percent are other (figure 8.2).

The UCLA report found no measurable difference between suburban and rural students in their likelihood of reporting gang presence and that the total percentage of students reporting the presence of gangs at school increased from 21 percent in 2003 to 24 percent in 2005. The percentage of students at

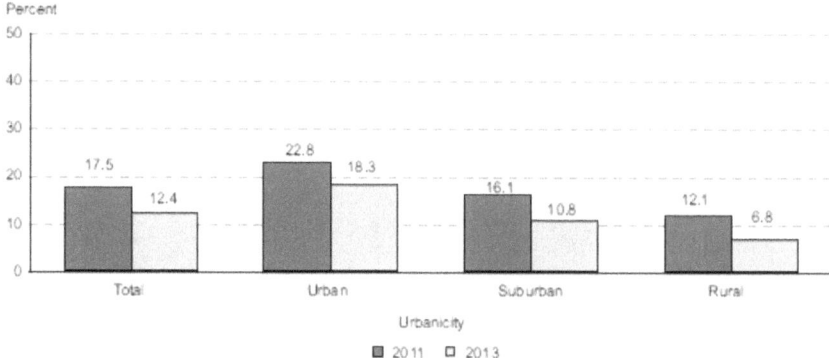

Figure 8.1 Students Reporting Gangs at School by Urbanity 2011–13. *Source*: School Crime Supplement to National Crime Victimization Survey, 2015.

urban schools reporting that gangs were present also increased during this period, from 31 to 36 percent. A survey of nearly 6,000 eighth graders in eleven cities known as gang localities found that more than 11 percent were currently gang members, and more than 17 percent said they had been at some point.

Howell and Lynch (2000) found that Hispanic and African American fifteen-year-olds from low-income households reported the highest prevalence of gangs in schools. These students were more likely to attend public schools that were located in central cities with populations between one hundred thousand and one million, which were characterized by high levels of student victimization, security measures, and a large number of readily available drugs.

Howell and Lynch also found that students in mid-to-late adolescence who lived in household incomes with less than $7,500 at the time (2000) at home and who had been victimized personally were most likely to report gang presence. The most criminally active gangs were reported by fifteen- to seventeen-year-old students of either gender.

Naber et al. (2006) concluded their review of research stating that gang membership at school is higher among nonwhites, urban residents, and students from lower socioeconomic strata. Additionally, they say that gang activity is also positively correlated with the amount of drugs and other criminal activity at school. It is associated with increased dropout rates and decreased grades and achievement scores (figure 8.2).

Howell and Lynch found a strong correlation between the presence of both guns and drugs in school. Higher percentages of students reported knowing a student brought a gun to school when gangs were present in the school (25 percent) than when gangs were not present (8 percent). In addition, gang

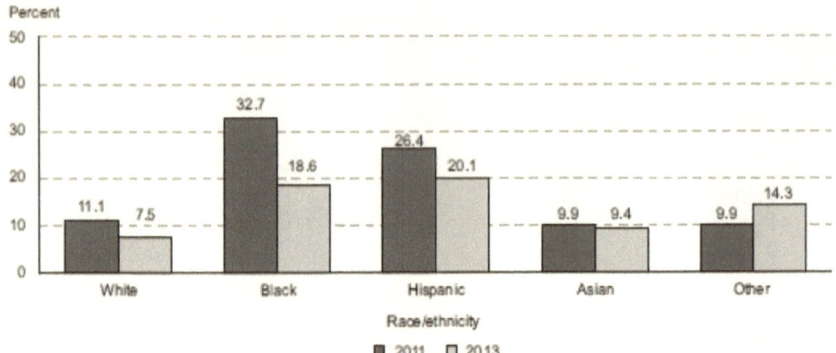

Figure 8.2 Percentage of Students Reporting Gangs at School by Race/Ethnicity 2011–2013.
Source: School Crime Supplement to National Crime Victimization Survey, 2015.

presence increased the likelihood of seeing a student with a gun in school. 12 percent of the students surveyed reported seeing a gun in school when gangs were present, compared to 3 percent when gangs were not present.

RISK FACTORS AND EFFECTS

Personal Risk Factors

The primary attraction of gangs is their ability to respond to student needs that are not currently being met in their lives, says Allen (1999). Gangs often provide these youths with a sense of family and acceptance, thus allowing them to disregard their true family he notes. Gangs attract members because they provide individuals with a sense of community, friends, a feeling of family, and support for survival.

Allen further notes that understanding how gangs draw youth into them can prepare schools and communities to better respond to them. He states that there are four factors that are crucial in the formation of gangs: first, youth experiences sense of alienation and powerlessness because of the lack of traditional support structures, such as family and school. This can lead to feelings of frustration and anger, and a desire to obtain support outside of traditional institutions.

Second, continues Allen, gang membership gives an individual a sense of belonging and becomes a major source of identity for its members. Gang membership affords a sense of power and control to these members and gang activities become an outlet for their anger. Third, he continues, the control of certain turf is essential to the well-being of the gang, which often will use force to control both its territories and members. And finally, recruitment of new members and expansion of territory are essential to remain strong and powerful.

To make a gang work, the UCLA report says, members actually pattern themselves after a family. It says that to truly understand a gang, it is necessary to look at the structure of the gang, who joins and why, and their chosen gang identifiers. In contrast to social clubs, the organizing structure is hierarchical, with leaders at the top, then hard-core members, then associates and wannabes. The gang acts as a powerful social network in controlling the behavior of members. This can limit their access to prosocial networks and cut individuals off from conventional pursuits.

Having a family member who is or was a gang member increases the risk. Lacking a sense of family at home, including fatherless homes, abusive homes, being raised away from parents, are all risk factors. As noted earlier, gangs provide a sense of family, support, and identity.

The UCLA report identified clusters of potential risk factors:

- Individual (prior delinquency, aggression, antisocial attitudes, alcohol and drug use, earlier precocious sexual activity)
- Peer group factors (peer delinquency, association with aggressive peers and gang members, street socialization)
- School (poor social performance, low attachment to teachers, feeling unsafe in school)
- Family (family violence, family history of gang association, lack of a positive adult role models, family disorganization)
- Community (social disorganization in distressed neighborhoods, high crime rate, strong gang presence, feeling unsafe in the neighborhood). (UCLA Center Report, 2011, p. 10)

The UCLA report cites Moore's description of the transition from typical adolescent groups to established youth gangs in terms of community conditions: a neighborhood where there is a lack of effective adult supervision; youngsters who have considerable free time not devoted to a prosocial activity; little opportunity for moving onto a good adult job; and gang members who congregate and operate.

Wright and Fitzpatrick (2006) say that for school-related risk, lower academic achievement is predicted to be associated with greater fighting. Family structures and peers also have a huge influence. Youth with greater personal and social assets are thought to be able to resist tendencies toward unhealthy and delinquent behaviors.

For personal assets, they note that high self-esteem is predicted to be associated with a lower frequency of fighting. In addition to individual assets such as self-esteem, the positive familial and school environments characterized by cohesiveness and involvement are instrumental in alleviating fighting and gang violence.

Ebensen et al. (2011) highlighted the differences between nondelinquent youth and delinquent and gang youth. They found that nondelinquent youth reported lower levels of commitment to delinquent peers, lower levels of social isolation, lower tolerance for deviance, and higher levels of commitment to positive peers.

Ebensen (with Deschenes in 1997) described a continuum extending from nondelinquent, to minor delinquent, to serious delinquent, to gang member. Based on delinquency scores, they categorized eighth-grade students into one of these four classifications. On every measure tested, gang members were significantly different from each of the other groups, but were clearly the most distinct from nondelinquent youth.

Gang members were more impulsive, engaged in more risk-seeking behavior and were less committed to school. They reported less communication with, and lower levels of attachment to, their parents. Many experienced multiple types of marginality, that is, a combination of disadvantages, including marginal ethnic and personal identities. These authors suggest that gang members are already delinquent before joining a gang and that delinquency increases dramatically during the time that they are in the gang.

Estrada et al. cite Stoiber and Good who say that the pathway to adolescent delinquent behaviors, such as becoming a gang member, is dependent upon a balancing act between risk factors that increase susceptibility and protective factors that enhance an individual's resistance and coping ability. They note that truancy, for example, is related to gang membership, drug use, and delinquency, and that early drug use has consistently been a predictor of gang membership.

School-Related Risk Factors

A 2007 UCLA Center report states that among the various reasons given for joining a gang, the two most common are social reasons to be around friends and family members already part of the gang, and for protection and the presumed safety that individuals believe gangs can give them. Taylor et al. (2007) find, however, that gang members are far more likely to be victimized and suffer greater number of victimizations than the nongang members in both general and serious types of violence. Bradshaw et al. (2015) point to research that shows that a history of violent and aggressive behavior and low attachment and commitment to school are important predictors of gang involvement.

Ebensen et al. consistently found that poor academic performance, feeling unsafe to and from in school, and associating with delinquent peers were among the strongest factors correlated with youth gang membership in addition to substance abuse problems and truancy. They note that these factors contribute to youth who are disconnected from school and to schools that view gangs as barriers to achieving their goals.

The UCLA Center report concurs and cites Howell who found that one of the strongest risk factors was achievement in elementary school, which in turn is related to low academic aspirations, a low degree of commitment to school, and teachers' negative labeling of youth.

Naber et al. (2006) cite Lawrence who found that the school environment can be fertile ground for gang member recruitment as well as for planning and coordination of gang activities taking place elsewhere. The presence of gangs in school is associated with student fear and victimization.

The UCLA Center report states that individuals who do not like school, whose school performance is poor, and who are not committed to education are more likely to engage in a variety of problem behaviors and more likely than others to be involved with gangs. This, too, provides schools with some insight as to potential approaches to prevention, which will be discussed later in the chapter.

Prosocial youth are more likely to be bonded to conventional norms and prosocial groups. Aggressive youth, on the other hand, are rejected by those groups and gravitate toward deviant peer groups. Thus, the report concludes, gang membership likely stems from weakened social bonds to conventional norms as well as the environmental factors such as urbanicity that reinforce delinquency.

Gangs and Bullying

Bradshaw et al. found that perpetrating bullying as early as the fifth grade predicted involvement in violence in early adulthood. They cited a recent longitudinal study of African American youth, which found bullying victimization to predict gang membership and higher aggression and delinquency trajectories. They describe a correlation between student perceptions of bullying in their schools and teacher reports of the presence of gangs. They describe a cross-sectional study of over ten thousand offenders that found that self-reported early perpetuation of bullying was predictive of gang membership.

They also found that bully victims fared the worst across all outcomes. They were almost twelve times more likely to have been a gang member and over twelve times as likely to have carried a weapon to school. The bullies were also at greater risk, they say, as they were approximately five times as likely to engage in these behaviors.

They note the overlap between bullying and involvement in violence, such as gang membership and concluded that youth with a prior history of bullying others, as well as those who were bullies and victims may be attracted to gangs and weapon carrying as a means of protection, particularly in urban contexts. They also found that bully/victims and bullies also had greater academic problems, including truancy and poor academic performance

Gangs and Substance Abuse

Swahn et al. (2010) found that gang members were significantly more likely than nongang members to have initiated alcohol early, to have reported a high prevalence of alcohol use, to have encouraged an alcohol-related physical fighting, peer drinking, drug use, selling, peer drug selling, and having seen drugs in their neighborhood.

They describe findings from the longitudinal Seattle Social Development Project, which showed that participants who were gang members (compared to nongang members) had a much higher prevalence of binge drinking (43 percent versus 24 percent), marijuana use (54 percent versus 26 percent), and drug selling (51 percent versus 9 percent).

Early alcohol use and marijuana use were both identified risk factors for joining a gang among adolescents and gang members reported an increase in frequency of drug use when they joined a gang. Swahn et al. also say that the prevalence of binge drinking appeared to be much higher among gang members and that certain contexts for drinking were unique to gang members and their specific subculture (e.g., gang initiation, funerals). Gang members who initiated alcohol earlier had a higher prevalence of alcohol use and alcohol-related physical fighting.

Over half of the gang members (50.9 percent) had initiated alcohol use prior to age thirteen compared to 22 percent of nongang members. Those who drank alcohol three or more times a week, or those who drank heavily three or four times per week, were significantly more likely to report being a gang member than those who did not drink. Those who fought due to drinking, and who reported that their peers were drinking, were also more likely to report being gang members.

Those who reported drug use and those who sold drugs were also significantly more likely to be gang members. The authors of this study concluded that peer drinking, peer drug selling, and having seen drug deals in the neighborhood were strongly associated with gang membership for both boys and girls. This confirmed the importance of peers and community context and understanding gang membership. We now turn to using these understandings to inform prevention efforts.

PREVENTION

Once again, we have seen with the other types of school violence prevention discussed earlier, expert recommendations predominantly focus on the public health model of universal interventions with primary, secondary, and tertiary approaches. The UCLA 2007 report says that with regard to primary prevention, it is important to remember that gang formation is not necessarily restricted to urban, economically disadvantaged areas. Gang members come from a variety of backgrounds, and that once youth join gangs, they engage in high levels of criminal activity.

Therefore, the report says, it is appropriate to focus on communities and youth exposed to the greatest risk factors. It notes that tertiary prevention programs, such as law enforcement crackdowns and gang suppression approaches, have shown little promise, and concluded that prevention efforts that concentrate only on individual characteristics will fail to address underlying problems.

The report goes on to cite Short's (1997) caution that, absent change at the macro level, forces associated with these conditions such as gang and criminal behavior will continue. Single approaches, whether based on prevention, suppression, coordination of agency programs, community change, or law enforcement, are unlikely to prevent gang formation or to be successful in stopping criminal behavior.

Ebensen et al. concur. Since delinquency generally precedes gang membership, they suggest that gang programs should not be limited to gang intervention or suppression. They agree that general prevention efforts that target an entire adolescent population may also prove beneficial in reducing youth gang involvement.

Prevention and intervention strategies that specifically target at-risk youth are also warranted, Ebensen et al. advise. They emphasize the importance of early primary prevention strategies and say that, if intervention efforts are to be successful, these efforts to prevent, intervene with, or suppress gangs must also be systematic, sustained, and based on local knowledge and research about predictors and causes of gangs and gang membership that is systematic and up-to-date.

Implications for Schools

Wright and Fitzpatrick (2006) indicated that to reduce fighting and potential gang involvement, parental monitoring, academic achievement, and school connectedness should be encouraged. They also emphasize the importance of child abuse prevention efforts, outreach to parents, and further efforts to reduce or eliminate the community factors that promote the proliferation of gangs.

Swahn et al. (2010) say that schools serve as a critically important resources for intervention and prevention efforts for gang members, especially those students in middle school who are still attending school. Early prevention efforts that target students in elementary and middle school appear warranted, as do screening measures for established predictors for dropping out of school.

They recommend that school staff who witness risk factors such as signs of alcohol and drug use consider asking about gang involvement and providing coping strategies for students in high-risk communities. Such staff needs to be appropriately trained to understand the risk factors, warning signs, and resources for these at-risk students.

Estrada et al. agree that schools are in a prime position to impact the student's choice of gang membership, and school violence behaviors through positive protective factors that include a teacher or other adult providing a connection, support, and safety. They advocate for providing more student connectedness and increasing support from adults. Perceptions of safety, too, will reduce the number of students who turn to gangs and violence. They point to the plethora of evidence-based programs that target school risk factors as promising ways to reduce school violence behaviors for all students, including those who are gang members.

The 2007 UCLA report found that high-school students who reported being involved with gangs were less exposed to many prevention activities than those who were not involved in gangs. This, the report says, suggests the potential for including more of the high-risk youths by actively seeking ways to include them.

Catalino, Haggery, Oesterle, Fleming, and Hawkins (2004) found that students with lower school attachment and commitment in fifth and sixth grade were about twice as likely to join a gang in adolescence. Students bonded to school in fifth grade were less likely to engage in any violent behavior between grades seven and age twenty-one. They point to another study that showed the odds of being violent at age eighteen were reduced for those students who had bonded to school in the ninth grade.

They also found that school bonding in middle school, and the pattern of bonding throughout middle and high school, also related to reduced levels of substance abuse in twelfth grade. A lack of school bonding during elementary and middle school was consistently related negatively to problem behaviors in their longitudinal study.

They recommend that school staff focus attention on reducing risk behaviors that include truancy, substance abuse, and risky, peer interactions that are directly related to school violence. They say that this approach would be more effective than punitive measures that solely target those students who are gang members.

They warn that school violence perpetration and victimization may be more apparent if the school is ill-equipped with inadequate resources or has a problematic environmental and organizational structure that struggles to control, truancy, substance abuse, and risky peer relations. The focus should be more on strategies that reduce risk and elevate protective behaviors and attitudes. Because gangs evolve from a variety of larger social issues, schools should consider developing a comprehensive approach that involves both community and school.

Suppression or elimination efforts have not been shown to be effective. The 2011 UCLA report states that the primary focus at both school and community levels has been suppression through dress codes in school uniforms, discipline related to bullying and fighting, collaboration with law enforcement, and zero tolerance approaches. These initiatives have had limited impact.

It notes that there is now increasing advocacy for a focus on enhancing school climate, so students can not only feel safe, but also experience the setting as positive. The goal, it says, is to develop a comprehensive system of supports that address barriers to learning and reengage disconnected youth.

Experts also point to the vital importance of communication between school and law enforcement. Such communication is essential for sharing information about the presence of gangs and the coordination of interventions as part of a comprehensive approach.

Implications for Communities

UCLA report notes that gangs are byproducts of their communities and that the community structure and capacity must also be targeted. A comprehensive system must focus on multiple facets:

- Community mobilization (involvement of local citizens, including former gang youth, community groups, and agencies in the coordination of staff within and across these agencies)
- Development of a variety of education, training, and employment programs targeting gang-involved youth; social intervention involving youth agencies, schools, faith-based groups, police and criminal justice organizations reaching out to gang-involved youth and their families, and linking them to needed resources
- Suppression (formal and informal social control procedures, including close supervision and monitoring of gang-involved youth by both community-based agencies and schools, as well as the juvenile and criminal justice systems). (UCLA Youth Gangs Report, 2011, p. 5)

The recommended emphasis is on developing and implementing a comprehensive intervention continuum that promotes healthy development and prevents problems; intervenes early when problems are noted; and addresses chronic and severe problems when they occur.

Ebensen et al. note that the problem with suppression approaches assumes that gang members commit crimes based on a rational decision-making process. In reality they are more spontaneous. While they say that there is no clear solution to preventing or reducing gang activity, some promising programs have been identified such as the G.R.E.A.T. Program described below.

And finally, schools need better communication with parents and families, many of whom do not have strategies and techniques to manage their children, according to one Fenger High School teacher. In a personal communication, he shared that many of the families of the students he worked with there did not have control over their children. Such families, many also living with violence and trauma, need more support and access and referral to social services such as counseling, which the schools cannot or do not provide.

PROMISING PROGRAM: GANG RESISTANCE AND EDUCATION TRAINING

Ebensen et al. describe the Gang Resistance and Education Training (G.R.E.A.T.) program, which originated in Phoenix, Arizona, in 1991. It was established to combat the growing problem of gangs there and is taught by a uniformed law officer in the schools. It is a nine-week program targeted at six and seventh graders under the assumption that gang activity begins around those ages.

The program goals include helping youth avoid gang membership, violence, and criminal activity and to develop positive relationship with law enforcement. G.R.E.A.T. officers teach students resistance skills in dealing with friends who try to get them to participate in violence, gang activity, and drug selling.

The initial program was subsequently revised (G.R.E.A.T. II) incorporating interactive teaching techniques in a skills-building, strengths-based approach, with lessons designed to address some of the known risk factors for gang involvement. In addition, the now-revised program was designed to be part of a more comprehensive school, family, and community approach. Law enforcement agencies are now encouraged to partner with other community organizations. The curriculum has thirteen lessons to teach life skills (e.g., communication and refusal skills, conflict resolution, and anger management) thought necessary to prevent involvement in gang behavior and delinquency.

Evaluation of the program found statistically significant effects for five of the nine variables examined. Specifically, the G.R.E.A.T. students compared to non-G.R.E.A.T. students were more likely to report positive attitudes about police, less positive attitudes about gangs, more frequent use of refusal skills, greater resistance to peer pressure, and lower rates of gang membership (Ebensen et al.).

The results for self-reported delinquency did not reach statistical significance, but the authors say that the direction of the findings favored a program effect. Several program-specific skills-building objectives also appeared to have been met, especially refusal skills. There were no statistically significant differences between the groups on measures of empathy, risk-seeking, and conflict resolution.

LESSONS LEARNED ABOUT GANG VIOLENCE

Gangs remain a vexing and dangerous problem today. Nationally, their numbers remain at about 30,000, small in proportion to the destruction to our communities and the disruption in our schools. Many are shocked to find that only 10 percent of urban students belong to a gang due to these impacts. Or that they are increasingly common in suburban and rural communities. Gang involvement is a response to a lack of connection, engagement, and prosocial involvement, and a perception of having few, if any, other options. Given that, approaches can be initiated to try to target and prevent vulnerable young people from taking that path.

Programs described here have proven that inroads can be made. They require the strong involvement of the community, especially between schools and law enforcement, but also between schools and families. If we are going to save more students from gang involvement and a criminal lifestyle, then investments must be made in these programs as well. Instead of schools viewing gang members as problems they need to get rid of, schools must embrace such students and offer them services and supports. The wider community must also commit to such children as valuable and worth saving.

Too often it is easier to turn our backs on situations, as has happened in Derrion Albert's case. Initially, due to the national—even international—publicity the tragedy received, his school received a visit from the heads of the U.S. Departments of Education and Justice. It then received a $1.6 million federal grant. At the time it had 1,290 students.

Then the world forgot about the students and the school. Today, due to the encroachment of charter schools and other community and demographic changes, Fenger High School has only 320 students. The federal monies have run out and class sizes, which, with the help of the federal grant, were reduced to twenty back in 2009, are now back to the previous average of thirty students. ACT test scores, which averaged were fourteen in 2009, remain at fourteen today.

The teachers and staff are still there, however. Their teachers still show up every day and care for, and about, their students. Yet teachers and staff members, too, are victims of school violence, too. One national study found that fully 80 percent of U.S. teachers reported at least one victimization in either the current or previous school year. How could that number be so high? And what is being done about it?

REFERENCES

Allen, B. (1999). Stop the Violence: Gang prevention in *Schools in Poverty & Prejudice: Gang Intervention and Rehabilitation.*

Bradshaw, C. P., Pas, E. T., Debnam, K. J., & Johnson, S. L. (2015). A Focus on implementation of positive behavioral interventions and supports (PBIS) in high schools: Associations with bullying and other indicators of school disorder. *School Psychology Review, 44*(4), 480–498. doi:10.17105/spr-15-0105.1

Catalino, R. F., Haggery, K. P., Oesterle, S., Fleming, C. B., & Hawkins, J. D. (2004, September). The importance of bonding to school for healthy development. *Journal of School Health, 74*(7), 252–261.

Ebensen, F. (2000). Preventing Adolescent Gang Involvement U.S. Department of Justice Juvenile Justice Bulletin, Washington, DC, September 2000.

Esbensen, F., Peterson, D., Taylor, T. J., Freng, A., Osgood, D. W., Carson, D. C., & Matsuda, K. N. (2011). Evaluation and evolution of the gang resistance education and training (G.R.E.A.T.) program. *Journal of School Violence, 10*(1), 53–70.

Estrada, J. J., Gilreath, T. D., Astor, R. A., & Benbenishty, R. (2014). Gang membership, school violence, and the mediating effects of risk and protective behaviors in California high schools. *Journal of School Violence, 13*(2), 228–251.

Gottfredson, G. D., & Gottfredson, D. C. (1985). *Victimization in schools.* New York: Plenum.

Henry, R. R., & Zeytinoglu, S. (2012). African Americans and teen dating violence. *The American Journal of Family Therapy, 40*(1), 20–32. doi:10.1080/01926187.2011.578033

High School Youth Risk Behavior Survey. 2011. Chart. Centers for Disease Control and Prevention, Chicago. http://apps.nccd.cdc.gov/youthonline/App/Results.aspx

Howell, J. C., & Lynch, J. P. (2000). Youth gangs in schools. Youth gang series. *Juvenile Justice Bulletin.* Department of Justice.

Jones, L. M. (2012). *A systematic review of effective prevention: Applying evidence-based practice in internet safety education initiatives.* Durham, NH: University of New Hampshire, Crimes Against Children Research Center.

Naber, P. A., May, D. C., Decker, S. H., Minor, K. I., & Wells, J. B. (2006). Are there gangs in schools? It depends on whom you ask. *Journal of School Violence, 5*(2), 53–72. doi:10.1300/J202v05n02_05

School Crime Supplement to the National Crime Victimization Survey. (2015). Washington, DC: U.S. Department of Education. Retrieved from http://nces.ed.gov/pubs2015/2015056.pdf

Swahn, M. H., Bossarte, R. M., West, B., & Topalli, V. (2010). Alcohol and drug use among gang members: Experiences of adolescents who attend school. *Journal of School Health*, *80*(7), 353–360. doi:10.1111/j.1746-1561.2010.00513.x

Taylor, T. J., Peterson, D., Esbensen, F., & Freng, A. (2007). Gang membership as a risk factor for adolescent violent victimization. *Journal of Research in Crime and Delinquency*, *44*(4), 351–380. doi:10.1177/0022427807305845

UCLA. (2007). Youth Gangs and Schools. Retrieved from http://smhp.psych.ucla.edu/pdfdocs/policyissues/youth%20gangs%20&%20schools.pdf

UCLA. (2011). Youth Gangs Report. Retrieved from http://smhp.psych.ucla.edu/pdfdocs/youth/youthgangs.pdf

Wolfe, D., Crooks, C., Lee, V., McIntyre-Smith, A., & Jaffe, P. (2003). Exposure to domestic violence: A meta-analysis and critique. *Clinical Child and Family Psychology Review*, *6*(3), 171–187.

Wright, D. R., & Fitzpatrick, K. M. (2006). Violence and minority youth: The effects of risk and asset factors on fighting among African American children and adolescents. *Adolescence*, *41*(162), 251–262.

Chapter Nine

Violence against Teachers and Staff

It was a typical day in 2007 for Frank Burd. He was a popular, involved high-school math teacher who had a reputation for going above and beyond for his students at Germantown High School in Pittsburgh, Pennsylvania. Two students became angry when he tried to confiscate an iPod and attacked him. One attacker was a fifteen-year-old ninth grader who was in the process of being transferred to an alternative school for students with discipline problems. Evidently after he confiscated the iPod from the student, the student followed him into the hallway. That student pushed him and another student in the hallway punched him in the face, knocking him down. Both were charged with assault and sentenced to juvenile detention centers.

The attack left Burd with a concussion, his neck broken in two places, and a brain injury. Afterward, he suffered from memory and concentration problems, depression, post-traumatic stress, and vertigo. Two years later he was still unable to go to work and was suffering from the continuing after-effects.

OVERVIEW

Violence against elementary and secondary teachers and staff is considered a serious problem, though little research has been conducted on it. The studies that have examined it, however, show that teacher and staff victimization is widespread and can have a tremendous impact on school climate, recruitment and retention of staff, and on teaching and learning. Significantly, Stewart and Robles Pina (2008) cite Hornig's finding that clean and safe schools were more important to teachers than the students' ethnicity, socioeconomic status, performance, or even an additional $8,000 in salary.

Espelage et al. (2013) affirm that violence directed toward teachers is a major problem in our schools warranting immediate research and policy reform. They say it has been understudied and has received limited media and policy attention, both here in the United States and internationally. They found in their investigations that student verbal aggression was the type of violence most frequently reported by teachers and staff members.

Espelage et al. note, however, that information on the extent of such victimization is critical for developing effective supports and interventions. It is critical for promoting positive school cultures and classroom climates, and enhancing staff satisfaction and student learning. They, too, found that a significant number of teachers experience victimization, with higher rates for less severe forms of victimization.

The CDC also concluded that there is scant research available, but the little that exists demonstrates that teachers and other school employees may be at increased risk for theft of personal property, verbal threats of physical harm, bullying, abuse, and physical assault injury.

Such victimization is often thought to be underreported, as teachers and staff may be unwilling to report such violence to police or school administrators. Negative publicity and backlash may discourage such reporting, too, though there is the threat of loss of a school's federal funds, at least over expulsion of students for firearms. While most victimization against teachers and staff is done by students, they can also be victimized by colleagues and parents. One study reported perpetration by students at 94 percent of victimizations, followed by parents at 37 percent, and then by colleagues at 21 percent (McMahon et al., 2012).

Bass et al. (2016), drawing on the work of several others, defined student violence against school employees as consisting of any one or more of the following: verbal insults, threats to injure, physical attacks, and sexual harassment. This research found that student violence victimization is linked to multiple adverse outcomes for school employees, including physical and emotional symptoms.

PREVALENCE

Just how common is such staff victimization in our schools? A U.S. DOE National Center for Educational Statistics (NCES) study found that 127,120 (4 percent) of public school teachers were physically attacked at school during the 2007–08 school year and another 222,460 (7 percent) were threatened by students with acts of violence.

The NCES study indicated that, in another previous study of 253,100 teachers, 7 percent of the teaching force surveyed in 2003–2004 reported being threatened or assaulted by students. According to a 2008 CDC report, teachers experienced thirty-nine crimes per 1,000 (including twenty-five thefts and fourteen violent crimes), but, as mentioned, that the true rate may be much higher.

Other reports (Dinkes, Kemp, & Baum, 2009) have found that urban schools had a somewhat higher reported rate of student violence than suburban schools, and that it was three times higher than in rural schools (77 percent, 67 percent, and 28 percent, respectively). They say specifically that urban teachers are more likely to be victims of violent crimes than suburban teachers (28 percent compared to 13 percent) and rural teachers (at 16 percent). African American teachers were more likely to be the victims of crimes than white teachers. Seven percent of elementary education teachers and 8 percent of secondary education teachers were threatened with injury, and approximately 6 percent of K–12 teachers overall were physically attacked in schools. Figure 9.1 depicts the range of threats and injuries through 2012.

A 2009 Institute for Educational Sciences survey found 11 percent of school principals reporting that students were verbally abusive to the middle- and high-school teachers. And, it found that although secondary school teachers were reported to be more likely than elementary teachers to be threatened with a form of physical violence, elementary teachers were reported to have been the actual victims of physical assaults (figure 9.2).

The APA conducted a major national survey of 12,000 K–12 teachers in 2013. It found that an astonishing 80 percent of teachers reported at least one victimization experience in the current or previous year, and of those, 94 percent reported being victimized by students. They found the percentage

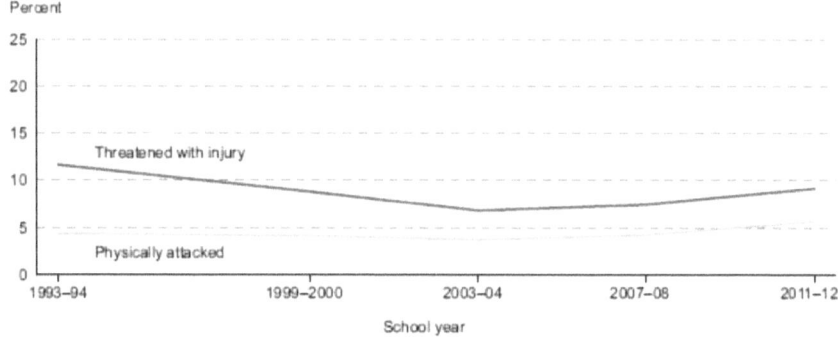

Figure 9.1 Percentage of Teachers Threatened or Injured by a Student in the Previous Twelve Months. *Source*: U.S. DOE Schools and Staffing Survey.

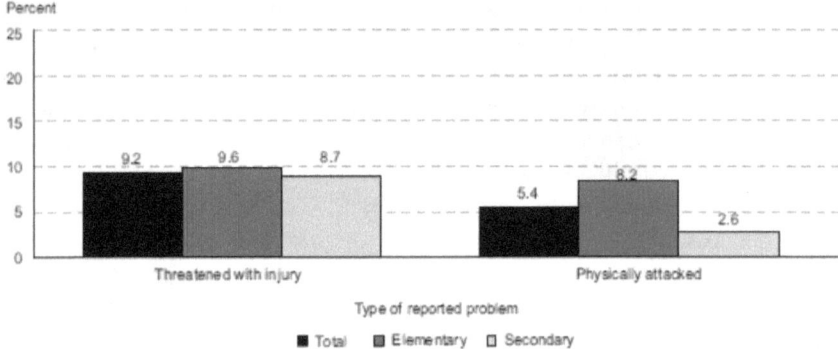

Figure 9.2   Percentage of Teachers Threatened with Injury or Physical Attack 2011–12. *Source*: U.S. DOE Schools and Staffing Survey.

of teachers who reported having experienced at least one harassment offense was 72.5 percent, with over 50 percent experiencing property offenses like theft or damage to property and 44 percent reporting physical attacks.

Regarding gender, male teachers were more likely than female teachers to be victims of violent crimes, at a reported rate of ten to one. McMahon et al. (2014) found that male teachers were more likely than female teachers to report obscene remarks, obscene gestures, verbal threats, and having a weapon pulled on them. Men were less likely to report intimidation, however, than were women, but there were no differences from property victimizations. Still, male teachers reported higher rates of victimization and most of the harassment offenses, including having a weapon pulled on them. Female teachers reported higher rates of intimidation.

These findings also revealed significant differences in victimization experiences across ethnic and racial groups for eight out of eleven offenses studied (obscene remarks, obscene gestures, verbal threats, intimidation, theft of property, damage to property, objects thrown, and physical attack not leading to a doctor's visit). African American teachers were less likely than white teachers to report victimization in those eight categories. Other studies have found a higher percentage of African American teachers experiencing threats and physical attacks. Latino teachers were less likely than white teachers to report obscene remarks or objects thrown at them.

Regarding demographic settings, teachers working in rural and suburban community settings were less likely to report harassment, property offenses, and physical offenses than teachers working in urban settings. These authors also found that schools in violent communities, which do not have positive organizational climates and do not effectively address such violence, experience more violence.

EFFECTS AND CONSEQUENCES

In 1976, Albert Bloch described the battered teacher syndrome characterized by symptoms including depression, high blood pressure, insomnia, and headaches. In addition to the physical trauma associated with being assaulted, say Stewart and Robles-Pina, it is difficult to adjust psychologically and as we saw with Frank Burd who chose to leave the profession. For those who have been victims and choose to stay, consequences include increased absenteeism, strained relationships, and an impact on the quality of their teaching.

Espelage et al. cite numerous studies emphasizing that educator-perceived victimization has been found to be associated with fear, physical and emotional symptoms, impacted peer relationships, and impaired work performance. Victimized teachers report of anxiety, depression, and other symptoms as a result of experiencing violence at school. These were related to lower professional functioning, lower efficacy in the classroom, and lower emotional and/or physical well-being.

There are other costs associated with teacher victimization, including lost wages, they say; increased Workmen's Compensation payments due to the distress, trauma, or injury; greater use of substitute teachers; lost instructional time and productivity; litigation costs; negative publicity and negative student outcomes. They say it also has impact on teacher recruitment and retention, and that such resulting attrition leads to negative effects on the students in the school.

Even the perceived fear of being a victim of violent crime has been shown not only to affect the way in which school staff perform their duties, but where they choose to work, and in some cases, their decision to change careers completely, say Stewart and Robles-Pina.

Bass et al. state that both traumatic and chronic experience of workplace violence can prompt immediate physiological and cognitive responses in individuals and that this can lead to greater physiological costs over time, like fatigue and exhaustion. They say that individuals classify an environmental event is either stressful or not. Then, depending on whether it is stressful, individuals engage in evaluations of how to best cope. If it is stressful, they appraise it in terms of potential threat, harm, and loss.

The consequences of an unsafe school setting are that school staff members are in danger of experiencing negative job attitudes, lower workplace productivity, decreased performance, increase sick leaves, high turnover rate, and intention to leave the profession. Obviously, these are all barriers to students' experience of safety, sense of school connectedness, and academic achievement as well.

PREVENTION OF VIOLENCE AGAINST SCHOOL STAFF

Prevention of violence against teachers and staff can be looked at from a school, classroom, and individual perspective. As with the other forms of violence discussed here, comprehensive, integrated, and multitiered service delivery models of prevention are recommended by the experts. Violence prevention programs have been found to be generally effective at reducing the more common types of aggressive behavior at school, though none of these programs typically addresses aggression against staff.

Espelage et al. agree that a multisystem approach is best for obtaining a comprehensive understanding for early detection and prevention of student disruptive and aggressive behaviors directed at staff. They say that effective interventions can be tailored to reduce or eliminate individual youth aggressive behavior patterns directed toward teachers and staff by using a three-tiered prevention model.

Espelage et al. advocate that schools need to have a clearly articulated plan for responding to students who are showing signs of behavior issues (secondary) as well as for those who have violated behavioral expectations (tertiary). Faculty and staff need to establish and implement real consequences for students who engage in rule violation. These consequences need to be reasonable, feasible, and proportional to the infraction. They recommend a multisystemic, multilevel approach that includes a broad framework of violence prevention that emphasizes self-assessment, training, and informed decision-making.

As noted earlier, zero tolerance approaches have not been proven to be effective, and often result in racial and gender discrimination. Punitive measures such as more security and increased security technology have been said to exacerbate feelings of social isolation, undermining teacher confidence, and increasing anxiety.

Cornell et al. (2004) state that developing a comprehensive threat assessment approach to school violence decreases the number of reported instances of school-related violence. Because it has been found that a majority of physical assaults on school staff occur when disciplining a student, as happened to Frank Burd at Germantown High School, individual teachers need to be aware of the issues surrounding the likelihood of a threat and be ready to respond to it.

An example of a threat assessment approach is the DANGERTOME Scale, which is designed to serve as part of an overall risk assessment approach. This scale is composed of ten risk factors presented as a mnemonic, which stands for delusions, access to weapons, noted history of violence, gang involvement, expressions of harm, remorse, closeness, overt or veiled threats of harm, myopic focus on harming others, and exclusion from others (Juhnke, 2010).

Juhnke says this scale is only to be used when someone is perceived as threatening, and that administration and scoring time are minimal. It also offers suggested actions on how to respond. He advises that it is critical to thoroughly investigate three areas: the *frequency* of violent threats toward the victim, the *intensity* of the threat, and the *duration* of the threat.

Espelage et al. have found that the effectiveness of teachers' classroom management skills is a strong indicator of the extent to which student violence is directed toward teachers. They say that student–teacher relationships characterized by conflict are also predictive of aggression and cite a study of associations between student aggression, teacher–student relationships, and academic achievement. Four hundred students were followed from kindergarten through fifth grade. The findings of that study indicated that the effect of general student aggression on student achievement was partially mediated by teacher–student relationships.

Stewart and Robles-Pina say that the way teachers perceive, process, and react to any form of school violence has significant implications. Assessing threats is complex, they say, and they recommend the ABC behavior model (antecedent–behavior–consequence) as a model that can help teachers in this instance. This model views knowing and understanding the antecedent–behavior–consequence continuum as a way to identify specific responses on the basis of observation and evaluation of what triggers the behavior.

Factors in a person's environment that precede and trigger the aggressive or violent behavior are considered the antecedents. Behaviors are the reaction of that person in response to the antecedent. These then lead to consequences that flow from the behavior. They say that this model empowers teachers to uncover patterns in student behavior to guide decisions about effective interventions.

One type of tertiary intervention that has been effective in decreasing negative student behavior is known as the functional assessment. It is based on individual observations of behavior of misbehaving students. Interventions are developed targeting the triggers for problem behavior. Rather than focusing on stopping the behavior from occurring, teachers and staff determine what the motivation behind the behavior is and develop interventions to address it. This and the ABC model are examples of evidence-based practices that should form the basis of professional development for staff in the areas of behavior and classroom management.

Effective behavior management strategies not only allow the teacher to have direct control at the teacher level, say Espelage et al., but put the teacher in a strategic position for control at the classroom level. They strongly recommend use of such social and behavioral programs to provide students with clear expectations and appropriate tools to resolve conflict. Such programs also enhance engagement and achievement.

Finally, they encourage teachers to consistently review the literature on student motivation and to implement strategies that lead to improved behavior, as motivated and engaged students are less likely to be aggressive. Cornell notes that structure, involvement, and autonomy support (i.e., giving students choices) also contribute to such student engagement, attachment, and involvement in school.

Implications for Schools

Interestingly, many researchers say that violence prevention programs are more effective in changing aggressive behavior when there is a focus on changing the classroom and school environments as well. And creating a positive school culture will likely reduce teacher and student victimization.

Teachers and staff are the key to early intervention because of their relationship with students. They are also the best first line of response, but many report that they need services and training for preventing and managing misbehavior and school violence. Therefore, part of any multileveled and multifaceted approach must include deep investment in professional development.

Staff need to learn the components of threat assessment, evidence-based behavior strategies, and preventing escalation of threatening behavior. They also need strategies for increasing and enhancing student motivation, bonding, and engagement. Understanding the impact of trauma on students is important also, as teacher support has been associated with improved relationships and lower aggression among students.

School leadership is vital as well, as organizational structure and social supports have been found to be both predictors and preventers of violence in the schools. Espelage et al. say that school leaders need to institute a thorough and inclusive investigation of any incidents, and take all the necessary steps to respond in a supportive fashion to affected staff members. Leadership decisions and responses are pivotal, they say, in preventive efforts and far-reaching with respect to issues like teacher recruitment and retention. They found that teacher perceptions of support from their administration were strong predictors of retention.

Gottfredson et al. (2005) studied of a nationally representative sample of teachers and students from 250 middle and high schools. A wide range of influences on teacher victimization, including school organization, school funding, and neighborhood characteristics, were assessed in this study. Results indicated that less teacher victimization was associated with consistent discipline management, as perceived by the students, and positive psychosocial climate as perceived by the teachers.

They also found that schools with greater concentrations of impoverished, African American students and African American teachers reported less positive psychosocial climates, which in turn were associated with greater teacher victimization. These results indicated not only that teacher victimization was predictable, but also that an overall climate of victimization was prevalent in many schools. They recommend that deliberate efforts be taken to consistently stabilize, review, and reteach district policy and procedures on violence against teachers and staff.

Prioritizing teacher and staff safety as well as student safety sends an important message of concern, and increases overall perceptions of safety in the school setting. And, just as school districts design strategic intervention policies and procedures to prevent such occurrences, they say, they must prepare staff to manage the aftermath of such occurrences (e.g., by establishing crisis response teams). Addressing staff psychological needs demonstrates the care and support necessary for psychological healing.

Bass et al. describe transformational leadership as a leadership approach that focuses on changing individuals and systems. They say that this type of leadership proactively shapes employee perceptions of their workplace and focuses on keeping employees motivated in the face of student violence. Transformational leadership enhances performance and reduces the level of staff burnout. They even say that schools with transformational leaders may even be safer places to work. This type of leadership will be discussed further in chapter 10.

Implications for Communities

Espelage et al. say that the community needs to recognize that the problem of school-based violence is everyone's problem and responsibility, and that aggression and violence in communities surrounding schools need to be addressed to prevent the spillover into the schools and classrooms. They advocate for strategies to be developed and implemented that foster collegiality among the key stakeholders so that responsibility is shared equally.

They also recommend that school site teams need to involve community stakeholders in creating safe zones inside and outside of schools, and ensure that adults have the skill sets to take ownership of all of the spaces within the school setting. This includes increasing resources for the schools and for the larger community that address issues such as poverty and unemployment, and strengthening community supports for at-risk students and their families.

Collaborations and partnerships between schools, community-based organizations, and law enforcement are also needed to prevent violence against teachers and staff. Effective collaborations can provide a coherent support structure for both victims of violence against staff and for the perpetrators. Just as with crisis intervention plans for intruder violence in school shootings, help may be needed from police and other first responders. This requires training in responding to students at risk, as well as knowledge and understanding of the school's protocols.

There are also legal considerations and remedies. In Wisconsin, for example, the Madison Teachers organization will institute a civil action against any student who threatens or hits an employee based on the Wisconsin stalking and harassment statute. That law makes it a crime for a person to assault someone or cause them to fear bodily injury. In Massachusetts, the union there utilizes state criminal statutes regarding assault and battery of a public official, which include school employees, as a felony. And in Michigan, a state law requires the expulsion of any student grade 6 and above who physically assaults a school employee (Simpson, 2011).

PROMISING PROGRAM: COMMUNITY OF CARING

According to information in the U.S. DOE's Exemplary and Promising: Safe, Disciplined and Drug-Free Schools (2001), the Community of Caring (CoC) is designated as a promising program for creating a positive school culture. The primary focus of the CoC program is to strengthen the decision-making skills that young people (K–12) need to avoid the destructive behaviors that lead to early sexual involvement, teen pregnancy, substance abuse, delinquent behavior, and dropping out of school. At the heart of the program are the following: caring, respect, responsibility, trust, and family. CoC has eight essential components: training and support, a facilitator, a coordinating committee, a comprehensive action plan, values across the curriculum, student forums, family and community involvement, and community service.

The components work together to structure the social climate to provide positive life experiences for students. CoC includes the following components: (1) student forums, which are one-day workshops for up to 150 students and adults to discuss problems that teens face and to identify solutions; (2) service learning projects for students; and (3) a family involvement piece that encourages parents to become engaged in schools through a list of possible activities. A coordinating committee plans the CoC program for its school by developing the action plan.

Reviewers highlighted the fact that school connectedness, a major part of the program, was considered by researchers to be a protective factor. Reviewers found the materials appropriate for diverse cultures, classes, and age groups. Evaluation results demonstrated numerous statistically significant findings that were sustained beyond one year, but added that the results were demonstrated with five high-implementation schools and their matched counterparts, a subset of the intervention group.

Results showed statistically significant effects favoring students in the program, with no effects favoring the matched comparison schools. Positive findings were found for outcomes measuring alcohol and marijuana use, delinquent behavior, and prosocial behaviors such as intrinsic academic motivation, task orientation toward learning, commitment to democratic values, acceptance of "out" groups, conflict resolution skills, and concern for others.

LESSONS LEARNED ABOUT VIOLENCE AGAINST TEACHERS AND STAFF

This chapter has covered a type of school violence that appears to be very significant and wide ranging. Not only does it impact victims and the perpetrators, but it has a corrosive impact on the school's climate, and the ability of the school to attract and keep highly qualified staff members. We know that teachers and staff believe that a safe school environment is more important than the type of school, the demographics of the student body, and even more pay.

As urban schools, many of which are embedded in extremely violent communities, experience more such violence, it is especially important to address this issue so that the neediest students, who need the best teachers, have access to them. It is important to remember, however, that violence against teachers and staff is not simply an urban school phenomenon.

Once again, we are told that experts believe that a universal prevention approach is the key. And while no one specific approach specifically targets violence against staff, we know many of the precursors and predictors of such violence. Now there are many more evidence-based programs that address those predictors, which can be part of a school-wide approach to reducing aggression and consequently reducing violence against staff at the same time.

Once again, we are told that school culture and climate play key roles in school bonding and student engagement, which are associated with decreased misbehavior and violence. Deeply knowledgeable and supportive staff members can create the necessary environment of respect, problem solving, and effective conflict resolution. They can, but do most schools achieve such cultures and climates? According to a 2016 Gallup poll on student engagement, nearly half of U.S. adolescents are disengaged at school, and a fifth actively disengaged. It appears there is a lot of work yet to do to reconnect with our children.

REFERENCES

Bass, B. I., Cigularov, K. P., Chen, P. Y., Henry, K. L., Tomazic, R. G., & Li, Y. (2016). The effects of student violence against school employees on employee burnout and work engagement: The roles of perceived school unsafety and transformational leadership. *International Journal of Stress Management, 23*(3), 318–336. doi:10.1037/str0000011

Cornell, D., Sheras, P., Kaplan, S., McConville, D., Douglas, J., Elkon, A. (2004). Guidelines for student threat assessment. *School Psychology Review, 33*, 527–546.

Dinkes, R., Kemp, J., & Baum, K. (2009). *Indicators of school crime and safety: 2008 (NCES 2009—022/NCJ 226343)*. Statistics, Office of Justice Programs, U.S. Department of Justice. Institute of Educational Sciences, U.S. Department of Education, and Bureau of Justice. Washington, DC: National Center for Educational Statistics.

Espelage, D., Anderman, E. M., Brown, V. E., Jones, A., Lane, K. L., Mcmahon, S. D., ... Reynolds, C. R. (2013). Understanding and preventing violence directed against teachers: Recommendations for a national research, practice, and policy agenda. *American Psychologist, 68*(2), 75–87. doi:10.1037/a0031307

Gottfredson, G. D., Gottfredson, D. C., Payne, A. A., & Gottfredson, N. C. (2005). School climate predictors of school disorder. *Journal of Research in Crime and Delinquency, 42*, 412–444. doi:10.1177/0022427804271931

Juhnke, G. A. (2010). DANGERTOME Personal Risk Threat Assessment Scale: An instrument to help aid immediate threat assessment for counselors, faculty, and teachers. *Journal of Creativity in Mental Health, 5*, 177–191. doi:10.1080/15401383.2010.485095

McMahon, S. D., Martinez, A., Espelage, D., Rose, C., Reddy, L. A., Lane, K., ... Brown, V. (2014). Violence directed against teachers: Results from a national survey. *Psychology in the Schools, 51*(7), 753–766.

McMahon, S. D., Todd, N. R., Martinez, A., Coker, C., Sheu, C.-F., Washburn, J., & Shah, S. (2012). Aggressive and prosocial behavior: Community violence, cognitive, and behavioral predictors among urban African American youth. *American Journal of Community Psychology, 51*(3–4). doi:10.1007/s10464-012-9560-4

Schools and Staffing Survey. Washington, DC: U.S. Department of Education, National Center on Education Statistics (NCES). Retrieved from https://nces.ed.gov/surveys/sass/

Simpson, M. D. (2011). *When educators are assaulted*. NEA. Retrieved from http://www.nea.org/home/42238.htm

Stewart, C. B., & Robles-Pina, R. (2008). Black and blue: The impact of nonfatal teacher victimization. *Journal of At-Risk Issues, 4*(2):9–15.

Violence against Teachers and Staff. CDC-NIOSH science blog. Retrieved from https://blogs.cdc.gov/niosh-science-blog/2008/04/14/teacher/

Chapter Ten

Reflections on Lessons Learned

CULTURE AND CONTEXT

School violence numbers have improved in recent years. Yet, there still remains much to do to increase awareness of the challenges and problems that we still face and to improve the lives of thousands of children who experience violence in their schools and communities.

Guns and Violence

One of the most vexing challenges our nation faces when it comes to violence in our schools is gun violence. As illustrated in the previous chapters, a child's access to guns is one of the most significant correlates to fatal victimization, whether it is suicide or homicide. Even after Sandy Hook, the American people did not enact legislation that would limit certain types of the assault weapons in any way. Yet, access to such weapons continues to result in violence in our schools, on our streets, and in our workplaces.

In addition to guns, we live in a culture of violence. It can be seen everywhere in the media. Whether it is the news, a violent TV show, or a movie, such violent media exposure does have an influence on our children. Many of the school shooters, for example, had excessive exposure to violent games and programs. Even today's notions of maleness seem to be tied into those images of violence. Just examining the changes in the kinds of toys and the size of the male action figures, and their guns, illustrates how this emphasis is inherent in our culture and incorporated into the development of our children.

Poverty and Demographics

Then we have the crushing issue of poverty. One of every five U.S. children lives in poverty. As we have seen, aggression and violence are more common in high-poverty urban centers. Our schools are simply a reflection of the larger community context. Family and street violence spills into our school hallways and classrooms. Too many young boys and men see no alternative but to turn to gangs for protection, to drugs for income, to violence to survive. Our nation must recommit and redouble its efforts to fight to eliminate poverty, which has such a disproportionate impact on our minority youth and families in urban areas.

We have also seen the disproportionate number of poor and minority students, particularly males, unfairly subjected to policies such as zero tolerance and disproportionately suspended and expelled. While having zero tolerance for things like bullying and sexual harassment is valid, leaders and school staff must be vigilant in fairly enforcing discipline policies. Too often such policies have been misused and abused at the expense of certain groups, such as African American males. Such institutionalized racism must be eliminated.

These are not issues that only affect disadvantaged minority urban children and families. In fact, as described here, some types of violence are greater in rural areas where there is a lack of education and resources available to help those affected. Suburban schools have their share as well. The nation was shocked, in fact, with a growing number of school shootings that were happening in suburban and rural areas. They were stark reminders that there are no boundaries when it comes to violence and that the stakes for not aggressively addressing it are very high.

Media and Its Impact

The media plays such an important role when it comes to issues of school violence. Many thought that Columbine had been oversensationalized by the media with its 24/7 coverage. Other impacts can be seen when it comes to suicide, with the danger of suicide contagion, depending on the way an incident is depicted in the media.

Schools in crisis need to have policies and procedures in place for dealing with the media and for preventing the media from overstepping into the situation, investigation, or the processing of the event by the students and families.

Mental Health and Stigma

Society must also overcome the stigma of mental health. Whereas most parents would not think twice about discussing their child's broken leg, a child's depression is a deep dark secret. So many of our young people are suffering from such depression and other forms of mental illness. Because of the stigma, because of their fear of rejection, because of the reluctance to talk to adults, and because of lack of resources for addressing their problems, many never receive help.

We have seen untreated mental illness spiral out of control, resulting in children and adolescents doing very impulsive, dangerous—and often preventable—things. Yet, with the proper resources and a knowledgeable and informed school staff, many of these undetected problems can be identified and these children provided help. Our schools still do not have enough mental health support for our children. There are still too few school psychologists and school social workers to meet the needs of children who are in such pain that they see no way out.

Their teachers do not have enough knowledge and understanding about the signs and symptoms of mental illness to be able to identify them and get them help. There is a desperate need for resources to prevent the kinds of tragedies that we have seen committed by individuals with untreated mental illness, which have escalated to the point of no return.

Cost to Society

And finally, we must consider the cost to society for *not* investing in violence prevention. The CDC estimates are that the social costs of child maltreatment alone in this country are $124 billion each year over their total lifetime. These costs include health care, child welfare, criminal justice, and lost productivity and earnings. The cost of untreated mental health problems is incalculable. There is the social emotional cost to the individual, of course. But there is a larger cost to society when a child is unable to develop and grow and learn and become a caring and responsible citizen.

RELATIONSHIPS AND CONNECTEDNESS

Parents and Families

Obviously relationships with parents and family members are fundamental to child development and the development of prosocial, positive behaviors. The early years are so important to the development of attachment and trust. Children with good relationships with their families are happier, more well behaved, and more likely to be engaged and successful in school.

Attachment theory describes a process through which interactions between parents and infants create working models for how a child forms social connections with others, say Catalano, Haggerty, Oesterle, Fleming, and Hawkins (2004). They say interactions between a child and caregivers build the foundation for bonding, a key to developing the capacity for motivated behavior. Attachment to parents has a positive effect in childhood and adolescence, and its effects last into adulthood. It also has positive effects on a child's resilience to adversity.

But the parenting skills that facilitate bonding, and other important developmental childhood tasks, do not necessarily come automatically either. Schools must do everything in their power to support, engage, and inform parents on effective parenting practices. They need to provide additional support for parents of children at risk of emotional or academic difficulties because, as we have seen, many parents and family members missed the warning signs of serious mental health issues. Armed with information, resources, and support, such family members can be keys to early identification of problems, resulting in early remediation.

Parents of teens, especially, have to be mindful of their essential role in their child's development. At a time when youth are pressing for more freedom, some parents do not monitor their children as much as necessary, yet that parental monitoring can make a huge difference. As the Fenger High School teacher noted, many parents did not have the knowledge or skills to control their teenagers, who were fighting for their independence in a very dangerous community. High schools need to be open and welcoming to parents as well because the job of supporting adolescents needs the intense involvement of both fronts.

Communities and Neighborhoods

Community members can play a vital role in providing support for children and youth. Neighbors, clergy, law enforcement, community organizations, and mental health providers all have an important role to play when it comes to supporting children. Awareness comes first, and while most citizens are generally aware of the impact of violence, many are not aware or engaged in communication and collaboration enough so that existing resources can be leveraged and maximized for purposes of prevention.

As we have seen, there are many programs that involve leadership from outside of the school, such as gang prevention, teen dating violence prevention, and bullying prevention. Real partnerships between entities and organizations enable us to surround our children with access to programs they may otherwise never be exposed to. They also provide them with access to other adults in the community who may be lifelines when they have no one at home.

Peers and Friends

Throughout this book peers have played pivotal roles, either as recipients, co-perpetrators, or bystanders to incidents of violence. They are really the first line of defense, as students turn to their peers more often than they turn to a parent or other adult. Too often peers have been aware of problems that their friends have been having (Reagan High School, Texas), their plans to do harm (Columbine High School, Colorado), or their access to weapons (Independence High School, Arizona). Too often, those peers have not taken that knowledge seriously, did not know what to do about it, and never reported it to adults.

We now have research that shows that awareness training can make a huge difference in students' understanding of problems such as bullying, suicide, and teen dating violence, the effects of those problems, and on what friends can do when they are faced with such situations. Peers have even been used as facilitators of many of these programs because of their credibility with other students. Many schools have initiated programs that include peer juries and other peer conflict resolution approaches to maximize this credibility.

Such programs must be incorporated into any universal school-wide prevention program. Not only are peers the first line of defense, they are tremendously affected by this violence as well. Even observing violence has an impact on the individual as well is on the entire school culture. The importance of the role the peers play and violence prevention must be central in the consideration of any school-wide approach.

SCHOOL POLICIES AND PRACTICES

School Bonding

Catalano et al. discuss how bonding to school has been shown to increase positive developmental experiences, decrease negative developmental experiences, and buffer the effects of risk for students. Once strongly established, they say, the social bond inhibits misbehaviors and increases the likelihood of conforming to its norms, values, and behaviors.

A lack of school bonding during the middle- and high-school years has been found to be significant and negatively associated with so many behaviors, which put students at risk: substance abuse, delinquency, gang membership, violence, academic problems, and early sexual activity. It is positively correlated to lower rates of drinking and smoking initiation and drug use.

Catalano et al. also found that students who bonded to school by fifth and sixth grades were less likely to become minor or serious offenders at the seventh grade. Girls who were more committed and attached to the school in grade

7 were less likely to initiate delinquent behavior between seventh and ninth grade. And among children from low-income families, school commitment, and attachment in fifth and sixth grades reduced the likelihood of their becoming offenders between grades 7 and 12.

School bonding in grade 8 was associated with greater likelihood of academic achievement and social skills. These researchers concluded that providing socialization skills to enhance the social environment of elementary school students resulted in more bonding with the school, which in turn led to enhanced academic achievement and reduced problem behavior.

So, since school bonding promotes academic success, reduces barriers to learning, and reduces health and safety problems, they say that a focus both on how children are taught and teaching children social and emotional competence are critical to achieving academic success. Doing this requires a focus on social and emotional competence as well as cognitive competence.

In addition to school-wide culture and climate enhancements, the classroom must be a place where students learn how to respect each other, solve problems, work through conflicts, take risks, and feel like they belong. Research-based classroom management and behavior management strategies can be drawn upon to help teachers facilitate both social-emotional learning and academic learning.

Teachers and school staff need to be constantly aware and vigilant about the tremendous responsibility they have. The far-reaching impact of a kind word of caring or concern on their charges can mean the difference between a child's decision to seek help—or not.

Student Engagement

Over and over again, student engagement and feeling of belonging to a school have arisen as protective factors for addressing the pain, isolation, anger, and rejection so many students carry with them and that forms the basis of so much school violence. Over and over again, research finds that the lack of student engagement results in disaffection with the educational process, the desire to drop out, and the misbehavior leading to aggression, leading to violence in the schools and in the community.

The *Indicators of School Crime and Safety* (2015) report found that the percentage of students with low school engagement who had ever been suspended or expelled (28 percent) was higher than the percentage of students with middle or high levels of school engagement who had ever been suspended or expelled (21 and 9 percent, respectively). Similarly, the percentage of students with a low sense of school belonging who had ever been suspended or expelled (28 percent) was higher than the percentage of students with a middle or high sense of school belonging who had ever been suspended or expelled (16 and 15 percent, respectively) (figure 10.1).

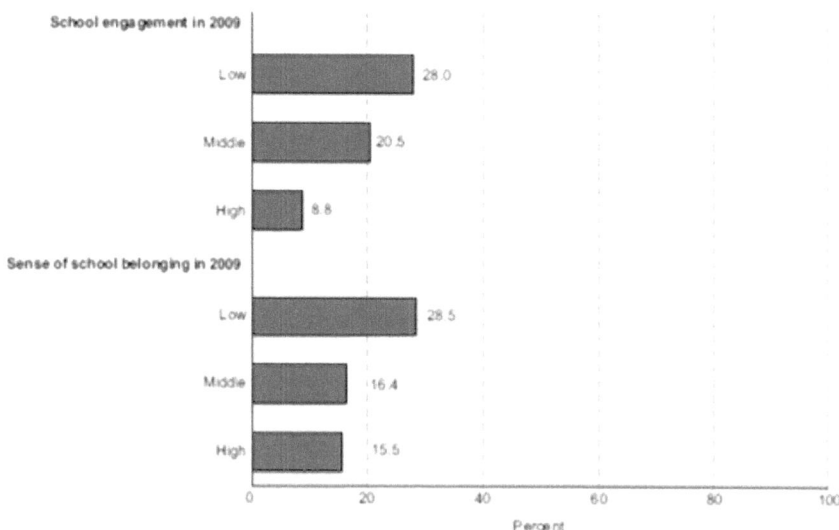

Figure 10.1 Percentage of Fall 2009 Ninth Graders Suspended or Expelled through Spring 2012 by School Engagement and Sense of Belonging: 2012. *Source*: U.S. DOE NCES, High School Longitudinal Study, 2009.

Student engagement it turns out is fundamental. Noted psychologist Abraham Maslow knew this many years ago when he put belonging just above the need for food and shelter on his hierarchy of human needs. If our students do not feel like they belong in school, they will turn on that school, its students, and its employees. They will attack that school and what it represents. They will feel like they have nothing to lose.

On the other hand, we see that students who are engaged and active, who feel cared about in their school, who like being there, and who have a relationship with at least one caring adult, are the students who thrive. These are the students who achieve and would not think of bullying another student or hurting a teacher. These are the students who finish school and go on lead happy and productive lives. They are not perpetuating the violence that we see happens too often and is passed on from one generation to another. Our schools have that awesome ability to stop the transmission of such intergenerational violence.

Culture and Climate

For virtually every type of school violence, we have seen the experts recommend school-wide approaches to violence prevention and improved and enhanced school safety. These universal approaches with their primary, secondary, and tertiary tiers of prevention are designed to impact a school's culture and climate. According to the Institute for Educational Research (IER),

168   *Chapter Ten*

school climate is a broad, multifaceted concept that involves many aspects of the student's educational experience. A negative school climate can harm students and raise liability issues for schools and districts. Negative school climate is linked to lower student achievement and graduation rates, and it creates opportunities for violence, bullying, and even suicide.

IER says that a positive school climate is the product of a school's attention to fostering safety; promoting a supportive academic, disciplinary, and physical environment; and encouraging and maintaining respectful, trusting, and caring relationships throughout the school community. The *Safe and Supportive Schools Model*, which was developed by a national panel of researchers and other experts, indicates that positive school climate involves:

- **Engagement**. Strong relationships between students, teachers, families, and schools and strong connections between schools and the broader community.
- **Safety**. Schools and school-related activities where students are safe from violence, bullying, harassment, and controlled-substance use.
- **Environment**. Appropriate facilities, well-managed classrooms, available school-based health supports, and a clear, fair disciplinary policy (IER Safe and Supportive Schools Website) (figure 10.2).

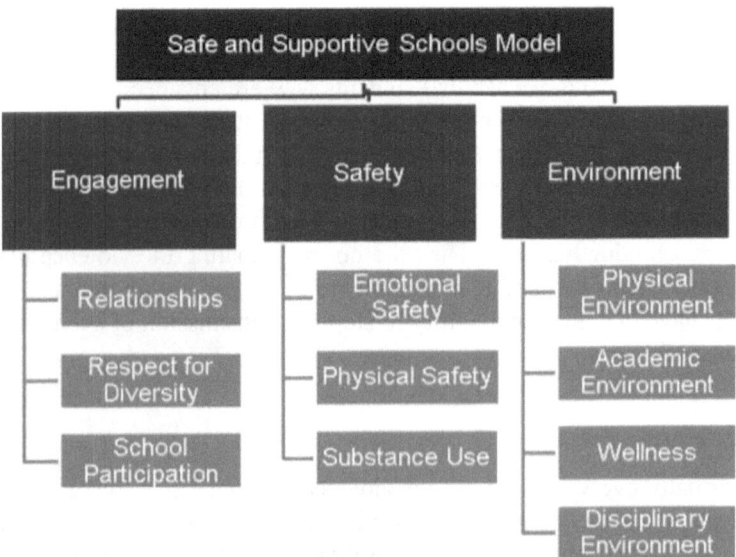

Figure 10.2   U.S. Department of Education Safe and Supportive Schools Model.

The antiviolence message has to pervade every aspect of the school in order for students to feel its impact and to feel safe. Every single adult in the building must have caring relationships with students, school safety, and violence prevention as top priorities.

But just having them as priorities does not mean that they follow them automatically. School staff at every level from the administration, to teachers, to janitorial and cafeteria workers need training. They need to be able to listen to their charges. They need to be able to recognize the signs and symptoms of student difficulty. They need to understand the effects of trauma or child abuse, and know how to treat a child and refer them for help. They need to know how to de-escalate conflict.

The skills are not magic, nor are they automatic. They take knowledge and practice, but they are worth the investment in creating and sustaining that culture and climate of warmth and caring for every child in the building. Not just the easy students, not just the popular students not just certain groups such as the athletic students. Every child in every school building needs to feel that he or she belongs there. They all need to feel safe, cared for, and able to turn to a caring adult when they have concerns.

Leadership and Decision-Making

School officials must make decisions based on both priority and resources. In addition to lack of resources (including money, support, and supervision), barriers to effective decision-making include leadership, competing priorities, overcoming denial about problems, buy-in to programs and interventions, and fidelity to research-based implementation. Savvy school leaders understand these barriers and plan for them.

It all starts with a will to plan and then a plan. The will to plan means honestly recognizing that problems exist rather than papering them over to protect the school's image. An audit of relevant data on absenteeism and discipline referrals, not to mention student achievement levels is where to start. And if a critical mass of staff is not attuned to the need, the leader(s) need to use that data to make a compelling case for making changes.

Curt Lavarello, executive director of the Florida-based School Safety Advocacy Council, said that many of the things that probably need to be done in school safety does not require writing a check, such as being present, getting to know the students. He says that he visits schools and finds metal detectors, door latches, bulletproof glass, but then he does not see an administrator for three hours. He advises that administrators have to engage and be present with the students (Williams, 2015). Being absent for much of the time speaks volumes.

In addition to great leadership, school-wide buy-in is imperative. Staff and community ownership of, and involvement in, planning greatly enhances the prospects of successful implementation and results. Once buy in is obtained, then a true commitment to implementing the selected program(s) with fidelity to the research on implementation for the program is necessary to have similar positive effects.

PROMISING PROGRAM: POSITIVE BEHAVIORAL INTERVENTION AND SUPPORTS

Positive Behavioral Intervention and Supports (PBIS) *has been adopted by over 5,600 schools throughout the United States. It uses a school-wide, tiered approach to applying behavioral interventions at different levels of intensity for students at different levels of need.*

Universal interventions focus on clarity of school and classroom rules and consistency of enforcement, and on screening for more serious behavior disorders. Group-based behavioral interventions are employed with the 5 to 10 percent of youths who do not respond to the universal interventions. In addition, intensive, individualized behavioral interventions are employed to manage the behavior of the small segment of the population that is especially at risk (Sugai & Horner, 2006).

PBIS *aims to prevent disruptive behaviors and promote a positive school climate through setting-level change in order to prevent student behavior problems systematically and consistently. Bradshaw, Pas, Debnam, and Johnson (2015) describe the model, which draws upon behavioral, social learning, organizational, and positive youth development theories. It promotes strategies that can be used by all staff consistently across all school contexts.*

PBIS promotes setting-level change as a means for systematically and consistently preventing student behavior problems and promoting a positive school environment. PBIS can serve as an overall framework for the integrated implementation of other evidence-based programs, such as bullying or teen dating violence prevention.

Staff and students work together to create a school-wide program that clearly describes positive behavioral expectations, provides incentives to students meeting those expectations, promotes positive student and staff interactions, and encourages data-based decision-making by staff and administrators. It aims to alter the school's culture and climate by creating both improved systems (e.g., discipline, reinforcement, and data management systems) and procedures in order to promote positive change in student and

Table 10.1 School Violence Prevention Approaches at a Glance

Violence Prevention Approaches	School Shootings	Intruders	Aggression/ Intimidation	Bullying	Suicide	Sexual Abuse/ Harassment	Dating Violence	Gang Violence	Violence/ Staff
Hardware									
Metal detectors	x								x
Fences		x							
Security cameras	x	x	x	x		x		x	x
Lighting	x	x	x	x				x	x
ID cards								x	x
Visitor sign-in								x	x
Locked doors	x	x							
Weapons hotline	x		x	x	x	x	x	x	x
Gates	x	x						x	
Electromagnetic locks	x	x							
Bullet-proof doors/windows	x	x							
Programs									
Bullying	x		x	x	x	x	x	x	x
At-risk	x		x	x	x	x	x	x	x
Anger management	x		x	x	x	x	x	x	x
Conflict resolution	x		x	x	x	x	x	x	x
Character education	x		x	x	x	x	x	x	x
Social skills	x		x	x	x	x	x	x	x
Peer assistance	x		x	x	x	x	x	x	x
Restorative justice	x		x	x	x			x	x
Peacekeepers	x		x	x	x			x	x
Suicide	x			x	x	x	x		

(continued)

Table 10.1 (continued)

Violence Prevention Approaches	School Shootings	Intruders	Aggression/ Intimidation	Bullying	Suicide	Sexual Abuse/ Harassment	Dating Violence	Gang Violence	Violence/ Staff
Teen dating									
Avoiding gangs			x				x	x	
Problem solving	x		x	x	x	x	x	x	x
Mentoring	x		x	x	x			x	
Policies and Procedures									
Lockdowns and drills	x	x							
Zero tolerance	x		x	x		x	x	x	x
Suspension			x	x		x	x	x	x
Threat assessment	x		x	x	x	x	x	x	x
Crisis planning	x	x			x	x	x	x	x
Codes of conduct			x	x		x	x	x	x
School-wide behavior management			x	x	x	x	x	x	x
School resource officers		x	x	x	x	x	x	x	x
Police patrols		x	x					x	x
Security staff		x	x			x	x	x	x
Increased staff supervision	x	x	x	x	x	x	x	x	x
Staff training	x	x	x	x	x	x	x	x	x
Student training	x	x	x	x	x	x	x	x	x
Parent training	x	x	x	x	x	x	x	x	x
Mental health resources	x		x	x	x	x	x	x	x
Reduced class size	x		x	x	x		x	x	
Communication systems	x	x	x	x	x	x	x	x	x

teacher behavior. The Tier 1 school-wide PBIS component is composed of the following seven critical features:

> *(a) Within the school, a PBIS team is formed that includes 6–10 staff members procedures ... (b) A behavioral support coach provides on-site consultation and technical assistance ... (c) Expectations for positive student behavior are defined and known by staff and students ... (d) Defined behavioral expectations are taught to all students ... (e) A school-wide system is developed to reward students who exhibit the expected positive behaviors ... (f) An agreed-upon system is created to respond to behavioral violations ... (g) A formal system is developed to collect, analyze, and use data for data-based decision-making. (Bradshaw et al., 2015, p. 2)*

Two randomized controlled trials demonstrated significant impacts on suspensions, bullying and peer rejection, as well as improved academic achievement and school climate.

THE LAST WORD

Retired Indianapolis Public Schools Police Chief Jack Martin gave three reasons why school security fails: "It can't happen here." "We can't afford it." "We don't have the time to do all that." They are also the three reasons to keep in mind when the going gets tough and there is no time and there are no resources. The executive director of the NASRO reminds us why we must never accept those excuses:

> I have come to realize that it does not take for long for us to forget the shock and the pain that tragedies (like Sandy Hook) bring. But we cannot afford to forget ... the families of the victims have not forgotten and they will never forget. We owe it to them to remain diligent and to do everything we can to prevent these types of tragedies in the future.

REFERENCES

Bradshaw, C. P., Pas, E. T., Debnam, K. J., & Johnson, S. L. (2015). A focus on implementation of positive behavioral interventions and supports (PBIS) in high schools: Associations with bullying and other indicators of school disorder. *School Psychology Review*, *44*(4), 480–498. doi:10.17105/spr-15-0105.1

Catalano, R. F., Haggerty, K. P., Oesterle, S., Fleming, C. B., Hawkins, J. D.. (2004, September). The importance of bonding to school for healthy development. *Journal of School Health*, *74*(7), 252–261.

Child Abuse and Neglect Cost the United States $124 Billion. Washington, DC: Center for Disease Control (CDC). Retrieved from https://www.cdc.gov/media/releases/2012/p0201_child_abuse.html

Safe and Supportive Schools Model, Institute for Education Research, U.S. Department of Education. Retrieved from https://safesupportivelearning.ed.gov/school-climate

Sugai, G., & Horner, R. R. (2006). A promising approach for expanding and sustaining school-wide positive behavior support school. *Psychology Review, 35*(2), 245–259.

Williams, K. (2015). *In controversial effort to stop violence, Ohio tries school barricades*. Retrieved from http://america.aljazeera.com/articles/2015/10/11/school-barricades-mass-shootings.html

About the Author

Deborah Lynch taught in urban elementary and high schools for twenty years. She also worked as an assistant director of the Educational Issues Department of the American Federation of Teachers for eight years. She was instrumental in the award of a $1.3 million MacArthur grant for an education reform and teacher leadership initiative to the Chicago Teachers Union and served as its president from 2001 to 2004. Lynch earned a PhD in public policy from the University of Illinois at Chicago and is currently an associate professor of graduate studies in the College of Education at Chicago State University.

www.ingramcontent.com/pod-product-compliance
Lightning Source LLC
Chambersburg PA
CBHW021850300426
44115CB00005B/99